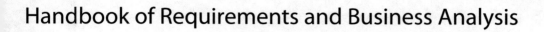

Handbook of Requirements and Business Analysis

Bertrand Meyer

Handbook of Requirements and Business Analysis

 Springer

Bertrand Meyer
Schaffhausen Institute of Technology
Schaffhausen, Switzerland

ISBN 978-3-031-06738-9   ISBN 978-3-031-06739-6   (eBook)
https://doi.org/10.1007/978-3-031-06739-6

Cover illustration: "Émailleur à la Lampe, Perles Fausses", plate from Diderot's and D'Alembert's Encyclopédie, by kind permission of the ARTFL Project at the University of Chicago.

This Springer imprint is published by the registered company Springer Nature Switzerland AG
The registered company address is: Gewerbestrasse 11, 6330 Cham, Switzerland

Short contents

Preface

If a system is a solution, requirements state the problem. Since a solution to the wrong problem is useless, stating the problem is as important as building the solution. Hence the centrality of requirements engineering — also known as business analysis — in information technology.

Good requirements are among the most treasurable assets of a project. Bad requirements hamper it at best and doom it at worst.

In software development as practiced today, requirements are more often bad than good. What passes for requirements in too many projects is a loose collection of "use cases" or "user stories", revealing the kind of amateurish process that used to plague other tasks of software engineering such as design, programming and testing. While these solution-side tasks have benefited from enormous progress in the last decades, on the problem side requirements remain the sick part of software engineering.

The goal of this book is to redress the balance so that the requirements you produce will support rather than hinder your projects. It is not a theoretical treatise but a Handbook, devised to provide you with concrete and immediately applicable guidance.

THE MATERIAL

You will find in the following chapters:

- 1: A precise definition of requirements **concepts**, and a classification of requirement kinds.
- 2: A discussion of general requirements **principles**.
- 3: A **Standard Plan** applicable to the requirements of any project.
- 4: A review of the **quality** attributes for requirements and associated **verification** criteria.
- 5: Precise guidelines on how to **write** effective requirements.
- 6: A description of how to obtain requirements, a process known as **elicitation**.
- 7: A discussion of **use cases** and other scenario-based requirements techniques.
- 8: A presentation of the **object-oriented** approach to requirements.
- 9: An introduction to **formal** requirements, using mathematical rigor for precision.
- 10: An important kind of formal specification, **abstract data types**.
- 11: What it means for requirements to be "**complete**", and how to achieve this goal.
- 12: How to make requirements a core part of the project **lifecycle**.

As befits a practical and compact Handbook, the discussion focuses on concepts and uses only short examples for illustration. A Companion Book, *Effective Requirements: A Complete Example*, develops the requirements of an entire industrial case study from start to end, using the concepts of this Handbook and the plan of chapter 3.

OBSTACLES TO QUALITY

Why has requirements quality continued to lag while other aspects of software engineering have advanced? Lack of attention is not the reason. There are thousands of articles on requirements engineering, conferences that have been running regularly for decades, specialized journals, and several good books (you will find references to them in the Bibliographical notes and further reading section at the end of this Preface). Their effect on how industry practices requirements is, however, limited.

One of the obstacles has already been noted: the belief, in much of the software world, that doing requirements means writing a few scenarios of user interaction with the system: "use cases" or "user stories". While helpful, such a collection of examples cannot suffice. If used as a substitute for requirements, it leads to systems that do not perform well outside of the chosen cases and are hard to adapt to new ones. The industry needs to wean itself from use cases and user stories as the basis for requirements, and start viewing them in their proper role: as tools for the *verification* and *illustration* of proper requirements, produced by more appropriate techniques.

Another impediment is the widespread distrust of "upfront" activities — specifically, upfront requirements and design— sown by proponents of agile methods such as Scrum. Along with the undeniable improvements it has brought to the industry's practice of software construction, the spread of agile ideas has led many people to believe that requirements as separate software engineering artifacts are a thing of the past, and that you can just rush into coding, writing user stories as you go. In reality, *some* upfront work is essential: in no serious engineering endeavor can engineers proceed directly to construction without a preliminary phase of analysis and planning. Good software practices include requirements, whether you write them before or during development. In fact, as you will learn (see "Requirements Elaboration Principle", page 25, and the lifecycle discussion of chapter 12), you should do *both*. The principles in this Handbook are equally applicable to agile and more traditional ("Waterfall") projects.

DESCRIPTIVE AND PRESCRIPTIVE

We may expect anyone discussing a branch of science or engineering to start by precisely defining the objects of study. Unfortunately, the requirements literature lacks such meaningful and systematically applicable definitions.

It often compounds the problem by failing to separate *descriptive* and *prescriptive* elements. To study any discipline, you need to learn the basic notions involved before you learn right and wrong ways of doing things. Speed is distance traveled per unit of time; only after giving this definition can you start prescribing speed limits.

In software engineering and particularly requirements engineering, the standard sources have not reached that level of maturity. They are as long on advice — not always buttressed by objective justifications — as they are short on usable technical information, and many an author seems to find it natural to claim a role of director of conscience for stranded souls. Consider this definition of "requirement" from the IEEE standard on systems engineering:

> **Requirement**: *A statement that identifies a product or process operational, functional, or design characteristic or constraint, which is unambiguous, testable or measurable, and necessary for product or process acceptability (by consumers or internal quality assurance guidelines).*

Although you would not guess it from its mystifying grammar (how does one parse "*product or process operational, functional, or design characteristic*"?), this definition is the result of years of work by an IEEE committee; numerous articles and textbooks cite it reverently. But it misses its purpose of defining the concept of requirements: it is instead trying to tell us what requirements *should* be (unambiguous, testable, measurable). Hold the preaching, please; first tell us what requirements *are*.

In its attempt at prescription, the definition is lame anyway: requirements quality involves much more than the criteria listed. In chapter 4 of this Handbook, devoted to defining requirements quality, you will find a set of fourteen quality factors. It is not possible to do justice to such a complex matter in the few lines of a definition. But consider the damage that this botched attempt at prescription does to the *description* (which should be the goal of a definition in a standard). If we only accepted "*unambiguous*" requirements as requirements, we would exclude many — probably most — requirements documents produced in practice. (Imagine a definition of "novel" specifying that the story must be absorbing, the characters compelling, the dialog sharp and the style impeccable. Bookstores would have to remove many titles from their "novel" shelves.) Requirements as we write them are human products; *of course* they will contain occasional ambiguities and other deficiencies! Not every one of their elements will be "testable or measurable". Perfect or not, however, they are still requirements.

Such confusion of the descriptive and the prescriptive is pervasive in today's standards. It mars what should have been the definitive standard on requirements (but ends up being pretty useless): the 2018 International Standard Organization's "Systems and software engineering — Life cycle processes — Requirements engineering", which you can purchase for some $300 to get such definitions as the following for "***requirements elicitation***":

> *Use of systematic techniques, such as prototyping and structured surveys, to proactively identify and document **customer** and **end user** needs*

(The underlined terms refer to other entries in the standard.) Requirements elicitation, covered in chapter 6 of this Handbook, is the process of gathering requirements from stakeholders. The cited definition only lists "*customers*" and "*end users*" as the source of needs, an obsolete view: it should refer to the more general notion of stakeholder (for which the standard actually has an entry!). The previous example used similarly imprecise and inadequate terminology by referring to acceptability by "*consumers*".

Even worse in the last entry is its failure to separate the definition of "elicitation" from the prescriptive fashions of the moment. Some committee member must have had a particular ax to grind: that *prototyping* is the best way to elicit requirements. (On prototyping for requirements, see 6.11, page 122 in this Handbook.) Another was pushing the idea of "*structured surveys*". They both got their two cents in, but at the expense of other widely used elicitation techniques (why leave out *stakeholder interviews* and *stakeholder workshops*, widely-used elicitation techniques discussed in chapter 6?). The result is a mishmash of partial prescriptions, not a usable definition.

The present text has a fair amount of advice, as one may expect from a Handbook. But it always defines the concepts first, and keeps the two aspects, descriptive and prescriptive, distinct. A prescriptive part, whether an entire chapter or just one section or paragraph, is marked at its start with the "Prescription" road sign shown here.

The first two chapters highlight the distinction: chapter 1 reviews and precisely defines the fundamental concepts of requirements; it is almost fully descriptive. Chapter 2 introduces general principles of requirements analysis and is almost fully prescriptive.

A BALANCED VIEW

One of the obstacles facing any serious discussion of software requirements is the dominance of two extremist schools with little tolerance for each other:

- "*Heavy artillery*": the more dogmatic fringe of the Waterfall, big-software-project school, which treats requirements as a step of the software lifecycle and insists that the subsequent steps cannot proceed until every single requirement has been spelled out.

- "*Guerrilla warfare*": the more dogmatic fringe of the agile school, which is suspicious of any "big upfront" activity (including upfront requirements and upfront design), and limits requirements to "user stories" (7.2, page 132), covering small units of functionality and written on-the-fly, interspersed with implementation.

Both extremes are unreasonable (and not endorsed by the wiser members of both schools). This Handbook takes a pragmatic stance on the place of requirements in the overall software development process. Two of the "key ideas" summarized in the next section, "*Just Enough Require-ments*" and "*Upfront **and** evolving*", reflect this flexible approach, which accommodates:

- Heavy-requirements processes, as may be justified for example in life-critical systems or others subject to strict regulatory processes.
- Light-requirements processes, as in web interface design or DevOps (12.4.3) projects.
- Anything in-between.

Each project is entitled to define the dosage of "a priori" and "as we go" requirements that best suits its context. This Handbook will, it is hoped, provide guidance and support in all cases.

KEY IDEAS

Successful requirements engineering demands a coherent approach with clear guiding princi-ples. Here is a preview of core ideas that this Handbook will help you master and apply.

A Standard Plan. Requirements in industry, when just using an ad hoc structure, often fol-low the model plan of a 1998 IEEE standard. While good for its time, it has long outlived its relevance; we understand far more about requirements, and today's projects are vastly more sophisticated, calling for a more sophisticated plan. The plan presented in chapter 3 consists of four "books" covering the *four PEGS of requirements engineering* (Project, Environment, Goals and System), with a chapter structure covering all important aspects. It has been tried on a num-ber of examples and fine-tuned over several years, with the goal of becoming the new standard.

A proper scope for requirements. Requirements are too often misconstrued as "the defi-nition of the functions of the system". Such a view restricts the usefulness of a requirements effort. This Handbook restores the balance by covering all four PEGS of the requirements plan. All are equally important. "*Project*" covers features of the actual development project, such as tasks, resources and deadlines. "*Environment*" covers properties with which the development must contend, but which are not under its control because they come from physical laws, engi-neering constraints or business rules. "*Goals*" covers the business benefits expected from the project and system. "*System*" covers the behavior and performance of the system to be built.

Requirements as a question-and-answer device. The maximalist view of an all-encom-passing requirements document, which must specify everything there is to know about a system (and in traditional "Waterfall" approaches, specify it ahead of any design or implementation), is in most cases expensive, unfeasible (as not all system properties *can* be determined early on), and over-reaching (as the project may not *need* to determine all of them early). Pushing this view on a project may lead to an equally damaging over-reaction from the team: a blanket dis-missal of the importance of requirements. More productive and practical is a view of require-ments as a technique for identifying key *questions* to be *asked* about the system, and *answering* these questions independently of design and implementation. This Handbook focuses through-out on this role of requirements as a question-asking and question-answering tool.

Not just documents. We will be less concerned with *requirements documents* in the traditional sense than with *requirements*. Elements of requirements appear not only in dedicated documents but in a variety of expected and unexpected places, from PowerPoint slide decks to emails. It is more productive to think of a repository (a database) of requirements, from which one can produce requirements documents if desired. The four books of the Standard Plan collect all necessary elements, across all four dimensions, but do not have to be written linearly.

Just enough requirements. Requirements are the focus of this Handbook, but they should not be the focus of software development. What counts is the quality of the systems you will produce. To reach this goal, you need to pay enough attention to requirements, but not so much as to detract from other tasks. This Handbook teaches how to devote to requirements the requisite effort — no less, and no more.

Upfront *and* evolving. The Waterfall-style extreme of requirements all done up-front then frozen, and the agile extreme of requirements (user stories) produced piecewise while you implement system components, are equally absurd. It is as irresponsible to jump into a project without first stating the requirements as it is illusory to expect this statement to remain untouched. The proper approach is to start with a first version (carefully prepared but making no claim of perfection or completeness) and continue extending and revising it throughout the project. This combination of up-front work and constant update avoids the futile disputes between traditional and agile views; it retains the best of both.

Requirements are software. Requirements are a software engineering product of the first importance, along with other artifacts such as code, designs and tests. They share many of their properties and can benefit from many of the same techniques and tools.

Requirements as living assets. As one of the fundamental properties they share with other software artifacts, requirements will inevitably undergo *change*. Correspondingly, they can benefit from *configuration management* techniques and tools for recording individual elements, their relations with others, and their evolution throughout the development process.

Taking advantage of the object-oriented method. The object-oriented style of decomposition structures specifications (of programs but also of systems of any kind) into units based on types of objects, rather than functions; then each function is attached to the relevant object type and the types themselves are organized into inheritance structures. This style has proved its value in the software development space, by yielding simple and clear architectures, facilitating change and supporting reuse. While it has long been known that the same ideas can also help requirements, they should be more widely applied in that space. This Handbook shows how to benefit from an OO style for requirements.

Taking advantage of formal approaches. Some parts of requirements demand precision, at a level that can only be achieved through the use of mathematical methods and notations, also known as formal. For most projects, the bulk of the requirements is informal — using a combination of English or other natural language, figures, tables... — but it is important to be able to switch to mathematics for aspects that have to be specified rigorously, for example if misunderstandings or ambiguities could cause the system to malfunction, with potentially grave consequences. This Handbook shows that formal approaches are not an esoteric academic pursuit but a practical tool for requirements engineering, and explains how to benefit from them in a realistic project setting.

GEEK AND NON-GEEK

The charm as well as the challenge of requirements engineering is that it straddles geek and non-geek territory. Requirements describe how a software project and the system it produces interact with their physical and business environment (non-geek), but must do so with enough rigor and precision to serve as a blueprint for development, verification and maintenance (geek).

The geek/non-geek duality is apparent in the existence of two competing terms: what some branches of the Information Technology (IT) industry call "requirements engineering" is known in others as "business analysis". While nuances exist between these names ("Requirements engineering, business analysis", 1.2.5, page 6), for the most part they express a difference of focus: engineering versus business.

This Handbook does not take sides. It is intended both for IT professionals ("geeks") and for non-IT stakeholders ("non-geeks") wanting to understand how to make projects meet their needs. It ignores industry borders and applies to projects in both the engineering and business worlds.

THE AUTHOR'S EXPERIENCES BEHIND THIS HANDBOOK

A technical book is usually one of: practical advice, by a consultant; course textbook, by an academic; research monograph, also by an academic; prescription of standard practices, often by a committee. This Handbook does not fall into just one of these categories, but has features from each. It benefits from the author's experience across several professional roles.

Part of this background is the author's practice as a **software project team leader**. A successful project must avoid two opposite dangers: unprepared coding (jumping too early to implementation, without taking the time to define requirements); and "*analysis paralysis*", whereby you become so bogged down specifying requirements down to the last detail that you have no time left to implement them properly. Experience teaches how much effort to devote to requirements so that they guide and protect the development without detracting from it.

Another experience — **helping projects while they are under development** — confirms what many published studies have shown: that some of the worst deficiencies in software systems come from insufficient work on requirements (rather than mistakes in the design and implementation of the software). It is amazing in particular to see how a distorted invocation of agile ideas can damage a project: "*We are agile! We don't do any requirements! We just start implementing and add user stories as we go!*". A sure way to disaster. Agile methods — often used in a misunderstood form — serve here as a convenient excuse for sloppiness and laziness. In agile and less agile projects a consultant can help a development team produce a much better system by prompting them, both upfront and throughout the development, to identify relevant stakeholders and devote the proper effort to requirements. This Handbook explains how to combine a significant but limited upfront requirements effort with a constant update and extension of the requirements throughout the rest of the development process.

Also part of the author's background for this Handbook is work as **software expert in legal cases**. Company C (customer) contracts out to company D (developer) to build an IT system. Things go sour and two years later they find themselves in court. C blames D for failing to deliver a working system, D blames C for failing to provide enough information and support. In comes a software expert, asked by the court to assess the technical merits. Sifting though tens of thousands of emails, meeting minutes, PowerPoint presentations, use cases, test reports and other project documents reveals major requirements-related problems. Sometimes they are the cause of the failure, sometimes just one factor, but they are *always* part of the picture. The flaws can be managerial (requirements did not receive enough attention); technical (requirements were not of good enough quality); human (D did not provide the right *business analysts*, C did not provide the right *Subject-Matter Experts* — see "Who produces requirements?", 1.10.2, page 16). In all cases, the expert's sentiment — kept to himself, since it's too late — is that the parties would have been better off devoting proper attention to requirements while the project was alive; and if they had to call on an expert, it would have been better to do so upfront (in the role of a project advisor, discussed in the previous paragraph) to secure the project's success, rather than now to help decide who pays and who receives millions in damages.

This Handbook benefits from numerous one-day or two-day **courses for industry** on requirements engineering and related topics, taught by the author to industry practitioners.

Also on the teaching side, the text relies on the author's **university courses** at ETH Zurich, Politecnico di Milano, Innopolis University and the Schaffhausen Institute of Technology on requirements engineering and more general software engineering topics (including agile methods). Such courses often include a development project with a requirements component. A particularly interesting experience was the *Distributed Software Engineering Laboratory*, taught for over a decade at ETH, and covering the challenges of software projects developed collaboratively across different sites. A key part of the course was a project conducted with several other universities and resulting in the full implementation of a system by student groups. Each group consisted of three teams located in different universities from different countries, with two or three students in each team. There is hardly a better way for students to realize the importance of requirements than when you have to interface your own part of the system with another written by people a few time zones away, from a different culture, and whom you have never met. Many students who took part in this experience have commented on how well it prepared them for the reality of distributed development (before Covid-19 made this setup even more prevalent), and how it helped educate them in fruitful requirements techniques.

BIBLIOGRAPHICAL NOTES AND FURTHER READING

The "Companion Book" mentioned on page viii is *Effective Requirements: A Complete Example* [Bruel et al. 2022].

Examples of the existing "good books" on requirements (page viii) include, on the practical side, [Wiegers-Beatty 2013], rich with examples from the author's practice as a consultant. On the more academic side, an important contribution is [Van Lamsweerde 2008] which covers the field extensively, focusing on goal-oriented requirements techniques; see also a textbook, [Laplante 2018]. Another requirements text is [Kotonya-Sommerville 1998]. [Pfleeger-Atlee 2009] is a general textbook on software engineering, but its almost 80-page chapter on requirements provides a good survey of the topic. Another software engineering textbook, older but still applicable, is [Ghezzi et al. 2002]. A classic text on software project management, [Brooks 1975-1995], includes some oft-quoted lines about the importance of requirements. An important source is the work of Michael Jackson and Pamela Zave, starting with an influential early paper, [Zave-Jackson 1997] and continuing with Jackson's own requirements books: [Jackson 1995] and [Jackson 2000]; a more recent compendium of the work of their school is [Nuseibeh-Zave 2010]. [Lutz 1993] is a classic study of software errors due to poor requirements.

The standards cited on page ix are the IEEE systems engineering process standard [IEEE 2005], and the ISO-IEC-IEEE requirements engineering standard [ISO 2018]. Another IEEE-originated standard is SWEBOK [IEEE 2014], the Guide to the Software Engineering Body of Knowledge. It still shows signs of immaturity (with such examples as "*a process requirement is essentially a constraint on the development of the software*", where "*essentially*", inappropriate in a definition, can only confuse the reader). It has, however, become more precise and rigorous over its successive editions (the latest one, referenced here, is the third) and serves as a good summary of accepted concepts of software engineering including requirements, the topic of its first chapter.

The Distributed Software Engineering Laboratory at ETH Zurich and elsewhere, initially called DOSE (Distributed and Outsourced Software Engineering), included a project developed collaboratively by students from different universities around the world, in which requirements played a key role. It led to numerous publications accessible from [DOSE 2007-2015].

ACKNOWLEDGMENTS

Special thanks are due the Schaffhausen Institute of Technology (sit.org) for providing an excellent environment for teaching and research. SIT is an ambitious new university destined to make a big splash in the technology world; this Handbook appears to be the first book produced by an SIT member since SIT's creation in 2019. It is important to express the key roles of Serguei Beloussov, the founder of SIT and definer of its vision, Stanislav Protassov, one of SIT's leading lights, and faculty colleagues Mauro Pezzè and Manuel Oriol.

Part of the context that led to this Handbook is the collaborative work, going back several years, of an informal research group on requirements whose members are spread between the University of Toulouse (IRIT, Université Paul Sabatier), SIT, and previously Innopolis University. The present work is in debt to the members of this group for many stimulating discussions and particularly for helping with the initial version of the taxonomy of requirements ("Kinds of requirements element", 1.3, page 6). They are Profs. Jean-Michel Bruel, Sophie Ebersold and Manuel Mazzara as well as Alexandr Naumchev, Florian Galinier and Maria Naumcheva.

The author's expert-consulting work in legal cases, and the resulting insights mentioned above, greatly benefited from collaboration with Benoît d'Udekem from Analysis Group.

The courses cited in the previous section yielded thoughtful comments by attendees, lessons from course projects, and insights from co-lecturers, teaching assistants and colleagues including, at ETH, Peter Kolb, Martin Nordio, Julian Tschannen and Christian Estler; at Innopolis, Alexandr Naumchev and Mansur Khazeev; at Politecnico di Milano, faculty members Elisabetta Di Nitto and Carlo Ghezzi in many thought-provoking discussions. A seminar at UC Santa Barbara in 2020 at the invitation of Laura Dillon and two talks in 2021, one for ACM, organized by Will Tracz, the other for IBM, at the invitation of Grady Booch, provided opportunities to refine the ideas and their presentation.

The author has had the privilege of being exposed early on and over the years to the work of pioneers in requirements engineering, people who really defined the field, and even in some cases to interact directly with them. Without in the least implying agreement, it is important to acknowledge the influence of such star contributors (a few of them not strictly in requirements engineering but in kindred areas, for example agile methods and software lifecycle models) as Joanne Atlee, Kent Beck, Daniel Berry, Barry Boehm, Grady Booch, Mike Cohn, Alistair Cockburn, Anthony Finkelstein, Carlo Ghezzi, Tom Gilb, Martin Glinz, Michael and Daniel Jackson, Ivar Jacobson, Capers Jones, Cliff Jones, Jeff Kramer, Philippe Kruchten, Bashar Nuseibeh, David Parnas, Axel Van Lamsweerde, Karl Wiegers and Pamela Zave. A number of them are members of the IFIP (International Federation for Information Processing) Working Group 2.10 on Requirements; attendance at one of their meetings provided many insights, as did regular participation in meetings of another IFIP committee, WG2.3 on Programming Methodology.

The friendly and efficient support of Ralf Gerstner at Springer, now for the third book in a row, is a great privilege.

The ETH Zurich library helped in obtaining the text of older articles. Alistair Cockburn kindly authorized using material from his book on use cases, [Cockburn 2001], for an example appearing in chapters 7 and 8; Bettina Bair kindly authorized reproducing her sample requirements document, devised for a course, [Bair 2005].

Comments received on early drafts of the text, particularly by from Mike Cohn, Lutz Eicke, Philippe Kruchten, Ivar Jacobson and Karl Wiegers, led to corrections and improvements.

Marco Piccioni provided support, comments and material over many years, and suggested exercises.The text immensely benefited from Raphaël Meyer's punctilious proofing. However much one would like to hope that no mistakes remain, chances are slim; the Handbook site referenced below will list corrections to errors reported after publication.

September 2022 (corrected printing)

HANDBOOK PAGE

Further material associated with this Handbook, including course slides, document templates for the Standard Plan of chapter 3 and links to video lectures (MOOCs) on requirements, is available at

requirements.bertrandmeyer.com

CREDITS

Cover picture: from "*Émailleur à la Lampe, Perles Fausses*" (lampwork enameler, imitation pearls), a plate in Diderot's and d'Alembert's *Encyclopédie* (1751-1766), by kind permission of the ARTFL Project at the University of Chicago.

Pages 168 and 178: detail from *A Pic-Nic Party* by Thomas Cole, Brooklyn Museum, photo by Bill Hathom on Wikimedia at upload.wikimedia.org/wikipedia/commons/0/09/Thomas_Cole%27s_%22The_Pic-nic%22%2C_Brooklyn_Museum_IMG_3787.JPG. See museum page at www.brooklynmuseum.org/opencoll ection/objects/1356.

RUP diagram, page 214: adapted from Wikimedia picture at commons.wikimedia.org/wiki/File:Development-iterative.png.

Contents

1

Requirements: basic concepts and definitions

The discussion of any technical domain starts with precise definitions of fundamental concepts.

1.1 DIMENSIONS OF REQUIREMENTS ENGINEERING

You may have come across such cursory definitions as *"requirements define what the system will do, independently of how it does it"*. That view, while still widespread, encompasses only one fourth of the picture. the "system" part. Requirements pertain to a *project* intended, in a certain *environment*, to achieve some *goals* by building a *system*. These four pegs, or PEGS (a mnemonic for Project, Environment, Goals and System) 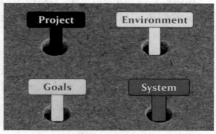 are the components of requirements engineering, and the basis for the study of requirements as pursued in the rest of this Handbook.

1.1.1 Universe of discourse: the four PEGS

Dimensions of requirements: Project, Environment, Goals, System
A **goal** is a result desired by an organization.
A **system** is a set of related artifacts, devised to help meet certain goals.
A **project** is the set of human processes involved in the planning, construction, operation and revision of a system.
An **environment** is the set of entities (such as people, organizations, devices and other material objects, regulations, and other systems) external to the project and system but with the potential to affect the goals, project or system or to be affected by them.

Goals cover the institutional dimension: what the organization commissioning the project expects to get out of it. The System should meet these goals, in a context defined by the Environment, and will result from carrying out a Project.

In the definition of "system", an "artifact" is a human-produced object, physical or — in the software case — virtual. While the primary focus in this Handbook is on software, the definition of "system" is general enough to cover systems encompassing both software and hardware artifacts.

© The Author(s), under exclusive license to Springer Nature Switzerland AG 2022
B. Meyer, *Handbook of Requirements and Business Analysis*, https://doi.org/10.1007/978-3-031-06739-6_1

1.1.2 Distinguishing system and environment

Do not confuse system and environment properties. The difference is easy to remember:

> **System versus environment**
> * A system property expresses a decision of the project.
> * An environment property characterizes objects from the physical or business environment, and is beyond the team's control (except to the extent that the system's operation may affect them).

For example:

* In an e-commerce system, *"only registered users can order a product"* is an environment property, defined by the company. The requirement that a non-logged-in user clicking "Purchase" shall be redirected to a login page is a system property (derived from that environment property).
* In a railroad crossing system, *"trains may be assumed to travel no faster than 200 km/h"* is an environment property. How long in advance of a train's arrival the gate must close is a system property (derived from that environment property).

As these examples indicate, domain properties often induce system properties. One of the criteria of good requirements (environment completeness, 11.4) is that system properties be compatible with environment properties.

In case of hesitation, remember this simple guideline: anything that the project is free to define is a system property; anything else (imposed on the project) belongs to the environment.

As a byproduct, the distinction between system and environment yields a clear definition of the difference between two system attributes: *safety* is the property that the system shall not harm the environment; *security* is the property that the environment shall not harm the system.

The Environment Principle, 2.3, will remind us of the importance of the distinction.

1.1.3 The organizations involved

The definition of the four PEGS covers the "what" of requirements. We must also consider the "who". A system is developed for a **target organization** by a **production organization**.

The more ordinary terms *"customer"* and *"developer"* are appropriate in the case of an IT company producing a system for a non-IT company. The general terms "target organization" and "production organization" include this case but cover more possibilities. For example, the production organization may be the IT division of the same company as the production organization; or a group with the right skills may serve as both production and target organization, producing a system that addresses its own goals. (There could even be a single person filling all roles, such as a researcher performing analysis of his or her own experimental data.) In all cases, requirements — as defined later in this chapter — will be necessary.

Another distinction (think of *haute-couture* versus *prêt-à-porter* in fashion) affects the relationship of the system to the target organization:

- A **bespoke system** is developed for a particular target organization, according to its explicitly stated needs. Synonyms for "bespoke" are "custom-made" and "tailor-made". Think of a payroll program built specifically for a company.
- A **packaged** product is developed for a mass market. Think of a smartphone app, or a desktop application such as Photoshop. Or, in contrast with the previous example, a general-purpose payroll package available for purchase by any company.

Here too, both kinds will need requirements. The big difference is that it is easier for a bespoke project to gain access to future users (and other stakeholders as discussed next). For a packaged product, the system must cater to possibly many current and future users, most of whom are not available to the developers or even known to them.

1.1.4 Stakeholders

Every system is built, directly or indirectly, for people. We must, however, avoid the simplistic view that requirements "reflect the needs of *users*". Users — also not a trivial notion — are just one of the groups of people who deserve consideration. All these groups have a stake in the project and are known as *stakeholders*. Like others, this concept requires a precise definition:

Stakeholders

The stakeholders of a project are the groups of people recognized by the project as having the potential to affect, or be affected by, the project, environment, goals or system.

(The environment, per its definition on page 1, is already restricted to properties that affect or are affected by the project or system.)

This definition is both broad and restrictive. It is broad because:

- It covers not individuals but *groups* of people. While a group can include a single person, as the target organization's CEO, the more typical stakeholder is a category of people defined by their function, such as student users in the case of a course management system for a university. (An *organization* can be a stakeholder; the definition covers this case since an organization is — among other things — a group of people.)
- It talks about "being affected by" as well as "affecting". Student users are an example of people affected by the system; the CEO (or other decision-maker) is an example of someone affecting the project and the system.

The definition is restrictive in insisting that stakeholders be "recognized" as such. If we remove this qualification, we get the notion of *potential* stakeholder. Whether we like it or not, projects do not always recognize all potential stakeholders as stakeholders. As a simple example, assume a system designed with only an English user interface; if it gets used worldwide, non-English speakers are potential stakeholders not recognized as stakeholders. All of us have had to use systems that were not designed in consideration of our specific needs.

A project may have many different stakeholders. It is important to identify them properly; section 1.10.1 of this chapter will cover this topic.

1.2 DEFINING REQUIREMENTS

Requirements are defined in terms of relevant *properties* and their *statements*.

1.2.1 Properties

Requirements will state properties of a project, environment, goal or system. Here the term "property" retains its meaning from in ordinary language, "*a quality or trait*" (Merriam-Webster), with one restriction: to keep things simple we limit ourselves to **boolean** properties, meaning properties which can only take the value "True" or the value "False".

Property

A "property" as used in requirements is a boolean trait of a project, environment, goal or system.

Sticking to boolean properties encourages precision and helps attain one of the quality objectives for requirements: *verifiability* (4.12). This rule is a matter of convenience and does not limit us in any essential way, since one can easily rephrase any non-boolean trait in boolean form. For example, instead of specifying a "color" property with possible values "red", "green" and "blue", we simply state that the color value has to be one of those; mathematically: color ∈ {red, green, blue}, a boolean property (see 9.2 for basic mathematical notations).

1.2.2 Statements

A property is abstract, in the sense that it does not depend on how anyone expresses it. To describe possible ways of expressing the property, we need another notion:

Statement

A statement is a human-readable expression of a property.

Do not confuse properties and their statements. Requirements consist of statements, since we cannot communicate a property without communicating a statement of it in some notation. What matters is the underlying property, but we need a statement to express it, and for the statement we must choose a notation.

For a given property, there are many possible statements expressing it. "*All humans are mortals*", for example, is a statement of a property. "*Tous les hommes sont mortels*" is a different statement, but of the same property, expressed in a different notation (French instead of English). Both are natural-language notations; it is also possible to use *formal* notations, meaning notations with a rigorous basis, coming from mathematics (chapter 9), as in

---

$\forall\, x: HUMAN \mid x.is\_mortal$

("for all x in the set *HUMAN*, x has the *is_mortal* property".) Or we can use a graphical notation:

A graphical statement

(A so-called Venn or Euler-Venn diagram, again expressing the same property.)

1.2.3 Relevance

A requirement is a statement, but not all statements are requirements. For a meaningful notion of requirement we need to exclude statements of *irrelevant* properties. It may be a property of the Project that three of the developers are called Clara, but that does not make it a requirement.

The notion of relevance excludes such properties and the corresponding statements:

Relevant property, relevant statement

A goal property is relevant. A property of the project or system is relevant if it can affect or be affected by a stakeholder. A property of the environment is relevant if it can affect or be affected by the project or system.

A statement of a property is relevant if the property is relevant.

"Affect or be affected by" for *project* and *system* refers to the definition of "stakeholder" (page 3). For completeness, the definition includes the notion of relevance for *environment* properties, although the environment was already so defined (page 1) as to imply relevance.

Goals, stating the objectives set by decision-makers from the organization responsible for the project, are relevant by definition. (It is of course not uncommon to encounter questionable goals. Requirements engineers are entitled to raise questions and ask for justification. The "*justified*" quality attributes for requirements, discussed in 4.2, addresses this issue.)

1.2.4 Requirement

With the preceding concepts properly identified, we can define what a requirement is:

Requirement

A requirement is a relevant statement about a project, environment, goal or system.

For example:

- "*The project shall produce a first release by 31 October 2023*": project requirement.
- "*All Web sites shall conform to GDPR*" (EU privacy rules): environment requirement.
- "*The Bridge Maintenance System shall limit bridge closures to no more than one night a month*": goal requirement.
- "*After 5 failed login attempts, access shall be blocked for 30 minutes*": system requirement.

1.2.5 Requirements engineering, business analysis

Requirements engineering is the task of developing requirements.

"Developing" includes not just producing an initial version of the requirements but updating it regularly, and managing the (possibly complex) set of requirements. As we will see in more detail in subsequent chapters ("Requirements Evolution Principle", page 23), we should discard the obsolete view of requirements as something you do at the beginning of a project and then use, unchanged, as a blueprint for design and implementation. New requirements can be produced, and previous ones updated, at all times through the project.

Business analysis is essentially a synonym for requirements engineering. A nuance does exist:

- Requirements engineering has a more technical connotation.
- Business analysis is more focused on the business goals.

In practice the terminology depends on which industry you are in: an aerospace project will typically hire requirements engineers, while a payroll project will look for business analysts.

In other words, the difference is mostly cultural. The jobs are essentially the same: producing a set of requirements for a project, its environment, its goals, and the system it will develop.

1.3 KINDS OF REQUIREMENTS ELEMENT

Requirements are of clearly recognizable kinds. The table on the next page lists the categories, in the order of requirements applying to goals, the project, the system, the environment, all four dimensions, and special cases. Sections 1.4 to 1.10 explain these categories in turn.

Many of the categories have a dedicated part in the Standard Plan for requirements presented in chapter 3, which provides additional details on their properties.

1.4 REQUIREMENTS AFFECTING GOALS

The Goals part of requirements covers properties of the organization commissioning the project. The main type of requirement here is simply "goal"; another kind, "obstacle", also belongs to this general category.

1.4.1 Goal

A **goal** is a need of the target organization, which the system must address. For example, "*increase by 20% the proportion of graduates finding suitable jobs 6 months or less after completing their studies*" (for a system matching university graduates with job offers).

1.4.2 Special case: obstacle

An **obstacle** is a goal consisting of removing or otherwise addressing a property of the current situation (prior to the project) that has negative consequences for the target organization. An example is "*the current manual operation of trains requires a minimum interval of 2 minutes between successive trains, preventing the tracks from operating at full capacity and making it impossible to meet the expected growth of traffic over the next 10 years*" (for a system devised to automate train operation and increase train frequency).

Categories of requirement			
Category	*Special cases*	**Abbreviated definition**	*Pertains to*
Goal		Desired result for the target organization	*Goals*
	Obstacle	Goal describing a property to be overcome	*(1.4)*
Task		Activity included in the project	*Project*
Product		Artifact needed or produced by a task	*(1.5)*
Behavior		Property of the operation of the system	
	Functional requirement	Outcome produced by the system or one of its components	
	Non-functional requirement	Property of how the system achieves an outcome	*System (1.6)*
	Example	Illustration of behavior through a usage scenario	
Constraint		Property imposed by the environment	
	Business rule	Constraint defined by an organization	
	Physical rule	Constraint imposed by laws of nature	
	Engineering decision	Constraint arising from technical choices	*Environment (1.7)*
Assumption		Posited property of the environment	
Effect		Environment property affected by the system	
Invariant		Environment property that must be maintained	
Component		Identification of a part (of the project, environment, goals or system)	
Responsibility		Assignment of behavior or task to a component	*All (1.8)*
	Role	Human responsibility	
Limit		Exclusion from scope of requirements	
Silence		Property that is not in requirements but should be	
Noise		Property that is in requirements but should not be	
	Hint	Design or implementation suggestion	*Documents (1.9)*
Meta-requirement		Property of requirements themselves (not of the project, environment, goals or system)	
	Justification	Explanation of a project or system property in reference to a goal or environment property	

1.5 REQUIREMENTS ON THE PROJECT

Task and product requirements specify properties of the project.

1.5.1 Task

A **task** requirement is an activity that is a component of the project. Examples are software design, user acceptance testing, domestic deployment, international deployment.

1.5.2 Product

A **product** requirement is the specification of an artifact as either:

- *Produced* by the project (specifically, by one of its tasks), as a test plan or a particular deployable part of the system.
- *Needed* by the project or one of its tasks; for example, the implementation task may require a particular software project management tool.

1.6 REQUIREMENTS ON THE SYSTEM

System requirements, and more specifically behaviors, are the only ones that would appear in a conventional, simplistic view of requirements as "a description of what the system must do". In the broader approach of this chapter they remain important, together with a few special cases: functional and non-functional requirements and "examples" of various kinds (use case, user story, test script).

1.6.1 Behavior

A **behavior** is the specification that the system must produce a certain outcome or behave in a certain way.

For example, in a text processing system: "the 'Justify' command applied to a paragraph shall result in all its lines having an equal number of characters".

1.6.2 Special cases: functional and non-functional requirements

A **functional requirement** expresses some of *what* the system must do. (Contrast with "effects" discussed in 1.7 below.) The paragraph-justification requirement is functional.

A **non-functional requirement** expresses some of *how* the system will perform. Typical examples of non-functional requirements include properties of performance (timing properties on operations, parameters of storage use or bandwidth), security and privacy.

1.6.3 Special cases: examples (scenarios)

An **example** is a behavior specification expressed not as a general rule (as should normally be the case) but in the form of an illustrative scenario for specific, representative cases. There are three fundamental forms of example:

- A **use case** specifies the scenario of a complete interaction of a user through the system, such as "cancel a previous order" in an e-commerce system. Chapter 7 covers use cases.

- A **user story** specifies the handling of a specific user need, such as logging in into the system. User stories are presented in chapter 7 alongside use cases.

- A **test script** describes a sequence of interactions with the system expected to produce a certain result. A test script includes a specification of the expected properties of that result, called a **test oracle**.

1.7 REQUIREMENTS ON THE ENVIRONMENT

Some requirements express properties of the environment, in terms of what the environment expects from the system and project, and what it provides to them. They include constraints, assumptions, effects and invariants.

1.7.1 Constraint

A **constraint** is a property of the environment that restricts what the system and project can do. An example Project constraint is "all programs developed for this project shall conform to the company's coding standards".

An example System constraint, for an auction site, is "for past auctions, the hammer price shall be displayed only to registered users". As explained under "special cases" below, constraints are of three kinds: business rules, physical rules, engineering decisions.

1.7.2 Special cases of constraints: business rule, physical rule, engineering decision

Constraints fall into three categories:

- A **business rule** is a constraint imposed by the target organization, the production organization, or another organization (such as regulatory authorities). An example for a bank transfer system is *"any purchase over EUR 5,000 requires two authorized signatures"*.

- A **physical rule** is a consequence of the laws of nature, such as maximum signal speed.

- An **engineering decision** results from an explicit choice of the project, rather than external considerations as in the previous two cases. A System example is the definition of the minimum and maximum network bandwidths that the system must support. A Project example is the imposition of a particular programming language (determined — maybe wrongly, but explicitly — by corporate standards rather than an analysis of the project's technical needs).

1.7.3 Assumption

An **assumption**, also known as a **precondition**, is a property that we expect the environment to fulfill; the construction of the system takes it for granted.

An example for a flight control system is *"all pilots can understand messages in basic English"*.

1.7.4 Distinguishing between constraints and assumptions

If you find yourself hesitating over classifying a certain environment property as a constraint or an assumption, use the following simple criterion:

- If the condition makes the work of the developers harder, it is a constraint; for example, in a software system relying on a network, *"the network can only guarantee a minimum bandwidth of 1 Mbit/s"*. (It makes the job harder because the system must be able to provide the functionality specified by System properties, even when impaired by low bandwidth.)

- If the condition makes the work of the developers easier, it is a assumption; for example, *"the available bandwidth will be 1 Mbit/s or more"*. (It makes the job easier because the system developers need not worry about operation under lower-bandwidth conditions.)

In this example, the situation for the developers of the *network* itself would be reversed: having to provide bandwidth at least equal to a specific threshold is a constraint; not having to provide more than a certain threshold is an assumption. The reason for the duality is that for a software system running on a network that network is part of the environment, whereas for the developers of the network the environment includes the systems that it must be able to support.

As another criterion, if the system developers can control the condition, it is an assumption; if it is imposed on them without them having any say, it is a constraint. The two criteria are closely related: if you can exert influence on a condition, it will typically be to make your job easier (assumption); conversely, if a condition makes your job harder (constraint), it is because you cannot remove or loosen it.

1.7.5 Effect

An **effect**, also known as a **postcondition**, is the specification of a change that operation of the system may bring to the environment. For example, the installation of a payroll system may change the day of the month on which employees are paid.

Do not confuse effects with behaviors, particularly *functional requirements* as defined in 1.6:

- The specification of a change brought upon by *an individual execution* of the system is a functional requirement. For example: running the payroll system will cause transfers to the bank accounts that employees have registered with the company.

- The specification of a change to *properties* of the environment, brought upon by the *deployment of the* system, is an effect. For example: when the system is put into operation, employees will be paid on the last working day of the month (whatever the practice was before).

1.7.6 Invariant

An **invariant** is an environment property that the system must maintain. In other words, it exists as both an assumption and an effect (precondition and postcondition); properties with this double affiliation will be categorized as invariants. Examples are:

- For a factory control system, including both sensors to measure the temperature and air-conditioning units to control it, the property that the system expects a temperature between 18 to 25 degrees Celsius (precondition) and maintains it in that range (postcondition).

- For a train control system, the property that a train can only start moving with the doors closed (precondition) and leaves them closed until arrival (postcondition). This invariant can also be formulated as a logic rule: whenever the train is moving, doors must be closed.

1.8 REQUIREMENTS APPLYING TO ALL DIMENSIONS

Requirements applying to all PEGS are of four kinds: component, responsibility, limit and role.

1.8.1 Component

A *component* requirement specifies that the project, environment, goals or system shall contain a certain part. Examples are: a component of the project (a case which yields its own category, "task", discussed below) or of the environment; one of the goals; a subsystem.

1.8.2 Responsibility

A *responsibility* requirement specifies a certain actor is in charge of carrying out a certain task (for a project requirement) or behavior (for a system requirement). "Actor" in this definition is a general term, which may cover:

- A system component, as in the responsibility requirement *"the input-output system ensures that the temperature value originally entered by the user, if validated, is in the allowable range of -20 to +40 degrees Celsius"*.
- A human actor, in which case the responsibility is also called a *role*, as seen below (1.8.4).

1.8.3 Limit

A *limit* requirement identifies aspects that fall beyond the scope of the system. This category seems paradoxical because we generally think of requirements as stating *positive* properties governing how to develop the project (through "tasks" as defined in 1.5.1 above), meet the goals, fit in the environment and define the system's "behaviors" (1.6.1). Limits are *negative* properties, protecting the project from matters it does not need to address.

As we will see ("Delimited", 4.9, page 62), good requirements clearly state where their scope stops. Consider a project to revamp a customer management system, which exists separately from a *prospect* tracking system — although the two are interfaced, if only to transfer information when a prospect becomes a customer. If the prospect system is also slated for redesign, but as a separate project, the requirements for the customer system should explicitly specify that changes to the handling of prospects are out of scope.

1.8.4 Special case: role

A *role* requirement specifies a human or organizational responsibility. For example:

- *"UI development shall be the responsibility of the Bangalore division"*, a Project role.
- *"Safety regulations for aircraft are as defined by IATA"*, an Environment role.
- *"The lead-tracking system shall be designed for use by marketing reps"*, a Goal role.
- *"Operation of the system for 24/7 availability shall be the responsibility of the central IT group"*, a System role.

1.9 SPECIAL REQUIREMENTS ELEMENTS

The preceding categories cover requirements corresponding to the definition of the concept (page 5): relevant properties of the project, environment, goals or system. The classification must also account for elements that commonly appear, or should appear, in requirements documents, but are not requirements in that strict sense since they are properties of the *requirements specification* itself (rather than of the project, environment, goals or system). They include silence, noise and meta-requirement.

The term **requirements element** covers both requirements and these new categories.

1.9.1 Silence

The **silence** category is — like "limit" in 1.8.3 — paradoxical since it describes something that the requirements do *not* include. An instance of silence is a property — pertaining to any of the PEGS — that the requirements should state, but do not. There are two sources of silence:

- The requirements gathering process, known as "elicitation", may miss an important need or feature in any of the four dimensions. Chapter 6, devoted to elicitation, will give some hints — only hints, there is no sure-fire recipe — on how to avoid missing important properties: see "Ask effective questions", 6.10.4, page 119.

- Requirements engineers may fail to record properties because everyone at the target organization considers them obvious — but they are not obvious to outsiders, including the developers. This phenomenon is discussed in "Uncover the unsaid", 6.10.1, page 118.

1.9.2 Noise

Noise is the converse of "silence": something that appears in the requirements documents, but should not.

Requirements documents often include discussions that are of no use as requirements (they are not "***relevant*** statement about a project, environment, goal or system"). Usually the authors include them to provide more context and explanations. Such attempts are laudable in principle but in reality self-defeating because they make the requirements bigger and more complex, forcing the requirements consumers — designers, programmers, testers — to rummage the requirements for the useful gems out of a plethora of unessential comments. A later discussion discusses the proper place of explanations ("Binding and explanatory text", 5.4, page 77).

A typical example of noise is repetition: an attempt to clarify the requirements by explaining properties in several ways. The resulting repetitions are often confusing, rather than helpful, particularly since the different phrasings may introduce involuntary contradictions and ambiguities. This phenomemon is an example of good intentions producing bad consequences. The "No-Repetition Principle", page 76, will enjoin us to avoid it.

1.9.3 Special case: hint

A **hint**, a case of noise made acceptable, is a suggestion for a design or implementation technique. Such techniques normally do not belong in requirements, where they risk causing *over-specification* (4.7.3, page 59), a form of noise. Sometimes, however, they can be useful, as long as they are properly characterized as suggestions for other activities of the project (design, implementation...) rather than actual requirements.

A discussion of this concept appears in "Design and implementation hints", 4.7.4, page 59.

1.9.4 Metarequirement

Unlike silence and noise, **metarequirements** cause no harm. They appear in a requirements document to bring information not about the project, environment, goals or system but about the requirements themselves.

Examples include section titles but also explanations of forward or backward references, such as "*networking protocols appear in section S.3.X*".

Noise and metarequirements are similar since both cover elements that do not introduce any actual requirement information (in the sense of properties of any of the PEGS). The difference is that noise is detrimental to the quality of the documents, whereas metarequirements can improve the requirements by helping readers navigate them.

1.9.5 Special case: justification

A **justification**, a case of meta-requirement, also called a *rationale*, is an argument explaining the reason for a property of the System or Project in terms of a Goal or of an Environment property. Examples are:

- "*The maximum allowed time of 100 ms for this input operation is necessary to meet the goal of immediate user feedback discussed in section G.4.X*" (justification by a goal).
- "*The presence of two signature fields follows from the rule on purchases higher than € 5000 (section E.3.X)*" (justification by an environment property, in this case a constraint).

1.10 THE PEOPLE BEHIND REQUIREMENTS

The previous sections explored the technical side of requirements, starting with the definition of the fundamental concepts (1.2) and continuing with the just explored classification of requirements. So far our only glimpse into human aspects was the definition of target and production organizations (1.1.3) and a first brush with the concept of stakeholder (1.1.4). It is time to explore the human side further with a discussion of:

- Who influences requirements: the *stakeholder* concept deserves deeper analysis (1.10.1).
- Who produces requirements: "business analysts" and "Subject-Matter Experts" (1.10.2).

1.10.1 Categories of stakeholders

We saw (1.1.4) that stakeholders are the categories of people with influence on or from the requirements, whose representatives may, as a consequence, have to be consulted. The most obvious stakeholders are "users", but they are not the only ones, and even that notion of user requires clarification. We now review the possible stakeholders in two parts, corresponding to the distinction between "target" and "production" organizations (1.1.3).

First, those on the side of the target (the organization that the system will serve):

Stakeholders on the target (customer) side	
Stakeholders	**Comments**
Users of future system (bespoke project)	The concept of "user" is not as simple as it sounds, since it can yield different categories of stakeholders. If you build a system for online learning, for example, you have at least two categories of users with very different needs: the instructors who prepare the courses and the students who take them. The requirements effort must identify these categories.
Users of future system (packaged system)	This category is similar to the previous one, but in this case the project does not directly have access to the users, although it may rely on test groups.
Users of existing system	Many projects today, whether bespoke or packaged, are not new ("*greenfield*" development) but replace or complement existing systems ("*brownfield*"). Their users should be consulted.
Client programmers	Along with a UI (user interface), many systems also have an API (program interface), enabling other programs to use their functionality. These programs' authors, called "client programmers", are stakeholders. In some cases — such as a system embedded in hardware, or a program library — there is no UI and client programmers are the only "users".
SMEs (domain experts)	Subject-Matter Experts (1.10.2) are people with expertise in the domain area covered by the system.
Purchasing agents	Particularly for bespoke projects, target organizations often rely on purchasing agents for all significant purchases, including software. They will have their word.
Legal department	Whether bespoke or packaged, projects involving an external organization will be governed by contracts. Waiting until the last minute to involve the legal department is a mistake.
Decision-makers on target side	Managers in the target organization will have to make key project decisions. In agile development, particularly Scrum, the "product owner" is the target-side representative entrusted with acceptance or rejection decisions for successive project deliverables.
Customers' customers	Particularly for bespoke projects, you may need to go to a second level of "users"; for example, if you build a reservation system for an airline, the airline's customers are also potential stakeholders.
Labor unions	Official employee representatives may need to be consulted if the system will affect people's work conditions.

Now stakeholders on the production side (the organization that builds the system):

Stakeholders on the production (development) side	
Stakeholders	**Comments**
Project manager(s)	The person or persons directing the development.
Testers	There is a close connection between requirements and tests, since a key goal of tests (specifically, of *acceptance* tests) is to ascertain conformance of an implementation to the requirements. Testers can be involved in particular to ensure that the requirements are *verifiable*, one of the quality attributes for requirements (4.12).
Documenters	Another close connection exists with documentation. One of the characteristics of good requirements is that it will be easy to turn them into user manuals. It is beneficial to involve people who will be responsible for the documentation.
Trainers	If the future system will require training, the people in charge of it are potential stakeholders, just as documenters are.
HCI experts	Experts in Human-Computer Interface, a field also known as *ergonomics*, are responsible for the quality of user interfaces (UIs, part of the more general concept of User Experience or UX). Requirements generally should not specify all UI details, but HCI experts can help ensure that they support the inclusion of a high-quality user interface, conforming to any UI standards defined by the target organization.
Developers	Requirements will have to be implemented. While they should remain *abstract*, that is to say, not influenced by premature implementation decisions, they should also be *feasible*. (These two properties will be among the criteria for assessing the quality of requirements, respectively 4.7 and 4.6.) Involving representatives of the development group — without letting them bias the requirements through implementation considerations — is important to avoid pie-in-the-sky system requirements that cannot easily be implemented.
Open-source community (for open-source project)	If the project is open-source, the developer community, which may include a mix of paid developers and volunteers, is an important potential source of input.

What should you retain from this long list of possible stakeholders? It should not
scare you into believing that your project will be doomed unless you have talked to
representatives of all the categories. Not every project needs to consult everyone.
Having a checklist of potentially relevant stakeholders simply helps you avoid forgetting some
important ones, then regretting it. This rule will appear as the Stakeholders Principle (2.2.1).

The discussion of requirements elicitation in chapter 6 discusses stakeholders further. See
in particular "Assessing stakeholders", 6.5, page 109, which introduces the notion of a "stakeholder map" for classifying stakeholders in terms of both their influence and their availability.

1.10.2 Who produces requirements?

More relevant than the distinction between "business analysis" and "requirements engineering"
(1.2.5) is a distinction addressing the human aspect. Who will write the requirements? Two categories of professionals are involved:

- **Business analysts** (abbreviated into "**BAs**" and also called *requirements engineers* depending on the application area) are requirements professionals, conversant with requirements
  principles and practices as discussed in this Handbook. They know how to produce quality
  requirements, but are generally not experts in a particular project's application domain (such
  as accounting, flight control, text processing...).
- **Subject-Matter Experts** ("**SMEs**"), also called "domain experts", are the ones with the
  domain knowledge (accountants, aviation engineers, publishing professionals...).

These functions are complementary. You generally will not find people with professional com-
petence in both: requirements engineering, a technical IT skill, the privilege of requirements
engineers; and a specific application domain, the prerogative of SMEs.

The profiles are typically very different. (The only significant exception is the case of a
pure-software-engineering project, such as a Web browser, a search engine, a compiler or an
operating system, for which the domain experts are software professionals.)

While SMEs are indispensable — without application domain expertise, you will not get a
satisfactory system — not all projects have a distinct requirements engineering or business
analysis staff. While larger ones usually do, sometimes the role is simply fulfilled by developers; typically not those who are just focused on implementation ("coders"), but team members
who are experienced enough to handle system-level tasks such as design and requirements.

Regardless of such *personnel* decisions, requirements engineering remains a distinct,
clearly defined *role*. This Handbook refers throughout to requirements engineers as the people
who, regardless of their job title, apply requirements engineering techniques to turn information provided by SMEs (and other sources discussed in section 6.3) into effective requirements.

Taking a more prescriptive tack, the discussion of the "Requirements Leadership
Principle", page 28, will explain that requirements engineers should take the lead in
the preparation of requirements documents. To make the process succeed, it is essential to establish a fruitful collaboration between requirements engineers and SMEs. Section 6.6
will provide guidance.

1.11 WHY PERFORM REQUIREMENTS?

It should be clear by now that the purpose of performing requirements extends beyond the simplistic notion of "specifying what the system should do". As a conclusion to this introductory chapter, here is a list of the benefits of performing requirements analysis. It is applicable to a requirements process of any kind: partial or exhaustive; light-touch or extensive; and (chapter 12) "upfront" or "agile".

Goals of performing requirements	
Goal	**Comment**
Understand the organization's goals	All actors in the project should keep in mind what the business objectives are, underlying all project decisions. The Goals book (see 3.4) collects them.
Understand the problem to be addressed by the system	What actual issues is the project meant to address?
Help plan the project	One of the outcomes of requirements is to help organize the project. (It will yield the Project book, 3.7.)
Prompt relevant questions about the problem, environment, goals and system	One benefit of studying requirements is to make sure that important questions about the future system (and the goals, environment and project) do not remain overlooked.
Provide basis for answering questions about the problem, environment, goals and system	Asking questions (the previous point) is good; answering them is better!
Decide what the system should do	This task corresponds to the traditional view of requirements. (It will yield the System book, 3.6.)
Decide what the system should not do	Just as important is the *delimitation* of the system's functions and scope. Good requirements make sure to define where the scope of the future system stops, and what problems it is *not* expected to address.
Ascertain that the system will satisfy the needs of its stakeholders	Every system is ultimately built for people. We have seen (1.10.1) a first list of the potential stakeholders. With a process leading to explicit requirements, stakeholders' representatives will be able to examine them and detect any mismatch with actual needs.
Understand fundamental environment properties	What are the constraints on the system? How will the system affect the business or physical environment? The Environment book (3.5) will collect this information.

Provide a basis for the development	The requirements — whether produced all upfront, as-you-go, or (more appropriately) in some combination of these modes — will provide the key reference for the design and implementation tasks.
Provide a basis for verification ("*Verification*" is an abbreviation; see "Terminology note" below.)	Being expressed in terms of stakeholder needs and environment properties, rather than implementation, requirements are the ideal reference for assessing the fitness of the system (once it exists) to its objectives. Again this observation applies both to a traditional "Waterfall" model (performing verification at the end) and to a more modern continuous verification process.
Provide a basis for evolution	No released system remains unchanged forever. While inevitable, evolution should proceed in a smooth and orderly way. Requirements — especially if continuously updated per the "Requirements Evolution Principle", page 23 in the next chapter — provide the right basis for controlled evolution.

All the listed benefits are important, but "*prompt relevant questions*" is highlighted because its essential role is not always recognized. One of the biggest sources of poor quality in software systems is the failure to ask the right questions at the right time — meaning by an analyst during requirements rather than by a programmer during development. This observation underlies one of the principles of the next chapter: "Requirements Questions Principle", page 22.

1-E EXERCISES

1-E.1 Silence and noise

A document prepared by Bettina Bair for a requirements course [Bair 2005] presents a sample requirements document covering a web-based sales system for a fictitious company. Imagine you are in the team tasked with implementing these requirements. Relying on your informal understanding of the problem domain, identify any cases of (A) silence (B) in this document.

1-E.2 Classifying elements of a requirements document

(Project exercise.) Consider again the sample requirements document in [Bair 2005]. Classify every sentence of that document into one of the categories of the table on page 7. In case of doubt, explain the reason for hesitating and the rationale for your final choice.

1-E.3 Constraints and assumptions

Give more examples of constraints and assumptions (1.7.1 to 1.7.4), from application domains of your choice. Explain your rationale for classifying each example as a constraint or an assumption.

BIBLIOGRAPHICAL NOTES AND FURTHER READING

The classification of requirements in sections 1.4 to 1.9 is based on [Meyer et al. 2019].

Many definitions of requirements still rely on the partial view that requirements specify stakeholder needs. For example a presentation of BABOK (see below), [Brennan 2015], defines "requirement" as "a usable representation of a need". Among the PEGS, such a view can cover Goals and System, but excludes the Project and especially Environment parts. That view was dominant in the early days of software engineering but was corrected by the seminal work of Pamela Zave and Michael Jackson, extended by Axel Van Lamsweerde. (The references appear in the bibliography section of the Preface on pages xv-xv.) Jackson and Zave explained that it is essential to distinguish between two kinds of properties:

- Properties of the part of the world (human processes in the case of business systems, physical laws and existing devices in the case of embedded, real-time and cyber-physical systems). They will be specified by *environment* requirements.

- Properties of the system under construction, specified by *system* requirements.

A key difference — see "Distinguishing system and environment", 1.1.2, page 2 — is that the developers of the system have control on properties of the second kind, through design and implementation decisions, but not on those of the first kind. (The Jackson and Zave papers originally used "*domain*" for environment and "*machine*" for system.)

[Rubens 2007] is a discussion of the nuances (see 1.2.5) between "requirements engineering" and "business analysis".

IIBA, the International Institute of Business Analysis, publishes the Business Analysis Book Of Knowledge or BABOK; the BABOK Guide version 3, from 2015, can be obtained from [IIBA 2004-2022]. An older version is available for download at [IIBA 2006]. An IIBA document on version 3 [Brennan 2015] defines business analysis as the combination of several interacting tasks: Business Analysis Planning and Monitoring; Strategy Analysis; Requirements Analysis and Design Definition; Requirements Life Cycle Management; Elicitation and Collaboration; Solution Evaluation. BABOK itself identifies 6 "core concepts" of business analysis: Needs, Solutions, Changes, Stakeholders, Value, and Contexts. (Note that the last one recognizes the role of the Environment part.) Inspired by CMMI (see the bibliographical notes to chapter 12, on page 227), BABOK version 3 defines business analysis techniques, a staggering 65 of them: 50 "general" and 15 "specific" techniques. Examples of general techniques are Concept Modeling, Data Mining, Prioritization, Risk Analysis and Management (see section 6.11.7 of this Handbook), prioritization (4.13 and 6.10.5) and Workshops (6.9). BABOK has the typical traits of an extensive standard document of several hundred pages produced by a large committee: in its effort to integrate many different viewpoints and not leave out any potentially valuable idea, it can be overwhelming; but it is useful as a exhaustive reference defining a compendium of techniques that various members of the industry have found beneficial to business analysis.

[Berry 1995] discusses the roles of requirements engineers (business analysts) versus Subject-Matter Experts (see "Who produces requirements?", 1.10.2, page 16), provocatively arguing that for requirements engineers *ignorance* of the target area is beneficial, since it prompts them to ask many important questions. (See the further discussion of this idea in a later chapter of this Handbook: "Uncover the unsaid", 6.10.1, page 118.)

On non-functional requirements, a reference is the work of John Mylopoulos and his colleagues; see in particular [Chung et al. 2000].

Planguage [Gilb 2005-2022] is one of the few approaches to requirements that gives a significant role to the Project part.

The list of reasons for performing a requirements process in 1.11 is updated and expanded from [Meyer 1997].

TERMINOLOGY NOTE: VERIFICATION AND VALIDATION

The software engineering literature often distinguishes between the "verification" and "validation" of a software artifact (such as program code, documentation, design) and uses the acronym "V&V" to refer to their combination. The distinction is that:

- Verification is internal: it ascertains that an artifact has, by itself, been built properly. A program, for example, should not produce arithmetic or memory overflows (which are undesirable — in fact, catastrophic — regardless of the purpose of the program). Documentation should be clear. Any failed test case should be retained in a non-regression test suite.

- Validation is external: it assesses that the artifact satisfies its purpose. The results produced by a program should be the correct ones. Documentation should accurately describe how the system functions. Tests should cover essential functions.

The difference is sometimes described as "*doing things right*" versus "*doing the right thing*".

Complicating the matter, different communities of the IT world use different conventions:

- In the software industry, "verification" most commonly denotes *testing* (performing V&V by executing a program on sample inputs and checking the results against expectations).

- In contrast, the programming research community tends to reserve "verification" for approaches to *proving* the correctness of programs. (While testing is dynamic, proofs are static techniques, meaning that they analyze the text of a program but do not execute it.)

Most comments about either verification or validation in this Handbook do not prejudge techniques (static or dynamic) and apply to both of the "Vs" of the traditional textbook distinction. For simplicity (and to avoid the repeated use of an acronym), **the text uses "verification" as an abbreviation for "verification and validation".**

A particular case is the verification of requirements themselves, covered in chapters 4 and 11 in connection with the concept of requirements quality. Here too the term encompasses both "Vs", since some of the quality criteria defined in those chapters ("consistent", "readable", "delimited"…) specify that the requirements should be by themselves of good quality, and others ("justified", "endorsed", "complete"…) that they should reflect organizational goals.

2

Requirements: general principles

The experience accumulated over decades of software engineering progress leads to a number of principles which hold the key to successful requirements. The present chapter introduces general principles; others pertaining to specific aspects of requirements appear in later chapters.

2.1 WHAT ROLE FOR REQUIREMENTS?

A first set of principles address the role of requirements in the software process: the need for requirements, their nature, their evolution, their form.

2.1.1 The need for requirements

Requirements Principle
Any successful project must involve a requirements effort.

As a reader of this Handbook having made it all the way to page 21, you probably do not need to be told that requirements matter. But the Requirements Principle is an opportunity to remind ourselves and others of some of the most important reasons *why* they matter, listed in the last section (1.11) of the preceding chapter.

The need for requirements arises **regardless of the development method**. Requirements are one of the tasks of the "software lifecycle", the succession of activities during a project. Numerous lifecycle models exist, discussed later in this chapter and in more detail in chapter 12:

- **"Waterfall"**: apply a fixed succession of tasks such as requirements, design, implementation and verification to the entire system. (As will be seen below, this model is almost never exactly applied in practice but is a useful pedagogical concept.)
- **"Agile"**: develop the system through short successive increments of functionality, called "sprints". (See the bibliographical section and chapter 12 for an overview of agile concepts.)
- And many others in-between and beyond.

The precise form of the "requirements effort" mentioned in the principle can vary, for example with a dedicated requirements phase early in the project in the Waterfall model, and the production of "user stories" in agile sprints; but the imperative of recognizing requirements as a separate task is one of the universals of software engineering.

© The Author(s), under exclusive license to Springer Nature Switzerland AG 2022
B. Meyer, *Handbook of Requirements and Business Analysis*, https://doi.org/10.1007/978-3-031-06739-6_2

2.1.2 The role of requirements

> **Requirements Questions Principle**
>
> Take advantage of the requirements process to ensure that important questions about the Project, Environment, Goals and System are raised and addressed at the proper time.

The underlying idea was already emphasized as one of the benefits of performing requirements ("*Prompt relevant questions*", page 17). Any project raises requirements questions of importance to stakeholders. Such questions may involve properties of the project, environment, goals or system. Examples in each of these respective categories are:

- When is the latest acceptable date for deploying the first version?
- What are the criteria for finding that a bank account is overdrawn?
- What are the criteria for suspecting that a customer is abusing the product-return process?
- How long will a "deleted" file remain available for restoring?

Sometime during the project, somewhere in the team, someone will have to answer such questions. At worst, the time will be implementation, the place will be the programming team, and the answerer will be a programmer. That worst-case solution is inadequate: programmers are influenced by implementation concerns and generally do not have the necessary information (domain experts and affected stakeholders do).

To avoid harmful requirements mistakes, the project must recognize the need for a requirements process. This need exists *regardless of the development method and model*.

2.1.3 The nature of requirements

> **Requirements Nature Principle**
>
> Requirements are software.

What is "software"? A narrow view confines the term to just program elements, also known as just "code", which have the following properties:

- Code describes a *computation*, to be executed by a computing device.
- Code is written by *people*. (Or, in some cases, generated by other code, including artificial intelligence tools, but still traceable directly or indirectly to human authors.)
- Code is expressed in a *precise notation*, as precise as mathematical notations.
- Code can be *combined* with other elements, up to amazingly high degrees of *complexity*.
- Code is subject to *change* (in part because it reflects human processes and human understanding of natural processes). Not for nothing does the name start with "soft".
- Code *interacts* with other elements, possibly many of them.
- Particularly because of the preceding two properties, code is subject to systematic recording of its content, properties and evolution in a database of software elements, a process known as *configuration management*.

- Code should satisfy correctness and other *quality* criteria.
- As a consequence, code is subject to *verification* (including validation, see page 20).

Remarkably, only the first feature (executability) is specific to code (*program* elements). All the others also characterize non-program artifacts of the software process, such as test cases, test plans, design specifications, design diagrams and many others. They are all software.

The Requirements Nature Principle tells us that requirements belong here too. Considering requirements as software has many consequences, which will recur throughout this Handbook, beginning with the next principle.

2.1.4 The evolution of requirements

> ### Requirements Evolution Principle
> Requirements are a living asset of any project, subject to evolution. They must be adapted and kept up to date throughout the project.

You should understand this principle in light of the traditional pedagogical device known as the "Waterfall model" for discussing the software lifecycle, which looks something like the following (the exact distribution of phases varies, but the general idea remains):

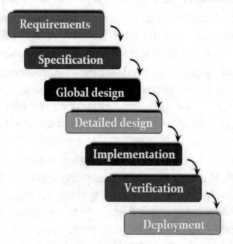

A waterfall model of the software lifecycle

Software development in this theoretical view is a fixed set of steps proceeding in sequence on the entire system, each to be completed before the next one starts and serving as the basis for it. "Requirements" is always one of the steps, usually the first as in the diagram (sometimes a "Feasibility study" step precedes it). The implication is that the requirements are frozen then and there; they serve as the definitive basis for design, implementation and verification.

The role of the Waterfall model is often misunderstood. No one in his right mind would recommend developing a significant system this way, and no project uses it in practice, since it is too rigid. The Waterfall is a *pedagogical* abstraction defining one end of a spectrum of development models, a strictly sequential variant; the other end is a completely unstructured process ("code first, think later"). Any successful software development model lies in-between these extremes, at good distance from both.

The Waterfall model also serves as a rhetorical device: if you are promoting your own development model, you can use the Waterfall as a foil. Because of its rigidity and impracticality, it will make almost any other approach shine in contrast. Proponents of agile methods have made ample use of that device, using the Waterfall as a strawman. (The agile lifecycle model involves successive increments of functionality called *sprints*, and will be studied in 12.4.)

The Requirements Evolution Principle rejects the naïve Waterfall idea of devoting a lifecycle step to the production of a requirements document that will thereafter remain frozen forever. Changes will occur, affecting all four elements of requirements:

- The project: just as no battle plan survives the first contact with the enemy, so does the best project plan face personnel changes and unforeseen events, both favorable and not.

- The environment: if human aspects are involved, as in the case of a business system, new regulations may appear, policies may evolve, companies may merge. For a cyber-physical system, although the laws of nature will not change over the duration of the project, engineering constraints, such as available hardware and bandwidth, may evolve.

- The goals: companies and stakeholders' policies and priorities fluctuate.

- The system: even the most careful analysis can fail to identify important functionality. Even for functionality correctly identified from the start, new ideas will pop up over time as a result of further thinking and of lessons drawn from initial implementation attempts.

The Requirements Evolution Principle enjoins us to treat the requirements as a living product. It is in line with the preceding principle, Requirements Nature, which told us that requirements are software: it is indeed a characteristic of software elements of any kind that they should be subject to change ("soft"). Projects cannot avoid change, but they can ensure that change is controlled, disciplined and orderly.

The strongest justification for the Requirements Evolution Principle is consideration of what happens if it is *not* followed. Pretending that the requirements are fixed, in the face of inevitable updates to the project, environment, goals and system, consigns the requirements to withering and oblivion. Once the developers find that *some* of the requirements elements are out of sync, developers cease to pay attention to *all* documented requirements, including the ones that are still relevant. Not only is the requirements effort wasted; ignorance of its valid elements can lead to bad project decisions and even disaster.

One such disaster is famous in the annals of software engineering. The 1996 loss of the Ariane 5 rocket launcher of the European Space Agency was traced to the code's failure to take into account a change to the environment (from Ariane 4): an extension to the allowed numerical range for an engineering parameter, the vehicle's "inertial bias". That change had been documented, but the implementation team missed it.

The Requirements Evolution Principle leads to the next principle, which expresses the need for both writing down requirements at project inception and updating them afterwards.

2.1.5 The place of requirements in the project lifecycle

Requirements Elaboration Principle

Produce an initial version of the requirements at the start of the project.
Update and extend these requirements throughout the project.

The role of this principle is to remove a spurious dilemma between:

- An exaggerated *Waterfall* view, considering that it suffices to produce early on a requirements document which becomes an immutable prescription for the rest of the project.

- An exaggerated *agile* view, considering that upfront requirements are useless: just start coding, and requirements will pop up on the fly as user stories implemented right away.

Both views are common, albeit in different communities; both are harmful. In their non-exaggerated variants, "upfront" and "continuous" forms of requirements are equally justified and equally necessary:

- Whatever naïve agilists might tell you, do take the time to write requirements upfront. Too many projects have failed because they neglected to include such an initial effort at understanding and documenting the key characteristics of the project, environment, system and goals, prior to any attempt at implementation.

- Whatever naïve traditionalists might tell you, do not treat the requirements as a sacred text, impervious to any changes after its initial approval. Treat them as a living asset of the project, always useful but always subject to updating.

The two forms complement rather than contradict each other. The Requirements Evolution Principle resolves any appearance of conflict by enjoining you both to:

- Devote sufficient effort upfront to produce a first version, good enough to start.

- Update the result constantly as more information is gained.

"Sufficient effort" means sufficient to produce a first version of the requirements, usually not complete but making it possible to get started.

The mark of a successful requirements process, and of the professional requirements engineer, is to strike the right balance between too little and too much upfront requirements work:

- Spend too little effort on upfront requirements, and you end up leaving aside key decisions that will come up during the implementation process, under the control of programmers, with the disadvantages mentioned above (2.1.1).

- Spend too much effort, and you get into "analysis paralysis", agonizing over every detail of a future system at the expense of actually building it.

2.1.6 The form of requirements

> ### Requirements Repository Principle
> Make requirements and all elements that provide requirements-relevant information available through a repository.
> Treat the repository as one of the key resources of the project; keep it up to date.

"Repository" is the accepted term for a database containing software elements (rather than a general database that may host data of any kind). Repositories support configuration management (the tracking of successive versions of every element, and retrieval of earlier versions.) GitHub repositories are among the most widely used.

To understand the scope of the Requirements Repository Principle, one should assess it against the older view that the requirements task in software engineering is all about producing a *requirements document*. This term appears only episodically in this Handbook because many modern projects cannot satisfy themselves with a single linear document. Among the reasons:

- Complex projects have several parts, each of which may need its own requirements specification, not necessarily easy to consolidate into a single document.

- It is often unrealistic to expect one document to encompass all requirements information. When a requirements document exists, it is seldom the sole source of knowledge about the project; relevant elements may appear in PowerPoint presentations, emails, Slack channels, Zoom session recordings and other places. Environment properties may come from external sources such as government regulations (for a business project) and scientific textbooks (for a cyber-physical project).

- Innovative approaches such as seamless development (8.7.8, 12.6) suggest, as part of quality policies, including as much as possible of the requirements information in the final code itself rather than as separate documents.

As we will see in the discussion of requirements quality ("Traceable", 4.8), one of the key quality factors is traceability, the ability to follow both the sources and consequences of requirements throughout the development. A frequent obstacle to traceability is the loss of "pre-requirements" information: communication that happened before the project officially started. Along with including the actual requirements as they get developed, the requirements repository should as much as possible record these pre-requirements elements.

What about the requirements document proper? In their standard form presented in the next chapter, the requirements are dispatched among four *books* corresponding to the four PEGS: Project, Environment, Goals and System. These books are themselves not necessarily linear but can be collections of elements from the repository. If a single linear document is required — imposed perhaps by company standards or regulatory agencies — software tools can help generate it from the contents of the four books and the repository.

2.1.7 Outcomes of requirements

Minimum Requirements Outcome Principle

The requirements effort must always produce the following elements.

For the **Goals**:
- Key business objectives (G.1).
- Key expected benefits (G.3).
- Key stakeholders (G.7).

For the **System**:
- Key functions (S.2).
- Overall division into clusters (S.1).

For the **Environment**:
- Key external constraints on the system (E.3).

For the **Project**:
- As essential guidance for the rest of the project: main tasks (P.4).
- Also as part of this guidance: main milestones (P.5).

The numbers in parentheses refer, in anticipation of the next chapter, to the corresponding parts in the Standard Plan for requirements.

The full scope and content of requirements — encompassed by the full Standard Plan — are much broader. Here we are talking about the minimum expectation from a requirements effort. You should particularly take it into consideration in a project whose sponsors impose strict agile tenets; the kind of person who cringes at the suggestion of any "upfront" activities such as requirements. Agility is good, but per the Requirements Elaboration Principle, it is unprofessional and harmful to reject upfront requirements entirely. You can use the Minimum Requirements Outcome to insist on the core upfront requirements elements which, agile dogma or not, should not be compromised. Producing these elements is not going to be a huge task (no "analysis paralysis" will result), but not producing them puts the project at risk:

- On the Project side, it would be unconscionable to skip the identification of key stakeholders, or the definition of a rough project plan (a guide for the rest of the project, not attempting perfect prediction), or an outline of the verification plan, particularly the test plan.

- On the Environment side, if the development team is not aware of key constraints, they may waste time and resources developing useless solutions.

- On the Goals side, unless everyone involved is aware of the key benefits that the organization expects from the system, the project risks spending its efforts on the wrong priorities.

- On the System side, it makes no sense to start out without stating the system's basic functionality and its division into major components. "Clusters" are the main parts of a system (such as a user interface cluster, a data management cluster, a logic cluster); the concepts are discussed in a later chapter ("The Cluster model", 12.5, page 217).

One element of the Minimum Requirements Outcome Principle deserves emphasis as part of any checklist of sound software project practices:

User Acceptance Test Principle
Use the requirements as the basis for the User Acceptance Test plan.

Rather than defining an independent rule, this principle repeats part of the previous one (in its Project component). It would be a mistake to wait until after development to think about user acceptance tests (often called UAT), which can be largely defined from the requirements.

2.2 HUMAN ASPECTS

The second set of principles identify the actors of the requirements process. They come directly from the discussion of human aspects in the preceding chapter: "The people behind requirements", 1.10.

2.2.1 Stakeholders

Stakeholders Principle
Identify all stakeholders whose non-involvement might imperil the project; involve them.

The preceding chapter gave guidance on how to identify stakeholders: see the definition of the concept ("Stakeholders", 1.1.4) and the list of typical stakeholders ("Categories of stakeholders", 1.10.1). The risk of not following the principle is to build a system without having identified in advance its impact on important groups of people. Much trouble can be avoided by recognizing that impact early, rather than experiencing a backlash after deployment.

Agile methods put the focus on "customers", either through the notion of a "customer representative" embedded in the development team or, in Scrum, by having a "product owner" in charge of making acceptance decisions after each sprint. These roles can be important, but there is no guarantee that one person can adequately represent the variety of perspectives that exist within an organization; they are not a substitute for the task of identifying all important stakeholders. (It is in fact one of the roles of the product owner to *arbitrate* between such views.) It will also be important to *assess* the relative importance of various stakeholders (6.5, page 109).

2.2.2 Authors

Requirements Leadership Principle
For all but small projects, requirements engineers (or business analysts) should lead the process of producing requirements.

In the preceding chapter, the section entitled "Who produces requirements?", 1.10.2, page 16, presented the two principal stakeholder roles associated with producing requirements: requirements engineers (or business analysts) and Subject-Matter Experts. They are equally important.

For small projects it does not really matter who writes the requirements, but for a significant project with representatives of both sides the requirements engineers should be responsible for writing the requirements. There are two reasons behind this rule:

- The obvious reason: requirements engineers know how to conduct a fruitful requirements process and produce quality requirements. SMEs know about their own business area.

- Perhaps less obviously, the risk that SMEs, being by their very qualifications versed in the current way of doing business, might (if left to their own devices) specify a system that simply reproduces old practices, including practices that are no longer justified in the new context. Requirements engineers, coming in with a different perspective and equipped with the experience of diverse projects, are less subject to the *"this is how we have always done things around here"* syndrome and may have a better shot at devising innovative solutions.

The Requirements Leadership Principle only suggests who should *lead* the requirements effort. Carrying out that effort requires the cooperation of both groups. With requirements engineers only, the risk would be the converse of the one just listed: that requirements engineers apply one-size-fits-all recipes that do not take account of the specifics of the organization and project. SMEs bring the indispensable specific expertise. But requirements professionals should have the final responsibility.

2.3 REQUIREMENTS ELICITATION AND PRODUCTION

> **Environment Principle**
> Distinguish between system and environment properties.

This principle follows up on an introductory discussion in the previous chapter, "Distinguishing system and environment", 1.1.2, page 2, which explained the difference between system and environment properties and the risk of confusing them. System properties are those under the control of the project; environment properties are beyond its reach, but fundamentally affect it.

In a software development project, you can decide (for an autonomous driving system) when to start slowing down automatically in response to posted speed limits, but you do not get to define the speed limits. You can decide (for an accounting system) the process for reporting income, but you do not get to define the tax rules.

Failure to distinguish clearly between the two kinds is a major source of confusion and actual errors in system development.

2.4 REQUIREMENTS MANAGEMENT

Traceability Principle

Throughout the project:

(T1) Record all the consequences of the requirements on the project and system.

(T2) Record the requirements sources of project and system elements.

The two parts correspond to tracking in two opposite directions: from requirements to their consequences in T1, from project and system elements to the relevant requirements in T2.

A more dogmatic version of the principle would state:

- *(T'1) Every element of implementation must relate to at least one element of requirements.*

- *(T'2) Every element of requirements must affect at least one element of implementation.*

We may call it the Perfect Traceability Principle. The rationale for it, assuming an ideal process, is strong:

- In theory, every requirements element must have some consequence in the system; otherwise it is just *noise* (1.9, page 12) and should be removed.

- In that same idealistic view, any element of the system — in particular, of the code — should follow directly or indirectly from some requirement. Think about it: the lowliest instruction in the code, say an assignment $i := i + 1$, only exists because it participates (even if at the end of a long chain of consequences) in the realization of something expressed somewhere in the requirements. Otherwise, what is it doing there?

This "Perfect" version of the Traceability principle, however, assumes that requirements are exhaustive. In practice, they usually will not be, but that is not a reason to discard the crucial concept of traceability. Hence the actual version of the Traceability Principle, which more pragmatically enjoins us to ensure as much traceability as possible:

- Forward traceability: tracking the consequences of every element of the requirements.

- Backward traceability: tracking the rationale for elements of the system and project, to check that they are not arbitrary but related to some element of the requirements.

We should, in particular, be on the look out for both:

- "Orphan" requirements, not having any visible consequence in the project and system.

- "Stray" functions in the system, not having any visible source in the requirements. They may be a sign of "creeping featurism" (also known as "scope creep"): gratuitous functionality being added for its own sake rather than as a response to actual stakeholder needs.

Traceability is ideally supported by tools, and is further discussed in the chapter on requirements quality, where it figures as one of the principal factors ("Traceable", 4.8, page 61).

2.5 REQUIREMENTS QUALITY

> **Requirements Effort Principle**
>
> Devote enough effort to guarantee requirements quality, but not so much as to detract from other tasks of the software development process.

This principle (which could also be called "Principle of Relativity", but a Web search suggests that the name may already be taken) puts in perspective all the requirements advice in the present chapter and other prescriptive parts of this Handbook.

There is no paradox here. Of course requirements quality matters, and the prescriptions that run throughout this Handbook are all focused on making you devote to requirements the attention and effort they deserve. But there is more to software engineering than requirements engineering, and more to software quality than requirements quality. The purpose of a software project is not to produce good requirements. The purpose of a project is to produce a good system. Quality in requirements only matters to the extent that it helps attain quality for the system.

For requirements, then, perfection is not the goal. The goal is good-enough quality, sufficient to obtain quality for the project and system as a whole without spending so much effort on the requirements ("*analysis paralysis*") as to detract from other tasks.

This observation is in line with an earlier principle: Requirements Evolution (2.1.4), which told us that we should reject two equally extreme opposite views, frozen upfront requirements ("Waterfall") and requirements-on-the-go ("agile"). We must have enough upfront material to start, but not so much as to cause analysis paralysis; and we should be prepared to extend and update them as the project unfolds. Similarly, we need to expend enough effort to obtain quality requirements, which the rest of the project needs, but not to the detriment of other factors of overall software quality.

Another example in the same spirit as the Requirements Effort principle is the previous principle, Traceability, which — instead of its "Perfect" version of 100% forward and backward traceability between requirements and (among others) code — retains a more pragmatic advice of carefully monitoring the relationship, both ways.

The good news is that the saying "quality is free" holds for much of the advice in this Handbook. Once you understand the principles, following the rules is a matter of professionalism and reason. Apply all the advice in the present chapter and subsequent ones, and remember to "leave good-enough alone" when exaggerated effort on the quality of the requirements would, in the end, damage the quality of the project and system they are intended to support.

2.6 OTHER PRINCIPLES

The present chapter has listed a number of general requirement principles. For completeness, here is the list of more specific — but equally important — principles which appear in the discussion of their respective areas of application in subsequent chapters of this Handbook:

- "Requirements Abstraction Principle", page 59: make requirements descriptive, rather than prescribing specific design or implementation choices.

- "Requirements Writing Principle", page 72: write requirements as you discover them.

- "No-Synonym Principle", page 74: call one thing by one name.

- "No-Repetition Principle", page 76: specify every requirement only once.

- "Reference Principle", page 76: use reference rather than repetition.

- "Explanation Principle", page 78: favor specifying over explaining, and mark explanations clearly as such.

- "Picture Principle", page 82: make sure every element of a graphical illustration has a clearly specified meaning.

- "Multiple Notation Principle", page 84: make sure that specifications in different notations complement (rather than repeat or contradict) each other.

- "Identification Principle", page 90: equip every requirements element with a unique ID.

- "TBD rule", page 92: observe strict practices for "To Be Determined" elements

- "Glossary Principle", page 107: provide definitions of all specific terms and acronyms.

- "Acronym Principle", page 109: in the glossary entry for an acronym, do not just give the expansion but also explain the concept.

- "Elicitation Coverage Principle", page 118: in requirements elicitation, cover all four PEGS.

- "Feasibility Prototype Principle", page 124: try out critically needed technology on a small scale to discover possible roadblocks early.

- "Prototype Principle", page 125: when using requirements prototypes, avoid raising any unwarranted expectations.

- "Scenario Principle", page 136: rely on use cases and user stories as help towards requirements elicitation and verification, not as requirements themselves.

- "Command-Query Completeness Principle", page 209: make sure that the System description determines the effect of every operation on every property of the affected objects.

- "Not-All-Sprints-Are-Created-Equal ("NASACE") Principle", page 222: even if project iterations have a uniform duration, adapt their composition to various phases of the project.

2-E EXERCISES

2-E.1 Limit cases

The Requirements Elaboration Principle (2.1.5) states that a successful requirements process results from a tradeoff between two extremes: requirements-upfront-only (Waterfall-style), and requirements-only-as-you-go (agile-style). Can you think of specific project types or circumstances in which the tradeoff should be strongly tilted towards one of these extreme variants? Give examples for both, and explain the rationale for your assessment.

2-E.2 Stakeholders

(This exercise refers to the Stakeholders Principle from 2.2.1.) A dating site is updating its software. Who are the stakeholders?

2-E.3 Requirements quality

In line with the Requirements Quality Principle (2.2.1), give examples (either abstract or based on your project experience) of cases in which it is necessary or at least legitimate to sacrifice requirements quality for the greater benefit of the final system's quality. Explain the rationale. To specify the aspects of requirements quality being sacrificed, you may refer to the analysis of requirements quality factors in chapter 4.

BIBLIOGRAPHICAL NOTES AND FURTHER READING

In this chapter and elsewhere in this Handbook, you will find references to **agile methods**, a set of approaches which in the last two decades have profoundly reshaped — mostly although not entirely for the better — how the industry produces software. The best known are *eXtreme Programming* (XP), which started the agile movement, and *Scrum*, which dominates it today. Instead of organizing the development into successive activities (requirements, design, implementation…) applied to an entire system, agile methods split it into "sprints" of a few weeks at most, each devoted to adding an increment of functionality all the way to full implementation. Agile development is, true to its name, more flexible than traditional development in some respects, but in others it is actually stricter; *timing constraints*, in particular, are non-negotiable. If a sprint runs out of time before having implemented all expected functionality, you never extend the sprint, but keep its fixed time slot; you then convene a "retrospective" meeting to decide whether to drop the missing functionality altogether or move it to subsequent sprints. A detailed study of agile methods is beyond the scope of this Handbook, which only covers them in relation to requirements (see "Rescuing Agile and DevOps", 12.4, page 215 in the last chapter).

Classic references on agility are [Beck 2005] on Extreme Programming, [Poppendieck 2010] on Lean Development and [Schwaber and Sutherland 2012] on Scrum. For a general tutorial on agile methods, see [Meyer 2014]; while much of the agile literature advocates the use of particular agile methods, this reference takes a neutral attitude and presents a critical analysis.

A 1970 article, [Royce 1970], introduced the Waterfall model (2.1.4) — by criticizing it.

One of the first references to promote an incremental approach to requirements (2.1.4, 2.1.5) is [Southwell et al. 1987], as cited in [Christel-Kang 1992].

[Jézéquel-Meyer 1997] analyzes the Ariane 5 software-induced disaster (page 24).

A classical article, [Gotel-Finkelstein 1994], showed that a key factor of requirements traceability is the need to keep track of what the authors call "pre-RS" (pre-Requirements-Specification) elements: information that was provided prior to the official start of a requirements process but has a strong influence on the requirements. This observation is one of the justifications for the Requirements Nature Principle (2.1.6).

3

Standard Plan for requirements

The concepts and principles of the previous two chapters lead to a division of the requirements into a "*Standard Plan*" made of four parts covering the four PEGS of requirements engineering. The present discussion explains what should appear in each of them.

To use the Standard Plan and its variants, you have access to free resources on this Handbook's web site including templates in major text-processing formats.

The reference for requirements documents has long been the structure outline defined in a 1998 IEEE standard, a response to the simpler needs of systems in another era. The present Standard Plan is a replacement, designed to meet the challenges of today's ambitious projects.

3.1 OVERALL STRUCTURE

We saw in 1.1.1 that requirements have four major dimensions or PEGS: Project, Environment, Goals, System. The Standard Plan correspondingly includes four *books*. Each book is divided into *chapters* (not to be confused with chapters of this Handbook), themselves made of *sections*. The table below gives the list of books and chapters, with the details coming next.

The four books of requirements	
Project (P)	**Goals (G)**
P.1 Roles and personnel	G.1 Context and overall objective
P.2 Imposed technical choices	G.2 Current situation
P.3 Schedule and milestones	G.3 Expected benefits
P.4 Tasks and deliverables	G.4 Functionality overview
P.5 Required technology elements	G.5 High-level usage scenarios
P.6 Risk and mitigation analysis	G.6 Limitations and exclusions
P.7 Requirements process and report	G.7 Stakeholders and requirements sources
Environment (E)	**System (S)**
E.1 Glossary	S.1 Components
E.2 Components	S.2 Functionality
E.3 Constraints	S.3 Interfaces
E.4 Assumptions	S.4 Detailed usage scenarios
E.5 Effects	S.5 Prioritization
E.6 Invariants	S.6 Verification and acceptance criteria

B. Meyer, *Handbook of Requirements and Business Analysis*, https://doi.org/10.1007/978-3-031-06739-6_3

3.2 FRONT AND BACK MATTER

The preceding standard structure covers the actual content of the books. Companies typically have specific practices regarding internal and external documents. For that reason, each book may include, in addition to the chapters listed on the previous page:

- Front matter, before the first chapter.
- Back matter, after the last chapter.

Typical *front matter* may include:

- Title of the book (usually occupying the entire first page, with the following elements typically making up the second page).
- A general reminder about the project, a mention that the current book is one of four covering that project, and references to the other three.
- Date of publication of first version and of current version; revision history.
- Table of contents and any other appropriate tables, such as a table of illustrations. (But not the glossary, which is part of the contents: chapter E.1.)
- Copyright notice, intellectual property, distribution information, restrictions on distribution.
- Approval information. (Some organizations require every document to be approved by authorized executives, and sometimes to include an actual signature. This practice has specific relevance to one of the requirements qualities: "Endorsed", 4.14, page 68.)

Some of these elements might instead appear in the *back matter*. Another typical back-matter element is an index. Front and back matter are *metarequirements* as defined in 1.9.4, page 13.The remainder of this discussion ignores front and back matter and focuses on the rest of the four requirements books, consisting of the chapters listed in the overall plan of 3.1.

3.3 USING THE PLAN

The following observations help understand the scope of the recommended plan and use it effectively in practice.

3.3.1 Forms of requirements conforming to the Standard Plan

The term "book" does not imply a traditional requirements process all focused on producing a linear "requirements document" (here with four parts). In accordance with the Requirements Repository Principle (page 26), requirements can consist of many elements, such as textual documents, PowerPoint slides, use cases, emails and others, as long as they are all recorded in a repository. The division into books means two things:

- Every such element should be marked as belonging to (exactly) **one of the chapters of the Standard Plan** as listed in the present discussion.
- It should be possible to obtain, for each book, a **linear form** — a single document, akin to a part of a traditional requirements document. If the actual requirements elements are scattered in various places accessible from a repository, **tools** can produce the linear form.

This Handbook's site provides templates (HTML, MS Word, LaTex…) for writing the linear forms directly, and tools to help produce linear forms from scattered elements.

3.3.2 Customizing the plan

Many organizations have specific requirements practices and recommendations. The plan is designed to support tailoring the requirements to such policies within a common framework:

- The first two levels, consisting of **books** (P, E, G, S) and **chapters** (P.1, P.2…, E.1 etc.) are universally applicable. That part of the structure should remain as given in 3.1.
- Starting with third-level **sections** (e.g. P.1.1), every organization can refine the structure to fit its specific requirements and software engineering practices.

3.3.3 Mutual references

The books may reference each other, but not arbitrarily. The following diagram shows which books may refer to which. (It only governs the chapters of substance, ignoring the front and back matter as introduced in 3.2.)

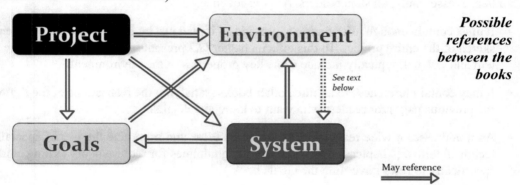

Possible references between the books

The rules and explanations are the following:

- The Project book may refer to all the others.
- The Environment book normally does not refer to the Goals and Project books, since the existing environment predates the project. (But all others may refer to it, as implied by the definition of "environment" at the onset of this Handbook in 1.1.1: *"the set of* [external] *entities* […] *with the potential to affect the goals, project or system or be affected by them"*.)
- The dotted downward arrow signals an exception to the preceding rule: the Environment book may refer to the System to describe possible changes to the environment's properties caused by the system. In a payroll system, for example, the environment defines payroll practices; but the system may by itself bring changes to the payroll process, requiring the Environment book to describe these changes. Such cases may appear only in chapters E.5 and E.6 ("effects" and "invariants") of the Environment book.
- The Goals book must be self-contained except for possible references to the Environment. It is indeed essential to explain the goals independently of how the Project plans to achieve them and how the System will meet them.

- The other way around, the descriptions of both Project and System will refer to the Goals.

- The System book must not refer to the Project book, since it is necessary to describe the system independently of when and how it will be developed.

- The other way around, the Project will reference components of the System, in particular as part of the development schedule and tasks (P.3, P.4).

The following sections give more details about the books, in the order Goals, Environment, System, Project.

3.4 THE GOALS BOOK

Goals are "*needs of the target organization, which the system will address*" (1.5). While the development team is the principal user of the other books, the Goals book addresses a wider audience: essentially, all stakeholders. As consequences:

- It must contain enough information to provide — if read just by itself — providing a general sketch of the entire project. To this effect, chapter G.3 presents a short overview of the system and G.1 will typically include some key properties of the environment.

- It may contain references to all three other books (satisfying the restrictions of the figure on the previous page) for readers who want to know the details.

- As it addresses a wide readership, it should be clear and minimize the use of specialized technical terms. (Chapter 5 is devoted to style guidelines for requirements writing, and 5.9 specifically to rules governing the Goals book.)

Here is the structure of the Goals book with an explanation of the role of each chapter:

Goals book (G)	
Chapter	**Contents**
Front matter	Control information (3.2).
G.1 Context and overall objective	High-level view of the project: organizational context and reason for building a system.
G.2 Current situation	Current state of processes to be addressed by the project and the resulting system.
G.3 Expected benefits	New processes, or improvement to existing processes, made possible by the project's results.
G.4 Functionality overview	Overview of the functions (behavior) of the system. Principal properties only (details are in the System book).

G.5 High-level usage scenarios	Fundamental usage paths through the system.
G.6 Limitations and exclusions	Aspects that the system need not address.
G.7 Stakeholders and requirements sources	Groups of people who can affect the project or be affected by it, and other places to consider for information about the project and system
Back matter	Control information (3.2).

Notes on the chapters of the Goals book:

- G.1 is a general introduction. It explains why the project is needed, recalls the business context, and presents the general business objectives. If the project's complexity requires a division into subprojects, that division should be stated here.

- G.2 describes the current situation, upon which the system is expected to improve.

- G.3 presents the business benefits expected from the successful execution of the project. This chapter is the core of the Goals book, describing what the organization expects from the system (hence its highlighting in the table).

  Together, G.1, G.2 and G.3 describe the rationale for the project. It is important to state these justifications explicitly. Typically, they are well understood at the start of the project, but management and priorities can change. Later on, executives may start questioning the project's value. Having a cogent writeup of its intended benefits can help save it from cancellation. Another use of these chapters, G.3 in particular, is to ensure that the project remains focused: if at some stage it gets pushed in different directions, with "creeping featurism" threatening its integrity, a reminder about the original business goals stated in those chapters will help.

- G.4 is a short overview of the functions of the future system, a kind of capsule version of book S, skipping details but enabling readers to get a quick grasp of what the system will do.

- G.5 presents the main scenarios (use cases) that the system should cover. The scenarios chosen for appearing here, in the Goals book, should only be the main usage patterns, without details such as special and erroneous cases; they should be stated in user terms only, independently of the system's structure. Detailed usage scenarios, taking into account system details and special cases, will appear in the System book, chapter S.4 (see below page 42).

- G.6 states what the system will *not* do. This chapter addresses a key quality attribute of good requirements, which we will see in 4.9: the requirements must be **delimited** (or "scoped"). G.6 is not, however, the place for an analysis of *risks* and obstacles, which pertain to the project rather than the goals and correspondingly appears in chapter P.6.

- G.7 lists stakeholders and other requirements sources. It should define stakeholders (1.1.4, 1.10.1) as categories of people, not individuals, even if such individuals are known at the time of writing; for example "company CEO" rather than the person's name. The main goal of chapter G.7 is to avoid forgetting any category of people whose input is relevant to the project.

To identify stakeholders, you should start from the detailed lists in "Categories of stakeholders", 1.10.1, page 13, which presents general categories applicable to many projects, on both the production and target sides. Starting from this common basis, every project may need its own customized list. See further discussions of stakeholders in chapter 6 of this Handbook.

Chapter G.7 also lists documents and other information that the project, aside from soliciting input from stakeholders, can consult for requirements information. Examples include: people who have relevant information (without being considered stakeholders of the project); documents predating the project, such as emails and minutes of meetings which discussed launching it; information about previous projects; documentation of existing systems in the marketplace pursuing similar goals; information about projects at competing organizations; industry standards; web sites providing background information. For a detailed discussion see "Sources other than stakeholders", 6.3, page 106.

3.5 THE ENVIRONMENT BOOK

The Environment book describes the application domain and external context, physical or virtual (or a mix), in which the system will operate.

Here is the structure of the Environment book:

Environment book (E)	
Chapter	**Contents**
Front matter	Control information (3.2).
E.1 Glossary	Clear and precise definitions of all the vocabulary specific to the application domain, including technical terms, words from ordinary language used in a special meaning, and acronyms.
E.2 Components	List of elements of the environment that may affect or be affected by the system and project. Includes other systems to which the system must be interfaced.
E.3 Constraints	Obligations and limits imposed on the project and system by the environment.
E.4 Assumptions	Properties of the environment that may be assumed, with the goal of facilitating the project and simplifying the system.
E.5 Effects	Elements and properties of the environment that the system will affect.
E.6 Invariants	Properties of the environment that the system's operation must preserve.
Back matter	Control information (3.2).

Notes on chapters of the Environment book:

- The glossary (E.1) introduces the terminology of the project; not just of the environment in the strict sense, but of all its parts. As discussed in a later chapter ("The glossary", 6.4, page 107), every organizational project has its own terminology, not always obvious to outsiders and in particular to developers; the glossary collects and defines the relevant terms.

- Chapter E.2 lists the elements of the environment that are relevant for the project and system. These components may include existing systems, particularly *software* systems, with which the system will interact — by using their APIs (program interfaces), or by providing APIs to them, or both. These are interfaces provided to the system *from* the outside world. They are distinct from both: interfaces provided by the system *to* the outside world (covered in S.3 in the System book); and technology elements that the system's development will require (covered in P.5 in the Project book).

- While all chapters are important, the table highlights E.3, Constraints, since this chapter defines non-negotiable restrictions coming from the environment (business rules, physical laws, engineering decisions), which the development will have to take into account. An example, in addition to those of 1.7, is the constraint that a system's user interface must accommodate screen resolutions as low as 1280 x 720 (HD) and as high as 3840 x 2160.

- E.4, Assumptions, defines properties that are not imposed by the environment (like those in E.3) but assumed to hold, as an explicit decision meant to facilitate the system's construction. An example, in addition to those of 1.7, is the assumption that available bandwidth (for a networked system) will be no less than 1 Gigabit per second. Another, to be compared with the preceding constraint example, is the assumption that the system *need not support* resolutions lower than 1280 x 720 or higher than 3840 x 2160. (A possibly risky assumption, especially the second part since screen technology evolves quickly, but one that may be necessary to enable prompt completion of the project.)

  If you ever hesitate between classifying a condition as a constraint or an assumption, go back to section 1.7.4, which gave practical criteria for deciding between these two cases.

- E.5 defines effects of the system's operations on properties of the environment. Where the previous two categories defined influences of the environment on the system, effects are influences in the reverse direction. 1.7 gave an example for a business system: the effect of a payroll system on the payroll process itself, such as changing the dates on which employees are paid. Another example, for an embedded system, is its maximum carbon footprint.

- E.6 defines invariants: properties of the environment that operations of the system may assume to hold when they start, and must maintain. In other words, influences in both directions. An example invariant for a train control system may be "doors must be closed whenever the train is moving". Any operation — for example, starting or stopping the train — may assume this property on inception, and it is also required to maintain it.

3.6 THE SYSTEM BOOK

Here is the overall structure of the System book:

System book (S)	
Chapter	**Contents**
Front matter	Control information (3.2).
S.1 Components	Overall structure expressed by the list of major software and, if applicable, hardware parts.
S.2 Functionality	One section, S.2.*n*, for each of the components identified in S.2, describing the corresponding behaviors (functional and non-functional properties).
S.3 Interfaces	How the system makes the functionality of S.2 available to the rest of the world, particularly *user* interfaces and *program* interfaces (APIs).
S.4 Detailed usage scenarios	Examples of interaction between the environment (or human users) and the system: use cases, user stories.
S.5 Prioritization	Classification of the behaviors, interfaces and scenarios (S.2, S.3 and S.4) by their degree of criticality.
S.6 Verification and acceptance criteria	Specification of the conditions under which an implementation will be deemed satisfactory.
Back matter	Control information (3.2).

Notes on chapters of the System book:

- S.1 lists the constituent parts of the system. Another term, which chapter 12 will use as part of the lifecycle discussion (see 12.5, page 217), is **clusters**. A cluster is a major subsystem. The cluster structure may be flat (for a simple system) or multi-level. For example, a web-based system may at the top level be split into "front-end" (Web interface) and "back-end", where the back-end has a data access cluster, a computation cluster and a business logic cluster.

- As the highlighting suggests, the bulk of the System book is typically chapter S.2, describing elements of functionality (behaviors). This chapter corresponds to the traditional view of requirements as defining "what the system does".

- Chapter S.3 specifies how that functionality will be made available to the rest of the world, including people (users) and other systems. These are interfaces provided by the system *to* the outside; the other way around, interfaces *from* other systems, which the system may use, are specified in E.2 in the Environment book (discussed in the comments part of 3.5 above.)

- S.4 describes typical usage scenarios, expressed for example as **use cases** or **user stories** (chapter 7 of this Handbook). Such scenarios are not by themselves a substitute for precise descriptions of functionality (S.3), but provide an important complement by specifying cases that these behavior descriptions must support; they also serve as a basis for developing test cases. The scenarios most relevant for stakeholders are given in chapter G.5 in the Goals book, at a general level; in contrast, S.4 can refer to system components and functionality (from other chapters of the System book) as well as special and erroneous cases, and introduce more specific scenarios.

- S.5 defines priorities, useful in particular if during the course of the project various pressures force the team to drop certain functions. Good requirements prioritize functionality, as discussed in "Prioritized", 4.13, page 67 and "Get stakeholders to prioritize", 6.10.5, page 121.

- S.6 defines the criteria under which the system will be deemed acceptable. Remember (terminology note on page 20) that this Handbook uses "verification" as shorthand for what is more explicitly called "Verification & Validation" (V&V), covering several levels of testing — module testing, integration testing, system testing, user acceptance testing — as well as other techniques such as static analysis and, when applicable, program proving.

3.7 THE PROJECT BOOK

Here is the overall structure of the project book:

Project book (P)	
Chapter	**Contents**
Front matter	Control information (3.2).
P.1 Roles and personnel	Main responsibilities in the project; required project staff and their needed qualifications.
P.2 Imposed technical choices	Any a priori choices binding the project to specific tools, hardware, languages or other technical parameters.
P.3 Schedule and milestones	List of tasks to be carried out and their scheduling.
P.4 Tasks and deliverables	Details of individual tasks listed under P.3 and their expected outcomes.
P.5 Required technology elements	External systems, hardware and software, expected to be necessary for building the system.
P.6 Risk and mitigation analysis	Potential obstacles to meeting the schedule of P.4, and measures for adapting the plan if they do arise.
P.7 Requirements process and report	Initially, description of what the requirements process will be; later, report on its steps.
Back matter	Control information (3.2).

Notes on chapters of the Project book:

- P.1 defines the roles involved in the project. "Role" was defined in 1.5 as a human respon-sibility. Some of the most frequent roles appeared in "Stakeholders on the production (development) side", page 15. Chapter P.1 of the Standard Plan also describes the actual personnel available, their characteristics, any constraints on their time — for example whether they are full-time on the project or also needed elsewhere — and conditions on the possible induction of further personnel throughout the project.

- P.2 exists because in practice not all technical choices in projects derive from a pure techni-cal analysis; some result from company policies (*"we only use open-source products"* or *"the policy is to use our own cloud storage system, not Microsoft, Google or Amazon solu-tions"*). While some project members may dislike non-strictly-technical decisions, they are a fact of project life and must be documented, in particular for the benefit of one of the qual-ity factors for requirements: "Justified", 4.2, page 49. P.2 addresses this need.

- The schedule in P.3 defines the project's key dates.

- The tasks and deliverables in P.4 define the project's main activities and the results they must produce, associated with the milestone dates defined in P.3. For a classic Waterfall-like project, the tasks correspond to successive steps such as requirements, design and imple-mentation, but the role of P.4 is more general. For example agile projects do not have a tra-ditional succession of phases such as requirements, design etc., but they have iterations or "sprints", and may have milestones and deliverables defined by a legal contract. As the highlighting suggests, P.4 typically makes up the core part of the Project book.

- Chapter P.5 lists external technology elements, such as program libraries and hardware devices, that the project is expected to require. Although the actual use of such products belongs to design and implementation rather than requirements, it is part of the requirements task to identify elements whose availability is critical to the success of the project — an important element of risk analysis (P.6 as presented next). It will also be advisable to per-form early checks of the actual availability and suitability of the technology ("Feasibility prototypes", 6.11.5, page 123).

- P.6 discusses risks associated with the project; it can include a SWOT analysis (Strengths, Weaknesses, Opportunities, Threats) for the project. It is essential to be on the lookout for events that could derail the project, and devise mitigation strategies. Two of the preceding chapters of the Project book yield sources of risk, since they express choices that may have been made without the benefit of a fully rational analysis: imposed technical choices (P.2) and external technology elements as just discussed (P.5). The analysis of risks in P.6 is dis-tinct from chapter G.6 of the Goals book (page 39), which covers limitations and exclusions of the system's goals, although it may need to refer to it. A later section of this Handbook discusses the topic of risk further: "Risk assessment and mitigation", 6.11.7, page 126.

- The Process and Report chapter, P.7, starts out as a plan for conducting the requirements elicitation process (covered by chapter 6 of this Handbook), but is meant to be updated as part of that process so that it includes the key lessons of elicitation; see sections 6.8 and 6.9.

3.8   MINIMUM REQUIREMENTS

It is reasonable to expect any project to produce requirements; the four-book structure presented in this chapter serves as a checklist for all the elements that may be needed.

Not all requirements efforts will fill in the entire structure at the same level of detail. In line with the general "Requirements Effort Principle", page 31, there is no reason to feel bad if the requirements are not textbook-perfect.

You should also, however, remember another principle, "Minimum Requirements Outcome Principle", page 27, which states the minimum that any project should have to show for its requirements efforts. Regardless of where your lifecycle model (chapter 12) lies in the spectrum from full-agile to full-Waterfall, these are the "upfront" elements which the project should have at its disposal before it can comfortably embark on other software development tasks.

Remember, too, that not all requirements are "upfront". Yet another principle, "Requirements Elaboration Principle", page 25, reminds us to continue working on the requirements as the project proceeds and accumulates new information about both the problem and the solution.

3-E   EXERCISES

3-E.1 Finding the right place

State the chapter from the Standard Plan (such as "P.1") to which each one of the following example requirements would belong:

- *"Some of the general constraints were defined in the preliminary meeting of 15 June 2022, available at"* [URL].
- *"The login record shall be implemented using MongoDB."*
- *"Here is the basic scheme of interaction for ordering a product:"* [followed by the description of that scheme].
- *"The project shall only use external software products available through an approved open-source license (GPL or Creative Commons)".*
- *"The product shall be available on mobile platforms as well as through an API."*
- *"Any use of cookies shall conform to the GDPR."*
- *"As a result of the introduction of the new payroll system, pay periods shall be standardized to monthly for all employees."*
- *"As the system depends on Windows 11 facilities, meeting the schedule depends on Microsoft fully releasing Windows 11 by end of October, 2021."*
- *"This function is considered critical to the deployment of the project."*
- *"Upon exiting a session, the system shall memorize the last explored directory as the restart point for the next session."*

3-E.2 Restructuring a requirements document

(Project exercise.) Consider the sample requirements document given in [Bair 2005]. Rewrite it as three books (excluding the Project book since the document does not address project organization) according to the Standard Plan of this chapter. (The document leaves out some figures, usually using a variable x, as in "*reduce the number of support calls from foreign customers by $x\%$*". Make sure to replace such placeholders by actual numbers.)

3-E.3 Devising a project plan

Referring again to [Bair 2005] (previous exercise), devise a suitable project plan for the system's development, and write it as a Project book according to the Standard Plan of this chapter.

3-E.4 Use cases in different places

(This exercise is about the Standard Plan discussed in the present chapter, but assumes familiarity with use cases, which you can obtain from reading chapter 7.) Consider examples of use cases from a standard reference such as [Jacobson 1992] or [Cockburn 2001]; alternatively, from an actual requirements document to which you have access. Starting from the criteria presented in sections 3.4 and 3.6, state which of those use cases would, in the Standard Plan, go into chapter G.5 of the Goals book ("*high-level usage scenarios*") and which into chapter S.4 of the System book ("*detailed usage scenarios*"). Explain the rationale for your decisions.

BIBLIOGRAPHICAL NOTES AND FURTHER READING

Until now, many industry projects have been applying a recommended structure for requirements document published in 1998 by a committee of the IEEE: [IEEE 1998]. Although it remains good (and short) reading, it does not measure up to the needs of the complex systems we develop today.

Gilb's Planguage work [Gilb 2005-2022] includes a systematic catalog of the elements needed in requirements specifications.

4

Requirements quality and verification

We expect to produce not just requirements but good requirements. There is no single criterion of goodness; part of the difficulty of the exercise is indeed that we must pursue several quality factors at once. Fourteen, as it turns out, discussed in turn in the following sections:

Quality criteria for requirements			
Attribute	*Applies to*	**Attribute**	*Applies to*
Correct (4.1)	*Environment, System.*	**Traceable** (4.8)	*all*
Justified (4.2)	*Project, System*	**Delimited** (4.9)	*all*
Complete (4.3)	*all*	**Readable** (4.10)	*all*
Consistent (4.4)	*all*	**Modifiable** (4.11)	*all*
Unambiguous (4.5)	*all*	**Verifiable** (4.12)	*Project, System*
Feasible (4.6)	*Project, System*	**Prioritized** (4.13)	*system*
Abstract (4.7)	*System*	**Endorsed** (4.14)	*all*

This entire chapter is prescriptive by nature: it helps you achieve the best possible quality. Emphasis on "*possible*": remember ("Requirements Effort Principle", page 31) that requirements quality is only a step towards the greater goal of *system* quality.

Even if we aim at high quality for requirements, it is impossible to reach perfection on all fronts. Tradeoffs will be necessary, as different criteria can pull us in opposite directions. "Unambiguous", for example, promotes meticulous requirements specifications, possibly using mathematics as discussed in chapter 9, which may hamper the "Readable" criterion.

Each section covers one of the factors. It starts with a definition, followed by subsections on: the factor's significance; how to *ensure* the factor; how to *assess* whether proposed requirements satisfy it; and *parts of the Standard Plan* that are particularly relevant to that assessment.

The factors are indeed designed to be **assessable**: it should be possible to ascertain (perhaps not rigorously but to a reasonable degree of comfort) that requirements possess them, or not. Non-assessable factors are of no use. We might for example wish requirements to be "*well-written*", but there is no such factor in the list since its assessment would be entirely subjective. The task of assessing whether proposed requirements satisfy the quality factors is known as **requirements verification**. (It should not be confused with the task of verifying a *system* against its requirements, covered by the "Verifiable" criterion in 4.12.)

© The Author(s), under exclusive license to Springer Nature Switzerland AG 2022
B. Meyer, *Handbook of Requirements and Business Analysis*, https://doi.org/10.1007/978-3-031-06739-6_4

4.1 CORRECT

> **Correctness**
>
> An Environment or System requirement is correct if it is compatible with actual project parameters, properties of the environment (constraints, assumptions, effects, invariants), organizational goals, and stakeholder expectations.

4.1.1 About correctness

The four reference points of the definition correspond to the four PEGS.

System requirements, gathered during the elicitation process (chapter 6), should reflect the actual needs of stakeholders to the extent they are compatible with the project's goals. Requirements on the environment should correctly describe environment properties (the four categories listed in the definition were defined in 1.7 with more details in 3.5).

4.1.2 Ensuring correctness

While there is no sure way to guarantee correctness (if domain experts give you wrong information, the requirements will be wrong regardless of the methods and tools you use), the key is to cross-check:

- If requirements are written by business analysts or requirements engineers from information provided by Subject-Matter Experts (SMEs), as discussed earlier ("Who produces requirements?", 1.10.2, page 16), have SMEs examine and approve them.

- Particularly for critical properties, avoid relying on a single source. Even experts can be biased or have holes in their expertise. Ask several SMEs rather than just one. This need is one of the reasons why, in the requirements elicitation process, stakeholder *workshops* (sections 6.7 to 6.9) are a useful alternative or complement to individual stakeholder interviews.

- Whenever you detect an inconsistency during requirements elicitation, do not brush it off but explore it thoroughly, going back to its cause, whether documents or discussions with stakeholders or both. An inconsistency may be a fluke or a misunderstanding, but it may also reflect a tricky feature of one of the PEGS, which should not go unresolved.

- As will be seen in the detailed discussion of requirements elicitation (6.10), a good elicitation process must ask the right combination of questions, including both specific questions ("*what are the criteria for approving product returns?*") and open-ended ones ("*did we miss any aspects of the product return process in the questions discussed so far?*").

4.1.3 Assessing correctness

The following guidelines help assess whether the requirements correctly reflect actual needs:

- Check the record of requirements elicitation, to ensure that all stakeholders have had their say. (Remember that stakeholders are not people but categories of people.) Note the importance of chapter P.7 of the Project book in the Standard Plan, "Requirements process and report", designed to start out as a plan for requirements elicitation and then to be updated regularly — as requirements interviews, workshops and other elicitation actions proceed — into a requirements elicitation report. Check it in particular against chapter G.7 of the Goals book, which lists stakeholders.

- Check that requirements sources other than stakeholders — also listed in G.7 — have been consulted. It is a common mistake to miss some of these sources, such as the legal contract (which may contain important conditions, whether the technical group likes them or not), previous systems, and decisions made in meetings that preceded the start of the project.
- Check the list of environment constraints (E.3 in the Standard Plan) against the functionality list (S.2) to make sure that no intended functionality contradicts a relevant constraint.

4.1.4 Parts of the Standard Plan particularly relevant to assessing correctness

- G.7 (stakeholders and requirements sources), to check that the project knows which stakeholders and other sources of information are relevant to ensure correctness.
- P.7 (requirements process and particularly requirements report), to check that these stakeholders had their say.
- G.2 (current situation), to check that the starting point is well understood.
- E.3 and E.5 (constraints from the environment and effects on it).
- S.5 (prioritization), to check that the requirements process has correctly assessed the relative importance of various elements of functionality.

4.2 JUSTIFIED

Justifiability

A Project or System requirement is justified if it helps reach a goal or satisfy a constraint.

4.2.1 About justifiability

Every element of the requirements affecting the project or the system should have a clear reason for being there. Justification can come from either:

- The goals, expressing why a system is being built. Everything in the system's functionality and in the project's tasks should ultimately represent a step, however minute, towards meeting them. Goals yield *positive* justifications: they express the ambition of the development.
- The environment, defining —as constraints (1.7.1) — limits to what the project and system can do. We can view such justifications as *negative*: they express limits on the ambition of the development. (Environment *assumptions*, for their part, are again positive; see 1.7.4.)

Requirements on the *project* should only include what is essential. It is all too common to impose restrictions — choice of programming language, reliance on specified contractors, use of a particular development method... — without good reasons (other than a particular manager's preference, or following current fashion, or repeating previous practice whether successful or not). Such premature choices are often political decisions masquerading as requirements.

You can seldom avoid this phenomenon completely (politics always plays a role in projects), but you must limit it in two ways:

- Be on the lookout for such non-technically-justified decisions, and remove them whenever possible. They needlessly constrain the project's freedom to make its own decisions later, based on analysis rather than prejudice.

- The ones that you cannot remove still need a justification, even if it is not purely technical.

As an example, company A might have made a strategic decision to use Microsoft products whenever available. The policy of company B is diametrically opposed: use open-source technology only. The reasons may be (in either case) primarily political rather than technical, but they are justifications all the same, and the requirements should state them explicitly, if only to avoid wasting time by letting project members unwittingly take initiatives that contradict the policy (and may need to be canceled later).

The Standard Plan has an explicit place for such non-technical justifications: P.2, "imposed technical choices".

Demanding that all *system* requirements be justified is the best defense against *feature bloat* (also known as "creeping featurism" and "scope creep"): the accumulation of requests for functionality that is not essential for future users. Feature bloat makes the project bigger and more complex, heightening the risk of delay and even failure. Time spent on non-essential features detracts from essential ones. In practice, the non-essential features often get discarded anyway when the going gets tough (see "Prioritized", 4.13, page 67 below); it is better not to include them in the first place. (Quote attributed to Steve Jobs: "*ideas are worth nothing unless executed*".)

4.2.2 Ensuring justifiability

To ensure that project requirements are justified, keep them to the minimum implied by the goals and constraints. In the development of the Project book, remove any element that does not follow from either of these sources. The Project part of requirements should define the context under which the project team will organize its work; it should not encroach on project management decisions that do not directly follow from requirements properties.

Similarly, throughout the preparation of the System book, make sure that every system requirement relates, directly or indirectly, to either a goal or a constraint.

4.2.3 Assessing justifiability

- For project requirements, check that there are no hidden assumptions. As noted above, it is common to have technical decisions motivated by non-technical reasons; regardless of any judgment on that practice, the requirements must document such cases explicitly (in P.2).

- For system requirements, check that every requirement can be traced back to either a goal or a constraint. Check in particular the record of requirements elicitation (chapter P.7 of the Standard Plan) for any vanity requirements that are of interest to just one stakeholder. Such personal preferences often creep into requirements, especially from particularly persistent and insistent stakeholders (in the worst case, "fellow travelers" as we will encounter them in "Assessing stakeholders", 6.5, page 109). They are respectable as they may reflect features that are important to those stakeholders, but the system development should focus on meeting the defined goals and can be considerably delayed or otherwise damaged by undue attention to specialized functionality that is not directly relevant to these goals.

4.2.4 Parts of the Standard Plan particularly relevant to assessing justifiability

- G.2 (current situation).
- G.3 (expected benefits), against which you should assess S.2 (functionality).

4.3 COMPLETE

Any requirement must, per the original definition ("Requirement", page 5), be *relevant*: of interest to some stakeholder ("Relevant property, relevant statement", page 5). Completeness is the other way around: all relevant properties should be in the requirements.

Informally, then, requirements are complete if they cover everything worth covering: all goals, all needed functionality, all environment constraints and effects, all needed project tasks.

Expressed this way, completeness sounds like unassessable wishful thinking. Complete with respect to what? How can we know all relevant properties? If we had their list, we could check the requirements against it; but that list would itself be a collection of requirements — maybe at a higher level of abstraction, but still subject to the same question: does it include all that is relevant? We would have only pushed the problem, not solved it.

Defining completeness is not as hopeless as this observation makes it sound at first. A number of useful practical criteria exist, each (ironically for the topic of completeness) partial, but all useful and, to a reasonable extent, assessable. Relying on them yields a workable definition:

> ### Completeness
> A set of requirements is complete, or not, along six criteria: document, goal, scenario, environment, interface and command-query completeness.

The topic is rich enough to deserve its own chapter (11), but here is a preview of the criteria:

- **Document completeness**: the requirements include all the expected parts, and shun improper use of "TBD" (To Be Determined) elements. (See the TBD rule in 5.8.)
- **Goal completeness**: they address all defined business goals.
- **Scenario completeness**: they include enough information to ensure that an implementation satisfying them will cover all identified usage scenarios (including use cases and user stories).
- **Environment completeness**: they take into account all environment constraints.
- **Interface completeness**: they specify interfaces to all relevant external elements.
- **Command-query completeness**: they define the effect of every operation on every observable property.

Details in chapter 11.

4.4 CONSISTENT

Consistency
A set of requirements is consistent if it contains no contradiction.

4.4.1 About consistency

If a requirement says green and another one says red, we have a problem. At some point a programmer will build the corresponding system part and resolve the contradiction. The programmer is not in the best position to make that decision; it should have been a requirements decision.

Even that case is the lucky one, because someone discovers the contradiction, and if the project uses a decent development process there will be standard procedures to resolve it, for example by going back to the requirements authors or domain experts (SMEs). The unlucky case is that *two* programmers implement separate parts of the system on the basis of contradictory assumptions, without even realizing that there is a contradiction; the system will be buggy.

A famous example in the annals of software engineering is the crash of the Mars Climate Vehicle in 1999, where most of the system used international units of measurement but one module used English units. If the sensor module measures a force in newtons per square centimeter and the processing module understands the same number as "pounds of force" (an esoteric unit used in the English system), we are in trouble. Trouble in this case meant that the mission crashed. Quoting from an article on the topic (see the bibliographical section): *"This navigation mishap pushed the spacecraft dangerously close to the planet's atmosphere where it presumably burned and broke into pieces, killing the mission on a day when engineers had expected to celebrate the craft's entry into Mars' orbit."* Further:

> The initial error was made by contractor Lockheed Martin Astronautics in Colorado, which, like the rest of the U.S. launch industry, used English measurements. The contractor, by agreement, was supposed to convert its measurements to metrics.

Although contradictions can creep into small sets of requirements, the main threat comes from requirements for complex systems, which can run up to thousands of pages and are written by several people, who may, as in the Mars Climate Vehicle case, work for different companies.

4.4.2 Ensuring consistency

The prime weapon against letting consistency creep into requirements is unity of direction. The tasks of *gathering* (eliciting) and *writing* requirements call for different criteria:

- It is normal in elicitation to involve a large number of people, including requirements engineers (business analysts) and SMEs. To some extent, the motto there is "the more the merrier", to avoid missing someone's important input. The process is broad and tolerant.

- Requirements writing (often interleaved with elicitation, as we will see in "When and where to write requirements", 5.1, page 71) should have a well-defined leader. To continue with clichés, too many cooks spoil the broth. The process is selective. One person or a small group should control it, and be familiar with all the requirements, not just individual pieces.

Even for a large project, in which it is difficult for a single person to master everything, responsibility for the final product should be concentrated.

Additional steps towards ensuring consistency:

- Devote appropriate attention to the glossary ("The glossary", 6.4, page 107), the central repository of project terms: make sure that it includes all the significant vocabulary of the project, and that the requirements themselves make systematic use of terms defined there. Inconsistencies often arise from different understandings of a given term.

- On the project management side, be on alert for the emergence of subgroups with an inward attitude and not enough communication with the rest. Such a phenomenon is a particularly risk in **geographically distributed** projects, for example projects involving outsourcing, with teams in different countries and of different cultures. Make sure to establish effective communication channels for bringing out and resolving possible misunderstandings.

4.4.3 Assessing consistency

The following techniques help assess consistency:

- Check the vocabulary of the requirements for adherence to the glossary.

- Check that the style of different parts of the requirements is similar. The style itself is a superficial feature, but *differences* in style often reveal deeper differences. If (for example) one chapter makes systematic use of bullet points and another uses enumerations in long paragraphs, they were probably produced by separate teams who did not coordinate enough and may have introduced more significant inconsistencies.

- Check the frequency of cross-references, both within books and between books. If books extensively refer to each other, we may deduce that their authors actually read the parts they reference and wrote their own parts in a compatible fashion. A paucity of cross-references may reveal that each part "reinvented the wheels" of the project.

- Check for requirements elements that are not specifications but explanations. Like repetition, explanations can be harmful, as discussed in detail in "Binding and explanatory text", 5.4, page 77; it is often desirable to remove them, as they only confuse the reader (see the analysis of the G&G specification in "The seven sins: a classic example", 5.10, page 93). Make sure any remaining explanatory text is clearly marked as such, complementing a precise specification (rather than serving as specification) and not contradicting it. You will find precise guidelines on explanatory text in section 5.4, summarized in the Explanation Principle on page 78.

- Check that if more than one notation is used — for example natural-language, graphical, tabular, mathematical — they do not contain contradictory elements. Detailed rules on combining notations appear in "Combining notations", 5.5.5, page 84.

4.4.4 Parts of the Standard Plan particularly relevant to assessing consistency

- E.1 (glossary): check that the definitions are non-contradictory.
- S.2 (functionality): check that the various elements of specified functionality are consistent.

4.5 UNAMBIGUOUS

> **Non-ambiguity**
>
> A set of requirements is unambiguous if none of its elements is so expressed as to lend itself to two significantly different understandings.

4.5.1 About non-ambiguity

Where the "consistent" criterion told us that two different requirements should not lead in two incompatible directions, "unambiguous" requires that *one* element should not lend itself to two (or — worse — more than two) different interpretations.

4.5.2 Ensuring non-ambiguity

As with consistency, a key tool to avoid ambiguity is the glossary. Direct all members of the requirements-writing team to limit the technical vocabulary they use to a well-identified set of terms and check that each has a clear definition in the glossary.

In using natural language, apply systematically the techniques of chapter 5, particularly "Style rules for natural-language requirements", 5.7, page 88. Make sure all requirements writers are aware of counter-examples (showing ambiguous usage, with words such as "user-friendly", "efficient" or "24/7 operation") and their suggested replacements, from the discussion in "Some examples: bad, less bad, good", 5.6, page 85. More generally, they should all be aware of the "The seven sins of the specifier", 5.2, page 72; it is good to analyze the "G&G" example presented there.

For delicate aspects of System and Environment properties, encourage the use of formal descriptions including Abstract Data Types (chapters 9 and 10), or tabular descriptions when appropriate. See the formal restatement of the G&G example in 9.5, page 171.

4.5.3 Assessing non-ambiguity

- Be particularly wary of pictorial explanations, bearing in mind their critique in "Graphical notations", 5.5.2, page 80. Every graphical convention — boxes, lines, arrows... — must have an explicitly documented semantics.

- Check for any deviation from the terminology defined in the glossary, and any technical term appearing in the requirements but not in the glossary.

4.5.4 Parts of the Standard Plan particularly relevant to assessing non-ambiguity

- E.1 (glossary): check that it includes definitions for the basic concepts used throughout the rest of the requirements.

4.6 FEASIBLE

> **Feasibility**
>
> A System (resp. Project) requirement is feasible if it is possible, within the constraints of the Environment and Goals, to produce an implementation (resp. schedule) that satisfies it.

4.6.1 About feasibility

System and project requirements are promises that something will be built, satisfying the specified properties and (for the Project part) by certain deadlines. Promises are dangerous, especially promises to be fulfilled by others, which is often the case in software development when requirements engineers (business analysts) are a separate team from the software developers.

4.6.2 Ensuring feasibility

One sure way to *damage* system feasibility is to set up a project structure that assigns requirements and the rest of the development to separate teams with little or no communication between them and, worse yet, belonging to different entities. For example:

- Assigning the requirements to consultants not employed by the company.

- In an outsourcing situation, having separate requirements and development teams in different countries or even continents.

In such setups, nothing really restrains the requirements engineers from specifying ambitious functionality that will please the decision-makers, since they will not bear the consequences of overreach. Someone else will have to design and implement a system, and will be blamed for delays and failures. Avoid this situation: even if requirements engineering is a distinct role calling for specific skills, keep the development team involved throughout.

Another threat to feasibility is the reliance on technical solutions that the project does not fully control: algorithms that have not yet been tried, and (particularly) external tools, required hardware, operating systems, APIs (libraries of components). For software dependencies, an important feasibility-enhancing technique is the **feasibility prototype**, a requirements-time mini-project meant solely to assess the readiness of a technology that the project plans to use. A discussion of this concept appears in "Feasibility prototypes", 6.11.5, page 123.

Part of the recipe *for* feasibility is mere professionalism. A good requirements team will know how to distinguish between pie-in-the-sky promises and implementable functionality. Requirements engineering, as noted, demands a distinctive set of skills, but they must include extensive programming and software architecture experience. Unless the requirements team understands software construction, it is bound to produce unrealistic requirements. This observation is part of the reason why this Handbook uses "requirements engineer" more frequently than "business analyst" even though the two terms cover closely related duties (1.2.5, page 6). Producing requirements is an engineering job, part of the more general category of software and system engineering, which also encompasses architecture and implementation. A requirements engineer must master these other disciplines, if only to produce realistic requirements.

The preceding observations are particularly relevant to the feasibility of System requirements. For the Project part, comparable risks exist of producing unrealistic schedules. This topic belongs to software project management rather than specifically to requirements; the bibliography section lists a classic reference.

4.6.3 Assessing feasibility

- Evaluate the software-development savviness of the requirements team and its effect on the realism of the proposed requirements.
- Systematically identify dependencies on external products, hardware or software, and other parameters beyond the project's direct control.
- Compare the system's scope, as defined by the requirements, to the functionality of previous systems built by the organization, competing systems, and commercially available tools.
- Determine whether the descriptions of the project's ambition (System part) and of the team size and deadlines (Project part) are of comparable quality, and consistent.
- If the system involves significant innovation, perform a risk and mitigation analysis (see "Risk assessment and mitigation", 6.11.7, page 126).
- Determine whether feasibility prototypes (6.11.5, page 123) have been produced for delicate parts, and their lessons properly analyzed.

4.6.4 Parts of the Standard Plan particularly relevant to assessing feasibility

- P.5 (required technology elements): check that any needed external tools or systems will actually be available.
- S.3 (interfaces of the system): check that it is possible to provide the right kinds of interface as will be needed by users and other systems.
- P.6 (risk and mitigation analysis): check that the risk analysis takes into account dependencies on external tools and any project or design decision that may prove hard to implement.

4.7 ABSTRACT

> **Abstractness**
> A System requirement is abstract if it specifies a desired system property without prescribing or favoring specific design or implementation choices.

4.7.1 About abstractness

The feasibility criterion demands that requirements should be implementable, but it does not mean that they will prescribe a *specific* implementation. Compare:

- *"The system shall display available products in order of increasing price."*
- *"Sort the product list by order of increasing price before displaying it."*

The first prescription is a proper requirement, the second is not. (*"Use the Quicksort algorithm to sort the list"* would be even more incongruous.)

The "abstract" criterion, particularly applicable to requirements on the System, expresses that requirements specifications must live up to their name: they must only specify requirements (per the original definition in 1.2.4: "*relevant statements about a project, environment, goal or system*"), and not venture into the realms of design and implementation. Remember this definition when writing requirements: they must express properties, not prescribe actions.

The difference may appear subtle, or even hair-splitting. Is it really important to distinguish between "*the displayed list shall be ordered*" and "*sort before displaying*"? Indeed it is. Even in the simple example above:

- When you reach implementation, it may turn out that at the corresponding program step the list was already sorted by price, because of an earlier operation. No need to sort it again.

- More generally, it is the programmer's responsibility to decide between (A) keeping the product list sorted at all times; (B) sorting it prior to displaying it; (C) keeping the list itself in some structure organized along other criteria, but sorting its *displayed* version, which may be a *copy* of a *part* of the list (and hence faster to sort).

These are implementation decisions. A requirements writer has no business preempting them.

System requirements should only tell the programmer about expected results. It can be tempting to go further and suggest implementation approaches, but such impulses generally cause more harm than good, for the simple reason that implementation parameters are only known at implementation time. Even when you believe, when writing requirements, that you *just see* how to do things, there is no guarantee that you do.

4.7.2 The difficulty of abstracting

To someone new to the field, ensuring abstractness might sound easy, trivial even, based on the assumption that describing a problem is easier than describing a solution. In software, however, it may be the reverse. Specifying *what* could be done requires a general effort of abstraction, which for many people is hard; it is often tempting to jump into *how* to do it — correctly or not.

Herein lies one of the paradoxes of requirements elicitation (the process of obtaining requirements from stakeholders, studied more extensively in chapter 6). In principle, the division of labor is clear: stakeholders help define the problem, and the project team builds a solution. In practice, some stakeholders are often more eager to tell you how to proceed than adept at explaining the goals. The two mindsets at play here are **descriptive** and **operational** reasoning. While design and implementation are operational, requirements should be descriptive.

Here is a simple example of the difference between descriptive and operational thinking: defining *alphabetical order*. Everyone can find a word in a dictionary and hence knows the concept at least pragmatically, but let us define it precisely. In this exercise:

- We assume that we understand the ordering between **letters**: E is *before* I, and so on.
- We are asked to define the notion of alphabetical order between **words**: (REQUIREMENTS is *smaller than* REQUIRING, and so on.

We must specify it precisely, as we would for a requirement in an unfamiliar application domain.

To avoid confusion we stick to the terminology of "*before*" for letters and "*smaller than*" for words (non-empty sequences of letters).

Experience shows that most people, asked to define under which conditions a non-empty word $w1$ is smaller than a non-empty word $w2$, will answer something like this:

When is a word "smaller" than another:
An operational attempt at a definition of alphabetical order

Consider the first letters x and y of $w1$ and $w2$. If x is before y, then $w1$ is smaller than $w2$. If y is before x, then $w2$ is smaller than $w1$. Otherwise x and y are the same. Then if both $w1$ and $w2$ have length 1, they are equal. If only one of them has length 1, it is smaller than the other. Otherwise, they both have two or more letters; remove their first letters and repeat.

This form is operational. It tells you what to do and is in fact an algorithm, not a definition. In contrast, a true descriptive definition (see also exercise 4-E.2, page 69) is:

When is a word "smaller" than another:
A proper definition of alphabetical order

$w1$ is smaller than $w2$ if and only if for some non-negative integer n all these conditions hold:
S1 $w1$ and $w2$ have length n or more.
S2   If $n > 0$, $w1$ and $w2$ have the same respective characters at positions from 1 to n.
S3   Either $w1$ has length n and $w2$ has length at least $n+1$, or they both have length at least $n+1$ and the $n+1$-st letter of $w1$ is before the $n+1$-st letter of $w2$.

Here is a visualization on two examples (corresponding to the two cases of condition S3):

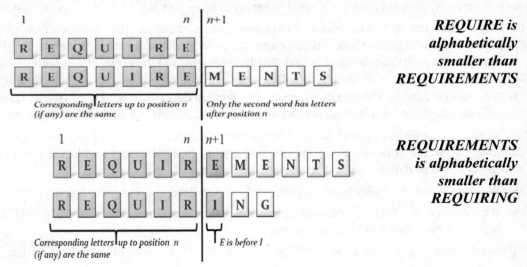

(Exercise 9-E.4, page 183 asks you to turn this definition into a "formal" specification.) The critical difference between the two specifications is not that one of them uses a bit of elementary mathematics, but that the first is operational, telling us how to proceed, whereas the second one is truly descriptive, giving us an actual *definition* of what it means for a word to be "smaller" than another.

A descriptive style is generally appropriate for requirements:

Requirements Abstraction Principle
Express requirements without prejudice to design and implementation.

4.7.3 Overspecification

Violations of the abstractness criterion are cases of *overspecification*, the inclusion in the requirements of properties that should not be there, because they result from premature design or implementation decisions. In the classification of requirements elements, overspecification is a form of *noise*, the general term for elements that appear in requirements documents but do not express proper requirements ("Noise", 1.9.2, page 12). Overspecification is a particularly obnoxious kind of noise, because:

- It confuses developers by presenting as requirements, in other words as a part of the problem, what is in fact one among possible solutions.

- Because it is written in ignorance of other elements of design and implementation, it may prescribe the *wrong* solution.

- It is often a cover for an inability (or laziness) to describe the real need, at the right level of abstraction.

Operational thinking indeed comes more naturally to many people than descriptive specifications. But that is precisely one of the reasons why we need requirements engineers and business analysts, trained to resist operational urges and produce unbiased specifications instead.

4.7.4 Design and implementation hints

Sometimes the requirements writer does have insights into desirable design or implementation decisions. It is not always appropriate to repress them; after all, they might be good. The danger is to confuse them with proper requirements elements.

The classification in requirements in chapter 1 expressly reserves ("Special case: hint", 1.9.3, page 12) a category for these insights: **hint**, a subcategory of "noise". Overspecification is also noise, but, like most other forms, should be tracked and removed. Hints, in contrast, are acceptable as long as you expressly mark them as such and separate them from actual requirements. A typical example would be:

Hint: while the precise choice of database system shall take place in phase 3 of the project [a reference to the schedule, appearing in P.3 in the Project book], *the incident database shall have to accommodate objects of widely different kinds and sizes. Experience with the previous version of the system has shown that the use of a relational database imposes unacceptable constraints and performance limitations. The solution probably lies in a NoSQL database such as Mongo DB.*

The author of this extract has avoided polluting the requirements with a prescription of the form *"The incidents database shall be a NoSQL database"* or, even more overspecifying, *"shall use Mongo DB"* (which would only be justifiable as part of an explicit policy decision, as part of chapter, P.2, "Imposed technical choices", in the Project book). In the "Hint" form shown above, the requirements writer shares an insight, but separately from the requirements proper, hence avoiding overspecification.

Such implementation hints should — like explanations, see "Binding and explanatory text", 5.4, page 77 — use a specific format distinguishing them from proper requirements elements.

4.7.5 Beware of use cases

As discussed in a later chapter (7), use cases do not suffice as requirements. One of the reasons is that when used in that role they lead to an operational style which can favor overspecification. The corresponding chapter develops these observations.

4.7.6 Ensuring abstractness

Enforce a discipline limiting requirements to specifications — not design, implementation or tool choices. If you find prescriptions that violate this rule but may have some usefulness, turn them into explicit design, implementation or tool hints as discussed above.

Make sure (after reading the discussion of use cases in chapter 7 of this Handbook) that use cases only play a role of *checks* on requirements (in chapters G.5 and G.5 of the Standard Plan). If you find use cases purporting to serve as requirements, demand of the requirements writers that they move to a higher level of abstraction by going from use cases to actual requirements.

4.7.7 Assessing abstractness

- Scan the requirements for elements which, instead of specifying functionality, venture into how to implement it in some particular way. Telltale signs are imperative descriptions emphasizing sequences of actions that the system must perform. They may reflect genuine ordering constraints, but may also over-interpret logical constraints as timing constraints (see "Logical constraints are more general than sequential orderings", 8.7.2, page 150).

- Look in particular for elements of functionality specified solely through use cases. They do not inevitably entail overspecification, but often do.

4.7.8 Parts of the Standard Plan particularly relevant to assessing abstractness

- P.2 (imposed technical choices), to make sure that the list is complete.
- S.2 (functionality): check that the style is descriptive rather than operational.

4.8 TRACEABLE

> **Traceability**
>
> A Goals, System, Project or Environment requirement is traceable if it is possible to follow its consequences, both ways, in other project artifacts including design, implementation and verification elements.

4.8.1 About traceability

The definition states that traceability works both ways, from requirements to other artifacts and in the reverse direction:

- Any element of the requirements must have some consequence in other artifacts of the project. The most obvious example is functionality-to-code traceability: for any element of functionality specified in the System description (chapter S.2 of the Standard Plan), there must be at least some part of the code that implements all or part of it. Otherwise the requirement would just be noise. As another example, a use case may yield a test case, a verification artifact. The observation generalizes to other kinds of requirements: if a requirement is useful, it must have some consequence in the actual products of the project.

- The other way around, elements of design, implementation and tests should follow from requirements elements. Making this rule absolute would mean that the requirements are all-encompassing, which is generally asking too much (as we saw in 2.4 with the "Traceability Principle", page 30). Still, we should try to ensure, as much as possible, that any such element, added during the development of the system, either can be traced back to an existing requirement or causes a corresponding update to the requirements.

Traceability helps ensure another quality factor (discussed in 4.11 below): modifiability. Software is by nature "soft": everything can change — requirements, designs, implementations… — and over the course of a project many things *will* change. One of the main consequences of traceability is to enable the recording of dependencies between project artifacts of many different kinds, so that if any element at any level changes it is possible to obtain immediately a list of the other elements that the change might also affect.

4.8.2 Ensuring traceability

Traceability is one of the requirements properties that tools can greatly enhance. A number of commercial tools support recording and tracking links between requirements and other project artifacts. A widely used one is DOORS ("Dynamic Object-Oriented Requirements System", today part of IBM's software engineering offerings), a comprehensive traceability framework letting users link requirements with each other and with different artifacts. For object-oriented requirements (chapter 8), the Eiffel Information System makes it possible to instrument both code and external documents (Word, PDF) to refer directly to each other, recording for example that a certain routine (code) implements a certain functionality (requirements document).

Such tools only help if the project applies a systematic discipline of recording the connections between requirements and other artifacts.

4.8.3 Assessing traceability

The use of traceability tools, or not, is a first test of how seriously the project takes traceability. Other signs include:

- Systematic identification of all requirements and elements related to requirements, through a consistent identification scheme (see "Document completeness", 11.1, page 205).

- An iterative development process, which helps decrease the temporal and conceptual distance between a requirements idea and its realization.

4.8.4 Parts of the Standard Plan particularly relevant to assessing traceability

- The Goals book, particularly G.3 (expected benefits): check that the advertised benefits are specified, so as to allow tracing their consequences throughout the project.

- S.2 (Functionality): check that every element of functionality clearly relates to a goal as expressed in the Goals book, particularly G.3. Also check that these elements, which specify the functionality precisely, are consistent with the functionality overview in G.4.

- S.6 (verification and acceptance criteria): check that the criteria explicitly relate to the goals and functionality.

4.9 DELIMITED

Delimitedness

A set of Goals or System requirements is delimited if it specifies the scope of the future system, making it possible to determine what functionality lies beyond that scope.

4.9.1 About delimitation

Requirements define, in the Goals and Systems parts, what the system must do. It is also important to clarify what the system is not expected to do. The process of producing a payroll may reveal deficiencies in the accounting database (see the anecdote in "Uncover the unsaid", 6.10.1, page 118); that is not a reason to start redoing accounting as part of payroll. A project to build a web site may reveal that a mobile app would nicely complement it; that is not a reason to let the project wander into apps. Such cases of scope creep (or "creeping featurism") can derail a project.

The question is not whether the extra functionality is justified but whether it fits in the project. If it is not part of the initial scope, the project should be adapted, including its requirements, and reevaluated as to feasibility (4.6), costs and schedule. The conclusion may also be that developing the extensions requires starting a new project.

To help ensure the "delimited" criterion, the Standard Plan includes a dedicated chapter, G.6, "limitations and exclusions", the place to specify what (often interesting) functionality does not lie within the project's scope.

4.9.2 Ensuring delimitation

The best guard against scope creep is to apply a discipline — particular in the Goals book, which determines everything else — of explicitly naming functionality that could be misconstrued as covered by the project but is not.

Goals and System requirements are typically positive. Not only positive but imperative: the system *shall do* this and *shall do* that (see "Be prescriptive", 5.7.6, page 91). Do not hesitate, particularly in the Goals book, to include negative statements to guard against scope creep.

When — in the middle of a project already fighting to meet its schedule, as all projects do — the assault of some over-enthusiastic stakeholders (including "fellow travelers" as we will encounter them in 6.5), or the discovery of functionality offered by competing products, build up the pressure to include "just a little" extra stuff, you will be able to point out that the endorsed requirements explicitly ruled out such extensions.

4.9.3 Assessing delimitation

- Check that the requirements include a meaningful chapter G.6 (Limitations and exclusions), describing functions that the system *could* meaningfully include but will not.
- Check that each element of functionality explicitly follows from one or more of the Goals. Here the pursuit of delimitation concurs with the pursuit of traceability (4.8).

4.9.4 Parts of the Standard Plan particularly relevant to assessing delimitation

- G.6 (limitations and exclusions): the principal place for stating what the system's development should not consider.
- S.2 (functionality): check this chapter to make sure that the functionality it specifies all follows from goals (particularly G.3, expected benefits) and does not add its own scope creep.

4.10 READABLE

Readability

A requirement is readable if it can be readily understood by its intended audience.

4.10.1 About readability

The mention of the audience in the definition highlights that readability depends on who reads the requirements. Natural language is an obvious example: Chinese text is very readable to a Chinese reader and very unreadable to someone who does not know the language. More generally, readability will depend on the level of training of the requirements' expected readership.

Beware in particular of the use of the readability criterion as an argument against special notations, such as formal (mathematical) notations, discussed in detail in chapters 9 and 10 of this Handbook. Special notations do require appropriate training, but to people having undergone such training they are just as readable as natural language. They can even be *more* readable since they are free of the noise, ambiguities and some other deficiencies of natural language (as will be reviewed and illustrated in "The seven sins of the specifier", 5.2, page 72).

4.10.2 Ensuring readability

Make sure that, regardless of project pressures, all requirements texts are written carefully, helped by available text-processing facilities including tools for spelling and grammar correctness. The goal is not to be pedantic; the application of proper language rules is a sign that the texts have been prepared with a focus on quality. While quality of content matters most, quality as a whole stars with quality of form.

Outside of the Goals book, special notations are not by themselves, as just observed, enemies of readability, but you must make sure that they are properly documented and that the relevant stakeholders receive appropriate training to understand them.

Graphical illustrations can help readability, but only if handled carefully. In particular, they must complement the textual specifications and never contradict them. They must always have clear semantics. We will study graphical specifications, their advantages and their limitations in "Graphical notations", 5.5.2, page 80.

Special readability considerations apply to the Goals book of the Standard Plan because its intended readership is broader: not just members of the technical team but a wide range of stakeholders, decision makers and outsiders. It should be written in plain language with particular attention to clarity; graphical illustrations are often appropriate there, while notations requiring specific training are generally not suitable.

More generally, an entire chapter of this Handbook (chapter 5) is devoted to techniques for writing clear, useful requirements. Enforce its principles throughout the requirements effort.

4.10.3 Assessing readability

- It does not take long to determine whether the general writing style of requirements documentation is so-so, or of professional quality. The injunction to use correct grammar and spelling applies to all chapters, however technical; there is no excuse for sloppiness.

- Check that the various parts of the Standard Plan are filled properly, with a good understanding of their respective roles and no confusion. For example, limitations go into G.6 (limitations and exclusions), not P.6 (risks and mitigation); constraints and assumptions (E.3 and E.4) should not be confused (see the disambiguating criteria given in section 1.7, page 9).

- Check for undue use of acronyms.

- Check that all technical terms and acronyms are defined and explained in the glossary.

- Check that graphical illustrations clearly explain all symbols and conventions (for example in captions) and follow the rules of "Graphical notations", 5.5.2, page 80.

- If any parts of the requirements use a special notation (such as a formal language, see chapter 9), check that tutorials and training are available (as part of the setup for the project and the responsible organization).

- Check that every requirements element using such a special notation applies it correctly, following its rules (or describes and justifies any deviations from its standard usage).

- More generally, check that the requirements texts follow all the requirements writing advice and principles of chapter 5 of this Handbook.

4.10.4 Parts of the Standard Plan particularly relevant to assessing readability

- E.1 (glossary).

- The Goals book, as a whole but particularly G.2 and G.3 (current situation, expected benefits), for clarity in conveying the essentials features of the project to all stakeholders.

4.11 MODIFIABLE

> **Modifiability**
>
> A set of requirements is modifiable if it can be adapted in case of changes to Project, Environment, Goals or System properties, through an effort commensurate with the extent of the changes.

4.11.1 About modifiability

There is an easy part and a hard part to modifiability of requirements. The easy part follows from good text-processing practices, ensuring that one can painlessly update elements and move them around. The hard part has to do with the structuring of the requirements, particularly system functionality (chapter S.2 of the Standard Plan).

4.11.2 Ensuring modifiability

For the "easy part", rely on automatic text-processing mechanisms for the identification and numbering of all individual elements. The rule here is never to make an exception to this discipline, for example by numbering the elements of a list manually. Resist the temptation.

For the "hard part", **object-oriented techniques** have been the principal solution used on the design and programming side to ensure modifiability of systems. Chapter 8 of this Handbook explains how requirements can also obtain modifiability benefits through the application of the same general techniques, leading to the concept of object-oriented requirements, whereby the architecture of requirements is based on object types and their relations.

4.11.3 Assessing modifiability

- Check that all elements are identified by automatic mechanisms facilitating updates.

- Check that the description of functionality (S.2) organizes the specification of individual functions around the types of objects to which they apply.

4.11.4 Parts of the Standard Plan particularly relevant to assessing modifiability

- Environment book and System book (particularly S.2).

4.12 VERIFIABLE

Verifiability
A System (resp. Project) requirement is verifiable if it is expressed in such a way as to allow determining whether a proposed implementation (resp. the sequence of events in the actual project) satisfies it.

The present discussion of verifiability will concentrate on the system part (project verifiability belongs to project management more than specifically to requirements engineering).

4.12.1 About verifiability

Verifiability is closely related to a central concept of the philosophy of science, falsifiability, due in particular to Karl Popper, according to which a scientific theory is not meaningful unless it is possible (if only in thought) to devise a test that would invalidate it. In software, similarly, it is generally easier to demonstrate that an implementation does not satisfy a requirement than to demonstrate that it does. The positive demonstration would requires fully formal requirements (chapter 9). When no such formal description is possible, making a negative demonstration possible is already a good sign of verifiability.

4.12.2 Ensuring verifiability

The rest of this Handbook presents, throughout the discussion, techniques and guidelines for avoiding vague, unassessable, motherhood-and-apple-pie requirements (*"the user interface shall be user-friendly"*!) and instead producing precise requirements against which it is possible to evaluate an implementation. Note in particular:

*   In the chapter on how to write requirements, the list ("The seven sins of the specifier", 5.2, page 72) of typical pitfalls such as noise and wishful thinking, which hamper verifiability, and the detailed advice on how to use a precise and effective style for writing requirements ("Style rules for natural-language requirements", 5.7, page 88).
*   In the chapter on formal methods (chapter 9), techniques for using mathematical specifications to guarantee precision, and examples of their application.

4.12.3 Assessing ("verifying") verifiability

"Verifying verifiability" implies neither paradox nor recursion but simply denotes assessing whether requirements are written in a way that will make it possible, once a tentative implementation becomes available, to verify that it conforms to them.

Many of the determinants of verifiability are those also affecting unambiguity (4.5) and, to a lesser extent, readability (4.10): requirements should be precise and amenable to falsifiability.

4.12.4 Parts of the Standard Plan particularly relevant to assessing verifiability

*   The Environment book, in particular the constraints chapter, E.3, to make sure that environment constraints are well understood).
*   The description of system functionality in S.2.

4.13 PRIORITIZED

Prioritization

A set of System requirements is prioritized if it includes for each of them a specification of its importance relative to the others, making it possible to make informed decisions if events in the course of the project make it necessary to renounce some functionality.

4.13.1 About prioritization

One of the most common — but easily avoidable — mistakes in devising system requirements is to throw in all desirable features without any clear statement of their relative importance. The feasibility criterion (4.6) rules out unbridled wishful-thinking ("kitchen sink") requirements, but does not suffice to guarantee that the project will deliver the essential functionality. (See also the "Second-system effect" in exercise 6-E.1, page 126.)

What functionality is "essential"? Potentially, all of it; at least, every element of functionality is likely to be essential to *some* stakeholders. Given environment and budget constraints, the project will have to retain some elements and renounce others. The choice should be a viable tradeoff between the desirable and the feasible. It is not, however, the end of the story. Things happen to projects. Promised budgets get cut. Unexpected technical problems arise (for example with external tools, as discussed in a later chapter: "Feasibility prototypes", 6.11.5, page 123). Project members get sick or leave and replacements are not up to par. The competition releases a product and you have to deliver your own new version earlier than expected to avoid losing market share. Enough reasons — although there may be more — to drop functionality.

It is common for a project to encounter such circumstances, but they carry a considerable risk: the decision to sacrifice some elements of functionality and retain others, made under fire, may turn out to be wrong and cost the project dearly. A well-run project will have prepared for this eventuality at the proper stage: during the study of requirements.

4.13.2 Ensuring prioritization

The discussion of requirements elicitation (in the chapter following the present ones) reviews techniques for prioritizing system requirements in a dedicated section: "Get stakeholders to prioritize", 6.10.5, page 121. As noted there, it is often sufficient to classify requirements into three categories: critical, important, nice-to-have.

The Standard Plan has a chapter of the System book devoted to prioritization: S.5. It is the responsibility of the requirements effort to make sure that whenever S.2 introduces elements of functionality each gets a clear indication of priority.

4.13.3 Assessing prioritization

- Check that every element of functionality in S.2 includes a corresponding priority specification in S.5.

4.13.4 Parts of the Standard Plan particularly relevant to assessing prioritization

S.2 and S.5.

4.14 ENDORSED

> **Endorsement**
> A requirement is endorsed if it has been approved by all the relevant decision-makers.

4.14.1 About endorsement

All the previous criteria apply to the contents of the requirements. Endorsement (our last one) involves the people who are either responsible for the requirements or affected by it. It is relatively simple to ensure, but indispensable.

To be of value, requirements should be approved by all the key stakeholder representatives, particularly two of them:

- The person, often called "product owner", officially representing the future user community. The product owner will be responsible for accepting or rejecting successive iterations of the software, and hence should endorse the requirements. (The term comes from agile methods such as Scrum, which have a specific view of requirements, but every project, regardless of its process-management method, has a person filling this role or a similar one.)

- The development team's head, who will bear responsibility for implementing the system.

Requirements are a contract between (among others, but most importantly) the two groups of stakeholders these people represent: those who need the system and those who build it. The goal of mutual endorsement is to identify any discrepancies early, before development begins.

Not only identify them, but, in almost all cases, resolve them. The only exception is a case of a discrepancy to which the parties cannot find an agreed solution, perhaps because the joint decision is "let's try out and see what works". But in that case, which should remain rare, the mutually endorsed requirements should include a clear description of this state of affairs.

4.14.2 Ensuring endorsement

Make sure that key stakeholder representatives sign off on all major requirement documents; specifically, every book in the Standard Plan. Make sure that every disagreement is recorded and its statement also signed off by the responsible parties.

4.14.3 Assessing endorsement

- Check that every major document, in particular every book of the Standard Plan, has been approved in writing by the key stakeholder representatives.
- Check that all such endorsements are applicable to the latest versions of the documents.
- Check that any disagreement has been recorded and the record also approved.
- Check that all such approvals are formal and attested by an actual signature.

4.14.4 Parts of the Standard Plan particularly relevant to assessing endorsement

Front and back matter of all the books, which contain official approvals.

4-E EXERCISES

4-E.1 Oppositions and tradeoffs

The introduction to this chapter (page 47) gave an example of two of the quality factors —
"unambiguous" and "readable" — possibly opposing each other, as illustrated by the question
of whether to use a formal notation. Identify other examples in which two different quality factors, among the fourteen of this chapter, would pull in opposite directions. For each of them,
discuss what kind of tradeoff might reconcile the opposing factors.

4-E.2 Alphabetical order, recursively defined

Provide a non-operational definition of alphabetical order, an alternative to the "proper definition" on page 58 (part of "The difficulty of abstracting", 4.7.2, page 57), but not using any integer value (such as n in that definition). Instead, your definition can use recursion, that is to say,
rely on the application of the property itself, "*smaller*", on some parts of the words involved.

You may use the notions of head of a non-empty word (its first letter), its tail (the word that
remains if we remove the head), prefix of a word (any word that is an initial substring of it, such
as "REQ" for "REQUIRE", or the word itself in full), proper prefix (a prefix other than the
word in full), suffix, proper suffix.

4-E.3 Family relations

Assume that the "*child*" concept (as in "Harry is a *child* of Diana") is known, give a precise
specification of "parent", "sibling", "grandparent", "grandchild", "ancestor", "descendant",
"proper ancestor", "proper descendant" (where "proper" means not the original person), "first
cousin", "remote cousin", "aunt or uncle". Adding a notion of "gender", define "daughter",
"son", "sister", "brother", "granddaughter", "grandmother" (etc.), "aunt", "uncle". (See also
exercise 9-E.1, page 183.)

4-E.4 Salad definition

[Meyer 2012] highlights the difficulty of requirements by showing how elusive it is to define
such a simple and seemingly obvious everyday notion as "salad": the variety of its uses makes
it hard to pinpoint universal properties. After reading that article, choose a specific context
(specifying your choice explicitly and clearly) and, within that context, provide a definition of
"salad" in a form that would be suitable for a requirements document, for example as part of
its glossary (6.4). Include limitations (scoping).

4-E.5 Consistency

In the example requirements document of [Bair 2005], can you find any case of inconsistency?

BIBLIOGRAPHICAL NOTES AND FURTHER READING

[Harish 2021] (from a commercial site for a specific software product) provides a good description of the circumstances that led to the crash of the Mars Climate Vehicle; the quotations in section 4.4 are from that article. The original official report was [NASA 1999].

The notion of handover ("Ensuring feasibility", 4.6.2, page 55) is one of the form of "waste" analyzed and decried in the "Lean Development" branch of agile methods, presented in [Poppendieck 2003] and [Poppendieck 2010].

The classic text on software project costing ("Ensuring feasibility", 4.6.2, page 55) is [McConnell 2006], full of excellent pragmatic advice.

A good reference on the DOORS requirements system (as of 2011) is [Hull, Jackson and Dick 2011-a], extracted from a requirements textbook, [Hull, Jackson and Dick 2011]. For more recent extensions, "DOORS Next Generation", see [IBM 2021]. On the Eiffel Information System, see [EIS 2021].

The concept of falsifiability (4.12) is a central component of Karl Popper's study of science [Popper 1959].

[Mannion-Keepence 1995] contains a list of requirements quality factors under the acronym SMART (Specific, Measurable, Attainable, Realizable, Time-bounded).

5

How to write requirements

Requirements engineering is an act of intermediation: you gather requirements from stakeholders and other sources and put them in a form useful to the developers. The next chapter will explain how to gather ("elicit") requirements; this one explains how to write them.

Section 5.1 discusses when this writing process will happen, and where its results will appear (reminding us that in most cases we should consider not just a single "requirements document" but a set of documents). As a warning of the difficulty of the task, section 5.2 introduces the "seven sins of the specifier": common mistakes in requirements writing. 5.3 discusses the nefarious influence of repetition, and how to avoid it. A related issue, addressed in 5.4, is how to separate explanatory text from binding specifications. Requirements are not all written in natural language; 5.5 discusses the role of other notations such as graphics and tables. The remaining sections present rules for natural-language requirements. 5.6 criticizes and improves a few poorly written examples. Switching from "how not to" to "how to", 5.7 presents the fundamental style rules, and 5.8 explains how to handle "TBD" (To Be Determined) elements. Section 5.9 addresses the specific needs of the Goals part of requirements. (The other sections apply to all four "books" of requirements in the plan of chapter 3: Project, Environment, Goals and System.) The last section covers a classic example, small but instructive, showing how much one can err by not following the principles expounded in the rest of the chapter.

As with other prescriptive parts of this Handbook, remember to avoid the risk of perfectionism ("Requirements quality", 2.5): quality of requirements writing is but one component of quality of the requirements process, which itself is but one step towards quality of the final system — the goal that really matters. This chapter is not about enforcing perfection. It simply presents professional standards for requirements writing, whose application costs much less than the damage that poorly written documents will cause.

5.1 WHEN AND WHERE TO WRITE REQUIREMENTS

The two processes of gathering and writing down requirements do not need to happen (as sometimes suggested in older views of software engineering) as two successive steps. An iterative, interleaved scheme is usually more productive: gather some, write some, repeat.

Iteration provides a feedback loop. As you perform requirements gathering activities such as interviews and workshops, the very act of writing down what you are learning helps you identify forgotten questions, which you can try to fit into the next gathering step. The observation yields the first principle of this chapter:

© The Author(s), under exclusive license to Springer Nature Switzerland AG 2022
B. Meyer, *Handbook of Requirements and Business Analysis*, https://doi.org/10.1007/978-3-031-06739-6_5

> **Requirements Writing Principle**
>
> Start writing requirements as you gather them.

This advice is part of a general trend in modern software engineering — most vividly illustrated by the spread of agile methods — away from strictly sequential, Waterfall-like processes, towards more iterative ones. It is in line with the advice that the requirements process as a whole does not need to happen only at the beginning of the project, but should continue throughout development. (The more complete form of the simplified cycle given above would be: gather some, write some, *develop* some, repeat.)

Along with the "when" part, we must also ask *where* requirements will appear. Remember ("The form of requirements", 2.1.6, page 26) that we can seldom expect that all the wisdom about a complex modern project will fit in a single, linear "requirements document". Requirements information will appear in many different places, some of which are beyond the control of the project team and may in fact predate the project ("pre-requirements" as defined in 2.1.6).

5.2 THE SEVEN SINS OF THE SPECIFIER

Before getting to positive advice about requirements writing, we start with a list of deficiencies commonly found in requirements documents.

5.2.1 The Sins list

Some of the danger signals reviewed below are simply violations of desirable properties of requirements, discussed in the previous chapter and elsewhere in this Handbook. Grouping them into a separate list will help you remain alert to their occurrence when you encounter initial versions of requirements specifications, or are writing such specifications yourself. The table below lists these "Seven Sins of the Specifier", coming from a classic paper in the field. The following subsections provide further comments on some of the categories.

In the table's entries, remember that a "relevant property" is a feature of the Project, Environment, Goals or System that can affect stakeholders (the complete definition was in 1.2.3).

The Seven Sins of the Specifier	
Deficiency	**Definition**
Noise	A requirements element that carries no information on any relevant property (5.2.2). Variants: *remorse* (5.2.3); *repetition* (5.3).
Silence	The existence of a relevant property not covered anywhere in the requirements (5.2.2).
Contradiction	Two or more requirements elements that define a relevant property in incompatible ways. Variant: *falsehood* (5.2.4).
Ambiguity	A requirements element from which a reader may understand a relevant property in different ways. Variants: *synonyms* (5.2.5); *etcetera list* (5.2.6).

Wishful thinking	A requirements element that defines a relevant system property in such a way that it is not possible to determine whether a candidate solution satisfies it.
Overspecification	A requirements element that does not correspond to a relevant property, but to features of a possible design or implementation (4.7.3, page 59). An insidious variant is *operational reasoning* (see 9.5.4).
Dangling reference	A mention, in a requirements element, of a property that should be defined elsewhere in the requirements but is not.

The list does not include everything that can go wrong in requirements; after all, we had four-teen quality factors in chapter 4, not just seven, and each of them can — bad news — be vio-lated in several ways. We are focusing on requirements *writing*, not the full requirements process, and on particularly common mistakes which — here comes some good news — you can avoid if you are aware of them.

5.2.2 Noise and silence

Noise is frequent in requirements; so is silence. The reason is a human tendency to go for the easier task. Sometimes it is easy to add information that is not relevant but makes the specifier feel good, and tempting to forget aspects that are trickier to explain precisely. The blame for noise as well as silence can lie with either or both of:

* Stakeholders who babble about unimportant things and skip important ones. The remedy is to focus on stakeholders of highest value to the project ("Assessing stakeholders", 6.5, page 109) and keep asking them relevant questions ("Ask effective questions", 6.10.4, page 119).

* Requirements engineers or business analysts, who fail to ask some important questions. The remedy is to perform reviews and verification of requirements, in addition to the require-ments writers' self-assessment, to check the requirements for relevance and completeness.

5.2.3 Remorse

Remorse is a form of noise, which arises when a requirements document discusses a certain component (typically, of the System), and further in the text mentions the possibility that it might not exist. We will see an example below (5.6.3): a specification of an error report pro-duced by a program, and later on the note that if there is no error there shall be no such report. Reasonable enough, but coming too late! This practice, while common, causes confusion and uncertainty. The proper approach, to specify an optional component, is the logical one:

* Upon first introducing the component, mention that it is optional.

* At the same place, specify the conditions under which it will exist (for example, an error report shall be produced if and only if the processing produces at least one error, where the specification defines what exactly constitutes an error).

* Only then describe the properties of the optional component for the cases in which it exists.

5.2.4 Falsehood

Contradiction does not even need to include two statements at odds with each other. *One* statement can be wrong by itself. This kind of wrongness is not the same as the case of an incorrect requirement, in the sense of correctness, the very first of the quality factors (4.1). A requirement is incorrect if it does not reflect actual needs (for a goal, system or project requirement) or constraint (for an environment requirement). In requirements writing, a requirement is a falsehood if it includes a statement of a false property. We will see an example at the end of this chapter: a statement that a "line", in a text, is a sequence of characters (other than new-line) appearing between two new-line characters — plainly wrong since it does not cover the case of the first and last lines (which respectively have no preceding and ending new-lines).

The remedy against falsehoods is simple, although not miraculous: in addition to checking every piece of requirements against the actual intent (to ensure correctness) and against others (to avoid contradiction), make sure that it is internally (that is to say, just by itself) sound.

5.2.5 Synonyms

Ambiguity can arise from the use of multiple names for the same concept. As discussed in more detail below ("Repetition", 5.3, page 75), technical writing differs from literary writing in promoting rather than eschewing the use of a single term for a given concept. Referring to the same concept as "apparatus" in one paragraph and "device" in another may lead the reader to conclude that they denote different kinds of things. Hereby lies a principle:

No-Synonym Principle

In requirements writing, enforce a one-to-one correspondence between important concepts (of the project, environment, goals and system) and their names.

5.2.6 Etcetera lists

A frequent case of ambiguity is the "etcetera list": the enumeration of the variants of a certain notion, ending with "etc." or "and so on" or "and others". For example, *"the system shall provide user interfaces in English, French, Spanish, Mandarin etc."* To system developers, this list is confusing: should the system support any other languages, and if so which ones?

Such a phrasing is never appropriate. Instead of it, use one of the following two solutions:

- Give the complete list if possible. A little more work for the requirements engineer, but saves headaches and mistakes for the developers.

- If the definitive list is not closed at requirements time and the variants listed are just examples, say so by using the phrasing *"such as"*, *"including"* or *"for example"* and — importantly — indicating where the complete list will appear. In listing specific cases, make it clear whether they are just examples (you can then use *"such as…"*) or a required subset (*"including, but not limited to…"*). There is a difference between

> *The system shall provide user interfaces in languages such as (for example only) English, French, Spanish and Mandarin. The precise list of languages to be supported appears in the regularly updated Language Support List at https://…*

and

> *The system shall provide user interfaces in several languages including at least the following: English, French, Spanish and Mandarin. The full list appears in the regularly updated Language Support List at https://…*

The first is non-committal as it only gives examples and refers the reader to a dynamically evolving document (which could also be a chapter of one of the requirements books, since per this Handbook's principles requirements are a living product). The second also has this dynamic component but specifies a fixed minimum.

Either of these styles may be better depending on the circumstances, but the "etcetera" style is not acceptable.

Note that inheritance, in object-oriented requirements (chapter 8), provides an elegant way to add new variants to a predefined notion.

5.3 REPETITION

One of the forms of noise (the first of the "seven sins" of 5.2) is a common plague of requirements which deserves particular attention: repetition.

Why is repeating relevant properties bad? The answer is that it causes multiple forms of damage:

- Giving the same information twice is a waste of space, one of the reasons why requirements documents can become large and unwieldy. Unreasonably long documents make requirements harder to comprehend and may even lead developers and others to start ignoring them and miss key aspects of the problem.

- In practice, repeated elements are often not *exactly* repeated. Identical copy-paste does happen (and is to be banned, since a *reference* to the source is always preferable, as will be explained below); but most of the time repeated information is repeated in a slightly different way. Without the requirements writers realizing it, the different phrasings may either lead various readers (particularly, various developers) to understand a property differently, or lead some of them to wonder whether there is an inconsistency. It is better to ensure that all requirements are distinct, and that each clearly defines a property and its variants.

- Finally, repetitions cause trouble when requirements evolve, as they will ("Requirements Evolution Principle", page 23). Even if you have been able to root out contradictions among the initial duplicates or quasi-duplicates, it is hard to avoid the emergence of new ones as these elements start evolving and diverging.

The following principle reflects this analysis:

> **No-Repetition Principle**
> In requirements writing, never specify a property more than once.

This rule is sometimes known as "Single Point of Maintenance". In slogan form:

> Say it well; say it once.

The principle as stated applies to requirements documents. We have seen that requirements can integrate existing outside elements (such as emails and external documents). The project has no control over them; they may contain repetitions (and redundancies with internal documents). In the project's own documents, repetition is to be banned.

While the principle is strict and suffers no exception, it does not exclude some forms of redundancy which are not repetition in the proper sense and deserve special consideration:

- *Explanations* complementing the specification of a relevant property, although even this case should be handled restrictively (5.4 below).

- *Illustrations* of a property in a different notation, which are not repetition in the proper sense but do require care as well (5.3).

- *Refinement*: providing more detail on a property already specified in a general way. Refinement is not repetition but a presentation technique, avoiding the need to specify a complex property in just one chunk. For example the specification of wire transfers for a banking system might state "the rules in this section govern transfers to countries in Europe, as defined in paragraph Y", where paragraph Y states "*for the purpose of transfer rules in section X, 'Europe' shall denote the countries of the European Union as of 1 January 2022 plus Switzerland and […]*".

It is hard to find an excuse for true repetition since a suitable alternative is available: when you need to mention a relevant property (of the Project, Environment, Goals or System) that also appears somewhere else, you can choose one of the two places to state it, and in the other place *refer* to that statement. This observation leads to a companion of the above principle:

> **Reference Principle**
> Do not repeat: refer or refine.

Text processing systems help apply this principle. In the old days, populating a document with cross-references (as in "the *Seven Sins of the Specifier* appear on page 72 as part of section 5.2.1") was scary, because you knew that the slightest change would force you to update all references or risk releasing an error-ridden text. Today's tools automatically take care of the updating. Good requirements documents rely on this technology to make sure that every property is defined in one place, then used whenever needed through a reference to that definition.

A practical tip for such references:

Advice: formatting references to concept definitions

When using a requirements concept that has a precise definition elsewhere in requirements documents, use a consistent format, and (in an electronic version) make the reference a hyperlink to the definition.

A typical format convention is to underline such hyperlink references. For example (assuming this Handbook were a requirements document, which it is not):

Another way of stating that requirements documents should not include noise is to say that they should only specify <u>relevant properties</u>.

---

where the underlined part is a hyperlink to the definition of "relevant property" in 1.2.3, page 5. (Elsewhere, this Handbook marks hyperlinks with a different color rather than underlining.)

5.4 BINDING AND EXPLANATORY TEXT

The primary purpose of requirements is to specify properties of the Project, Environment, Goals and Systems. A committed requirements writer, intent on producing a useful document, will often feel an additional urge to *explain* the specification. Most of the time, this urge should be resisted.

"Most of the time" because a few specific parts of requirements do leave a role for explanations. In the Standard Plan of 3.1 they are the following chapters:

The only places where explanations are legitimate (in Standard Plan of 3.1)		
Chapter Title		*Why an explanation may be justified*
P.2	Imposed technical choices	It may be useful to recall the strategic decisions that stand behind some of these choices.
P.7	Requirements process and report	The description of how the requirements process will be conducted, and the report on how to proceed, may benefit from a more discursive style.
G.1 to G.3	Context & overall objective, current situation, expected benefits.	By their nature, these chapters have an explanatory spirit.
G.6	Limitations and exclusions	It may be useful to explain why some parts are not covered by the system.
S.5	Prioritization	Although mostly a specification, this chapter may spell out the reasons for some of the specified priority decisions.

Explanations appearing in these contexts often express "justifications", one of the legitimate kinds of requirement, introduced in 1.9.

Outside of these chapters, the focus of requirements documents should not be on explanation but on specification, descriptive and prescriptive. (Mostly descriptive for the Environment and Goals, mostly prescriptive for the Project and System.)

The temptation to explain comes from good intentions: requirements writers want to produce clear, helpful documents. The rationale for *not* yielding to this impulse is the same as for the ban on repetition (5.3): avoiding contradiction. Assume a specification, in an airline booking system, that only adult passengers may occupy seats on an exit row, and a supposedly helpful explanation that "*there is no guarantee that people 18 or younger will understand safety instructions*". In fact, the age limit defining an "adult" varies, and even if it is 18 it usually includes people of that exact age (whereas the phrasing "*18 or younger*" bars them — did you notice the discrepancy?). A programmer seeing the explanation might implement an incorrect rule.

The more you try to repeat things, the higher the likelihood that mistakes of that kind will creep in. The better approach is in most cases to make the specification clear and precise, so that it does not *need* an explanation. Specification beats explanation. Say it well; say it once.

For cases in which you feel the bare specification is too dry and does require explanations, you should limit the risk of confusion by clearly separating the two kinds of elements: those that specify, and those that explain. You will find a model for this approach in good *standards documents*. A standard is prescriptive: it sets parameters that an entire industry must follow. Often, the specification by itself is terse and hard to understand; explanations will be welcome. A common practice in standards is to mark explanatory text explicitly as such, using appropriate typographical conventions, so that only the non-explanatory parts have prescriptive value.

An example, extracted from the standard for the Eiffel programming language, appears on the next page. Note how the various official components are marked with their nature (definitions, syntax, validity), and how "informative text" uses a distinctive format. This is an excellent practice, recommended for all requirements, not just standards. It encourages requirements writers to reflect on what is truly binding on the developers and what is simply meant to help them. (A similar convention should apply to implementation hints, covered in 4.7.4, page 59.)

A note on the pragmatic side: of all the requirements writing advice in this Handbook, this one is among the least commonly applied in today's practice. But it is not particularly hard to enforce, and produces a significant benefit.

The following principle summarizes explanation-related advice:

Explanation Principle

E1 In requirements, favor specifications over explanations.

E2 When explanatory elements are indispensable, devote special care to checking that they do not contradict the specification elements, even in small details.

E3 In requirements texts (and other forms of expression of requirements), use a clear and explicit convention to ensure that any explanatory elements stand out as distinct from specification elements.

Levels of discourse in a programming language standard

8.9.18   **Definition: Check-correct**
An <u>effective</u> routine *r* is **check-correct** if, for every Check instruction *c* in *r*, any execution of *c* (as part of an execution of *r*) satisfies its Assertion.

8.9.19   **Syntax: Variants**
Variant $\triangleq$ **variant** [Tag_mark] Expression

8.9.20   **Validity: Variant Expression rule**   Validity code: *VAVE*
A Variant is valid if and only if its <u>variant expression</u> is <u>of type</u> *INTEGER* or one of its <u>sized variants</u>.

8.9.21   **Definition: Loop invariant and variant**
The Assertion introduced by the Invariant clause of a loop is called its **loop invariant**. The Expression introduced by the Variant clause is called its **loop variant**.

8.9.22   **Definition: Loop-correct**
A routine is **loop-correct** if every loop it contains, with <u>loop invariant</u> *INV*, <u>loop variant</u> *VAR*, Initialization *INIT*, Exit condition *EXIT* and body (Compound part of the Loop_body) *BODY*, satisfies the following conditions:

   1   {**True**} *INIT* {*INV*}
   2   {**True**} *INIT* {*VAR* $\geq$ 0}
   3   {*INV* **and then not** *EXIT*} *BODY* {*INV*}
   4   {*INV* **and then not** *EXIT* **and then** (*VAR* = *v*)} *BODY* {0 $\leq$ *VAR* < *v*}

Informative text

Conditions <u>1</u> and <u>2</u> express that the initialization yields a state in which the invariant is satisfied and the variant is non-negative. Conditions <u>3</u> and <u>4</u> express that the body, when executed in a state where the invariant is satisfied but not the exit condition, will preserve the invariant and decrease the variant, while keeping it non-negative. (*v* is an auxiliary variable used to refer to the value of *VAR* before *BODY*'s execution.)

End

5.5 NOTATIONS FOR REQUIREMENTS

A requirement is (1.2.4, page 5) *"a relevant statement about a project, environment, goal or system"*, where a "statement" is (1.2.2, page 4) *"a human-readable expression of a property"*. As was discussed in the introduction of these concepts, the "expression" of the property may take place in various notations, including:

- Natural language, such as English.

- Graphical notations, using either precisely defined rules such as those of UML (Unified Modeling Language) or ad hoc conventions (as in informal diagrams of system structure).

- Tabular notations. Tables can be useful to specify behavior that depends on combinations of various parameters. A typical example appears below.

- "Formal" notations, such as mathematical specification languages, or programming languages such as Eiffel, used for description (rather than implementation) purposes.

The rest of this section takes a look at the specific demands of each of these forms, then discusses (in 5.5.5) how to combine them.

5.5.1 Natural language

Natural language accounts for the bulk of requirements, in both longer traditional versions ("requirements documents" in "Waterfall" style) and shorter versions (use cases, user stories).

The advantages and limitations of natural language are clear. On the positive side, it is the only notation that everyone understands without specific training. It is flexible and lends itself to expressing nuances; it can be used for explanation (5.4) as well as specification. On the negative side, natural-language statements often lack the precision required for specifying delicate properties of complex systems. Also, natural language can be discursive and wordy.

Where you need precision, you can complement natural language by formal specifications (5.5.3 below and chapter 9). For high-level overviews, graphical illustrations (5.5.2) can help.

Natural languages as applied to requirements are not quite the same as in their everyday use. Different rules apply: some (although not all) of what is considered good style in a novel can be bad for requirements, while a novel written in good requirements style would make for awful reading. Where literary pieces benefit from variety and surprise, requirements texts call for regularity; a good requirements document should be boring. A later section of this chapter introduces the specific rules: "Style rules for natural-language requirements", 5.7, page 88.

Going beyond this observation, some requirements methods use restricted versions of natural language, allowing only certain turns of phrase. See the bibliographic section for pointers.

5.5.2 Graphical notations

Graphical illustrations can be a great help for understanding. They are particularly appropriate in the description of Goals, to give a general idea of possibly complex problems and solutions.

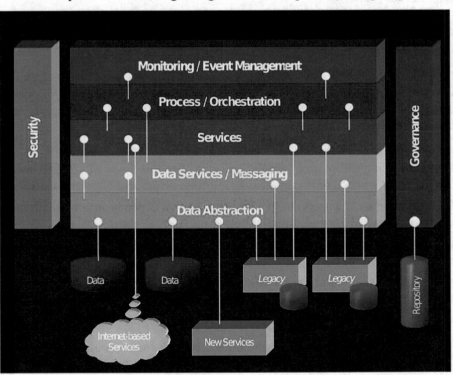

SOA meta-model (Source: Wikipedia)

Using pictures in requirements calls for caution. Too often (with the cliché that "a picture is worth a thousand words" as implicit cover) technical texts flash fancy graphics without bothering to define the precise conventions being used. Such boxes-and-arrows diagrams are particularly common in networking, as in the richly colored figure on the preceding page, from Wikipedia, describing components and connections of a Service-Oriented Architecture.

This example typifies the problems found in many graphical illustrations:

- What exactly does it mean to have a particular layer (such as "Services") above another ("Data Services / Messaging")? What is the implied relationship between them?

- What is the meaning of the white connectors between layers (the ones that look like tadpoles caught in a snowstorm)? If there is a general rule that each layer relies on the one immediately below, why are there three connectors between "Process / Orchestration" and "Services" just below and just two between "Monitoring / Event Management" and "Process / Orchestration"? Why do some connectors go through intermediate layers, such as from "Process/Orchestration" directly to "Data Services / Messaging" and from "Services" to "Legacy"? Are these cases violations of traditional information hiding rules?

- Why do some elements, such as "Legacy", appear twice? Is it a convention to suggest elements that may appear in two or more instances, such as "legacy" elements and (at the same level) "data"? But are we then to understand that there is only one of "New Services" and of "Internet-based services"?

- The layers are of different nature. The "Data Services / Messaging" layer offers APIs (program interfaces) for certain network services. "Data Abstraction", on the other hand, is just a methodological concept (see chapter 8). Layering apples on top of oranges is confusing.

- The role of the vertical boxes on the sides is unclear. They seem to suggest that Security and Governance apply across all levels (as "cross-cutting" concerns). Since it is hard to think of an endeavor of any kind in information technology — or, for that matter, any other field — in which this observation does not apply, it seems hardly essential to the specification of Service-Oriented Architecture. Assuming the boxes do merit their spots in the figure, their placement is puzzling: does Security cease to be a concern for the lower levels, such as "New Services", to which the box does not extend? Why is there a tadpole from "Governance", a strategic concern, to "repository", a technical artifact? (Presumably having a repository helps governance, but the repository will also help "Process/Orchestration", "Monitoring/Event Management" and just about all other horizontal layers. Puzzling.)

Pictures of that kind, as strong on impressiveness as they are weak on precise meaning, are common in technical documentation. They are prized because they give the reader a quick grasp of the structure of a system. This impression can, however, be deceptive.

If you use such pictures, you should pay particular attention to the **connectors** between elements of a diagram — typically, lines or arrows of some kind. Too often, diagram authors include an arrow to indicate that component A somehow relies on component B, or interacts with ("talks to") B in some way, or knows about B, or uses B, or is just related to B in some unspecified sense. Such vagueness is inappropriate in requirements. **Beware of boxes bearing arrows**.

Pictures can do more harm than good unless they explicitly state the meaning (also known as *semantics*) of all symbols. As an example (although not from a requirements document), the figure on page 139 at the beginning of section 8.3 of this Handbook uses two kinds of arrow (for the "client" and "inheritance" relations in object-oriented programming) and an asterisk symbol; their semantics is specified in the figure's caption.

Along with arrows connecting components, the symbols representing the **components** themselves need to have a precisely specified semantics. If you are variously using squares, rectangles, ellipses, circles and other shapes, make sure they correspond not to your whim but to distinct concepts, each explicitly stated.

If a set of a common conventions apply to several figures, you should — in line with the No-Repetition Principle — specify them in a single place (instead of repeating them in separate captions), and refer to that place in each figure.

In the exercise of making sure that each graphical symbol corresponds to a specific meaning, you will often be led to simplifying the figures. Colors are a typical example: after some initial exuberance, supported by the power of modern graphical design tools, you may realize that you are using too many colors without justification. A color change, like any other graphical convention, should represent a change of concept. Otherwise, go for the drab! Divert your artistic creativity to other pursuits; your requirements pictures may at the result be less exciting but they will also be less confusing and more useful to the people who really need them.

Summarizing graphics-related advice:

Picture Principle

Graphical illustrations in requirements texts must only use symbols — in particular those representing components and their connectors — with a precise semantics, defined in the illustrations themselves or in a common reference.

Every pictorial variation must reflect a semantic variation.

A complementary piece of advice is to ensure that there is no contradiction between pictures and texts (and other notations that may appear in the requirements). It is developed further in "Combining notations", 5.5.5, page 84 below.

5.5.3 Formal notations

For specifications requiring precision, human civilization has devised a solution: mathematical notation. "$\forall x: \mathrm{R} \mid cos^2(x) + sin^2(x) = 1$" is vastly superior to all other ways of expressing the same property (including the natural-language statement that "*the sum of the squares of the cosine and sine functions applied to any real number, the same for both, is always equal to one*").

Mathematics-like notations, known as *formal* notations, and the associated *formal methods* have gained ground for software requirements. They do not have to replace natural-language requirements entirely, but can complement them for parts that require precision. The important topic of formal specification occupies the entirety of chapter 9.

5.5.4 Tabular notations

Tabular notation is a variety of formal specification using a simple spatial representation, easily understood even by people who may be resistant to the use of usual mathematical formalisms.

Consider a specification that expresses the value of a certain property as resulting from one or (more interestingly) two other properties. In the Open Systems Interconnection (OSI) model, for example, various networking features such as error recovery and the ability to reinitiate a connection are available, or not, depending on the class of transport protocols, of which there are five, TP0 to TP4. The property of interest is "feature available or not?"; the two properties that condition it are the networking feature and the transport class.

Mathematically, this specification is a case of a well-known notion: a boolean-valued function *present* taking two arguments. We can state that *present* (*Error_recovery*, *TP0*) has value false, *present* (*Error_recovery*, *TP1*) has value true and so on. But a tabular representation — as used in the OSI Wikipedia page — also does the job, in a concise and readable form:

Feature name	TP0	TP1	TP2	TP3	TP4
Connection-oriented network	Yes	Yes	Yes	Yes	Yes
Connectionless network	No	No	No	No	Yes
Concatenation and separation	No	Yes	Yes	Yes	Yes
Segmentation and reassembly	Yes	Yes	Yes	Yes	Yes
Error recovery	No	Yes	Yes	Yes	Yes
Reinitiate connection[a]	No	Yes	No	Yes	No
Multiplexing / demultiplexing over single virtual circuit	No	No	Yes	Yes	Yes
Explicit flow control	No	No	Yes	Yes	Yes
Retransmission on timeout	No	No	No	No	Yes
Reliable transport service	No	Yes	No	Yes	Yes

[a] If an excessive number of PDUs are unacknowledged.

Classes of Transport Protocol (Source: Wikipedia)

Tables also work well for specifying functions of one argument (rather than two), as in the example (about the simplest possible one) of the negation function in logic:

a	**not** *a*
True	False
False	True

Tables often beat all other notations when you need, as in these examples, to specify the precise value of a function of one or two parameters, each of which takes one of a fixed set of values.

In addition to being readily supported by spreadsheet tools such as Excel, tables benefit from being easy to change as the understanding of the requirements advances or the requirements themselves change. (We may note here the connection with the software design and programming technique of "table-driven computation", which computes results not through a specific algorithm, hard-coded into the program, but by looking up a table. The table can be represented as data, easier to change than program text. In this case the concept of table is applicable to more than two dimensions.)

For requirements, tables lose their appeal for more than two parameters — except if one of the parameters only has a small number of possible values, in which case you can use several tables — and for parameters that take too many possible values, or have a continuous (rather than discrete) range. Within their scope of applicability, however, they can be an excellent requirements specification technique, more precise than natural language and more widely understandable than other mathematical notations.

5.5.5 Combining notations

The four kinds of notation just reviewed — natural language, pictures, mathematics and tables — are the principal ones available for specifying requirements. All have many variants (reviewed in a survey article cited in the bibliographical section). They are not exclusive; in particular, while natural language in some form remains dominant in the industry's practice, it benefits from complements in other notations, for example graphics for illustration and formal or table notations for elements that require a precise, rigorous specification.

The caveat here follows from the discussions of repetition and explanation (5.3 and 5.4). The risk to keep in mind is that requirements elements expressed in different notations lead to understanding a certain property in slightly different ways. Hence the rule, which extends the No-repetition and Explanation principles to the case of multiple notations:

Multiple Notation Principle

In requirements using more than one notation, make sure that the binding specification of every property unambiguously appears in only one of notations.

If elements in more than notation pertain to a common property, make sure that the requirements clearly indicate which one is binding, and label the others as explanatory.

(Again: *say it well, say it once*.) The binding specification could be in natural-language text, with a figure illustrating the concepts. In this case, the figure caption should state "This figure for explanatory purposes only; see specification in section x.y", or equivalent. Conversely, a figure or table could serve as a precise specification (like, in this Handbook, the diagram of possible references between books on page 37), and a text could comment on it; such text should be labeled as "informative", per the conventions illustrated in the standard extract of page 79.

Work on *multirequirements* (see the bibliographical section) goes further than the last principle by proposing a requirements methodology that interleaves descriptions at three levels: natural-language texts; formal descriptions in a high-level language; graphical representation.

5.6 SOME EXAMPLES: BAD, LESS BAD, GOOD

In the spirit of grammar and style textbooks (*"do not write: ..., write instead: ..."*), here are some examples of requirements writing that is subject to improvement. Most come from various authors' publications, listed in the bibliography section.

5.6.1 "Provide status messages"

An example cited by Wiegers and Beatty: *"The Background Task Manager shall provide status messages at regular intervals not less than 60 seconds."* Objections:

- Lower bound, but no upper bound! Is an interval of 5 minutes OK? An interval of two hours? Of a year?
- *"Provide status messages"*. Is it OK to flash the messages for a couple of seconds and let them go away (like Skype alerts on a desktop)? Probably not. We need to specify whether, how and how long the messages should stay.

Wiegers and Beatty's proposed replacement:

> *The Background Task Manager (BTM) shall display status messages in a designated area of the user interface:*
> - *The messages shall be updated every 60 plus or minus 10 seconds after background task processing begins.*
> - *The messages shall remain visible continuously.*
> - *Whenever communication with the background task process is possible, the BTM shall display the percent completed of the background task.*

This rewrite has some improvements:

- It corrects the two deficiencies listed above.
- It indicates that the user interface design must provide a place for the error messages, without overspecifying the form of that UI element.
- It identifies the mechanism being specified under a precise name (an acronym, "BTM", which should have an entry in the glossary, see 6.4).

It is not, however, itself immune to criticism:

- It is much longer. Is the four-fold increase in the number of words truly justified? Wordiness leads to huge, hard to manage and eventually ignored requirements documents.
- One mention is either incorrect or infeasible (remember "Correct", 4.1 and "Feasible", 4.6): since screen space is finite and fonts must be large enough for readability, one cannot keep all messages *"visible continuously"*. It should probably say *"accessible"* continuously (for example with a scroll list, although as noted there is no need to prescribe a particular UI style).
- The last part (about communication) is a new requirement, not deducible from the original. Maybe it is justified, but it also can raise a suspicion of overspecification.

Exercise 5-E.1, page 102 asks you to provide a replacement that addresses these problems.

5.6.2 The flashing editor

Another example cited and criticized by Wiegers and Beatty: *"The XML Editor shall switch between displaying and hiding non-printing characters instantaneously."* Criticism:

- When does it "switch"? Does it decide on its own accord one minute to display non-printing characters in a file, such as backspace, and the next minute to hide it? Probably not (editors are not expected to possess free will), but the trigger should be stated.

- "Instantaneously". What is instantaneous to me may seem like an eternity to you. Such words have no place in a proper requirements text.

Wiegers and Beatty's replacement, correcting these deficiencies:

> *The user shall be able to toggle between displaying and hiding all XML tags in the document being edited with the activation of a specific triggering mechanism. The display shall change in 0.1 second or less.*

Indeed better. At the risk of nitpicking, we note that there is no obvious need for both the verbs "toggle" and "trigger", and that *"with the activation of a specific triggering mechanism"* is noise: by definition, any operation that an editor provides to its user is available through "a specific triggering mechanism" — what else could one expect? Since everything is clear and the replacement remains fairly concise, we would probably leave it alone in an actual requirements document, but for the sake of perfectionism (in a deviation from the Requirements Effort Principle), exercise 5-E.1 asks you to improve the text further if you can.

5.6.3 Always an error report?

One more Wiegers-Beatty example: *"The XML parser shall produce a markup error report that allows quick resolution of errors when used by XML novices."* Its critique is left to the reader. The authors' proposed replacement is:

> *After the XML Parser has completely parsed a file, it shall produce an error report that contains the line number and text of any XML errors found in the parsed file and a description of each error found.*
> *If no parsing errors are found, the parser shall not produce an error report.*

This correction removes the ambiguous *"when used by XML novices"*, a vague, subjective criterion no better than *"instantaneously"* in the preceding example. Who is an XML novice? How do we know what it takes for error messages to enable such a user to correct the error? (We do not.) More modestly but more usefully, the revised version says what basic information the error message should provide. This replacement is still subject to discussion:

- It has opted for an error report produced only after full parsing. This property was not in the original. It may be overspecification, since it excludes the possibility of reporting errors on-the-fly. Why not leave this aspect open, as a user interface choice to be made later? What matters is that the parser will be able to process input containing syntax errors and detect those errors, not *when* it will report them.

- The new text correctly indicates (unlike the original) that the system should only produce an error report if there is an error. This property may sound obvious, but the phrasing of the original version implied that there would always be a report, which is probably incorrect.

- The way the new version adds this property, is, however, a case of the "**remorse**" syndrome in requirements documents. Remorse is the phenomenon of describing some element (of the project, environment, goals or system) as if its existence was a done deal, only later suddenly to state that it might not exist after all, leaving the reader confused. Technically, remorse is a case of *contradiction*: in the first paragraph we are told that the processing "shall produce" — strong words! — an error report, and in the second that maybe it will not. The damage is minor since the two statements are close to each other, but in a complex requirements specification they might lie further apart, or even in different documents, and cause misunderstandings.

Again, can you do better? (Exercise 5-E.1, page 102.)

5.6.4 Words to avoid

"Instantaneous" in one of the above examples is one of a number of words, of which "user-friendly" is perhaps the most annoying, that are useful in ordinary language and may sound nice — who would argue *against* making a system "user-friendly"? — but are too vague to merit a place in requirements texts. Here is a list; it is not exhaustive but gives the idea. Each entry explains why the term or terms are bad and, if possible, suggests a replacement.

A checklist of terms that have no place in requirements texts	
Words to avoid	**Why (and how to replace)**
About, approximately, around	Subjective terms, not useful in requirements. Instead, give a tolerance range, e.g. "*5 cm ± 0.2 mm*".
Acceptable, appropriate, satisfactory, suitable	Subjective terms. Instead, explain what concrete properties a value, parameter, solution etc. must satisfy.
Certainly	If it is certain, no need to state that it is. If not, make it so and stop babbling.
Clearly, obviously	Noise terms, not useful in requirements. Making things clear is better than boasting about clarity.

Definitely	Noise term, not useful in requirements. Remove.
And so on, etc.	Requirements should leave no room for ad-libbing by the reader. See "Etcetera lists", 5.2.6, page 74.
Fast, immediate, instantaneous, real-time	Subjective terms. Instead, give hard bounds for response time.
Many, several, some	Give precise values or ranges if available. Even the simple variants "zero or more", "one or more" etc. are better.
Much, very	Subjective terms. Instead, give precise criteria. Or, remove altogether.
Should	Requirements are not the place for timidity. The system either must do something, or is not required to do it. "Shall" is the conventional terminology.
State-of-the-art	Vanity term, even though it may sound attractive in Goals documents. Instead, define applicable standards and technologies.
User-friendly	Vanity term. Instead, develop and document user-interface guidelines.
24/7	Sounds really impressive, but pure wishful thinking. Replace by precise requirements on incident handling and failsafe modes.

In many of these examples, the underlying criterion, among the quality factors of chapter 4, is *verifiability* and the associated concept of falsifiability (4.12). A requirement of "real-time" response is not verifiable. A precise specification of acceptable response times is.

5.7 STYLE RULES FOR NATURAL-LANGUAGE REQUIREMENTS

Writing requirements is, before anything else, writing, and should follow the general rules of good writing. But it is a specific kind of writing, entirely directed at the success of the project and resulting system, and driven by rules reviewed below.

5.7.1 General guidelines

Requirements can only be effective if their recipients — particularly programmers and testers — understand and trust them.

Gaining trust requires achieving a good level of quality. If developers come across sloppy requirements, they may be tempted not to pay them enough attention. They will second-guess or bypass the requirements, making instead their own requirements decisions, right or wrong.

The guidelines in the table on the next page are the principal rules of writing for requirements specifications. The basic justifications are in the table; further comments appear after it.

Basic rules of requirements writing	
Rule	**Comments**
Use correct spelling and grammar	Using correct language hardly costs more, and reinforces trust in the quality of the requirements. See 5.7.2 below.
Get the structure right	Avoid piling up a loose collection of individual requirements; instead, think about the overall structure of documents, to help the reader grasp each of the PEGS in its entirety. Chapter 3 gives the standard structure.
Use simple language	Other than technical terms from the domain, avoid any phrasing that will delay understanding for some readers.
Define all terms	You cannot expect all readers to know the domain vocabulary. In particular, beware of acronyms and include all relevant terms in the glossary (6.4).
Identify every part	Every element of the requirements, down to every paragraph, should have a unique identifier enabling convenient retrieval. See 5.7.4.
Be consistent	The same conventions should apply throughout the requirements specifications. For example, a given concept should always be denoted by the same term. See 5.7.5.
Be concise	Resist temptation to achieve clarity through redundant explanations.
Be precise	Imprecision causes misunderstandings and bugs.
Be prescriptive	The Goals, Project and System books enjoin developers and other project members to produce certain results. They should give clear prescriptions.
Separate explanation from prescription	Sometimes prescriptions require explanation. The two styles should be clearly distinguished.
Define responsibilities (use active style)	A passive style ("X will be done") leaves room for ambiguity. An active style ("Y will do X") avoids it.

5.7.2 Use correct spelling and grammar

There can be no justification for spelling and grammatical mistakes in requirements documents. Any text-processing tool will spot misspellings and suggest replacements. Any standard style guide (see the bibliography section) will remind you of the basic rules of good writing.

Even with these tools, mistakes will creep in; the way to produce a correct text is to make sure every element is reviewed by one or more people other than the writer. Requirements, as noted in one of our very first principles, are software (Requirements Nature Principle, 2.1.3).

Modern software development imposes strict procedures for *program* elements: no code is accepted until it has been reviewed by people other than its developer. Requirements elements deserve a similar process.

Pragmatic note from the projects in the author's experience: most of the failed ones did not apply this rule (they had sloppy requirements). Most successful projects did: they devoted comparable attention to the more mundane parts of requirements writing as to the substance of the requirements and to the rest of the development effort. Professionalism starts with the basics.

5.7.3 Use simple language

Requirements must be precise and to the point. Short sentences are usually sufficient. Other than technical terminology defined in the Glossary (6.4), it is generally appropriate to use ordinary words rather than their more fancy equivalents. In addition to the obvious merits of simplicity, note that many development teams are international; not all readers of the requirements will be native speakers of English (or another language with international reach).

Here are a few examples (among many) of preferring simplicity over pomposity:

- A basic mechanism provided by a system is a "function"; no need to glorify it into a "functionality". The latter word means a set of functions. (The system offers a certain overall functionality, consisting of a number of specific functions.) There is in fact seldom any reason to use "functionality" in the plural.
- In listing what a system can do, you can talk about its "capabilities", but the simpler word "features" usually does the job.
- No need to use such verbs as "facilitate" when "allow" and "support" are both simpler and more precise.

And so on. You will not be able to avoid scary technical terms from the problem domain (Environment) and information technology practices (Project), collected in the Glossary (6.4), but for explanatory and prescriptive elements of the requirements the simpler the words the better.

5.7.4 Identify every part

> **Identification Principle**
>
> Every element appearing in requirements must have a unique number or key allowing unambiguous identification.

Every element of the requirements must have a unique identifier. In particular:

- All structural text elements, starting with books (if the project follows the 4-book plan of chapter 3) and continuing with chapters, sections, subsections and individual paragraphs, must be indexed as part of a uniform numbering scheme, such as G, G.1, G.1.1 etc. for the Goals book. Some projects apply this rule down to the level of individual sentences.
- All other elements such as figures must also have individual identifiers.
- The Identification Principle applies to all other requirements-relevant items present in the requirements repository ("Requirements Repository Principle", page 26).

5.7.5 Be consistent

The quality of a requirements text does not just follow from the individual quality of its successive elements. Just as importantly, they must follow a consistent style. Discrepancies will confuse the requirements' consumers.

Already necessary for short requirements, this property becomes essential for the complex requirements that many industrial systems demand. They will usually be the result of the work of a team rather than a single person, making it likely that in the absence of a strict discipline inconsistencies will creep in.

As a simple example, English-language system requirements often use "shall-style" to specify behaviors: "*If the temperature sensor detects a temperature above the maximum, the system **shall** raise an alarm within no more than one second.*" Shall-style is attractive to many requirements writers because of its firmly prescriptive nature, reminiscent of military or legal orders. In truth, it is not indispensable; in many cases, "*must*" or other variants would also work. But whichever one a project chooses, it should stick to it. Changing the convention from one part of the requirements to another confuses readers and can lead to misunderstandings.

The same rule applies to all aspects of documents, including more mundane properties of style; as two examples among many:

- If some bulleted lists are numbered, all bulleted list should be numbered.
- In English, choose American or British spelling, but do not use *color* (US) in one place and *catalogue* (British) in another.

One place where good requirements writing differs from good non-technical writing is the matter of repetition. Not repetition of the *properties* themselves specified in the requirements — the "No-Repetition Principle", page 76, warned us against this practice — but repetition of *words* in the text, as a style issue.

At school, we were told to vary terminology to avoid boring the reader. If you wrote that the mood was dark and want to insist, you might, according to such advice, call it "somber" the second time around. Well, maybe in a novel, but not in a requirements document. The terminology must be both precise and consistent. If (in the environment of your project) a vat is the same thing as a tank, call it a vat or call it a tank but stick to one name throughout. The developers reading the requirements as a guide to design and implementation need that consistency.

Synonyms do exist even in technical domains. It may be the case, for example, that some technical documents beyond your control, describing the environment of your project, use "vat", and others use "tank". What the requirements documents should do here is clear: help avoid the ambiguity by using one term only, but devote an entry of the Glossary to the other, as in: "*Tank: synonym for <u>vat</u>*", with a hyperlinked reference. (Nothing prevents you, in the "vat" entry, from adding "*also called tank*".)

5.7.6 Be prescriptive

The meek may be destined — albeit presumably long-term — to inherit the earth, but they do not write good requirements. Requirements should be firm, not timid. (Correction: they *shall* be firm.)

For the Project, state without hesitation what the tasks, assignments and milestones are; for the Environment, define the relevant properties with precision; for the Goals, make it clear what the organization expects; for the System, specify the expected behaviors.

5.8 THE TBD RULE

TBDs ("To Be Determined"), elements left out for later completion, are a plague of requirements documents. Strive to avoid them.

TBDs can be just an excuse for laziness and procrastination, leaving out some properties because they are hard to specify. They can be legitimate when they reflect that some information is not known at the time of writing and expected to become available later. Or that the requirements writers simply decided for now to focus on some elements and leave others to later.

That some property is "to be determined" does not mean, however, that we should say nothing about it. All too often one finds cursory and careless TBDs, as in example:

Triggering conditions for overheat alarm: TBD.

Such a form is unacceptable in a professional setting. TBDs must adhere to the following rule:

TBD rule

Any incomplete ("To Be Determined") mention in requirements must include:

1   Name of author declaring the property "tbd".
2   Date the property was found to be "tbd".
3   Date or project phase by which the indetermination should be resolved.
4   Importance of resolving it, one of: show-stopper, serious, desirable.
5   What will be needed to resolve it, one or more of: stakeholders to ask; documentation to consider; management decision (by whom?).

In addition, the requirements must include a **TBD list** with links to all TBDs.

For example:

Triggering conditions for overheat alarm: TBD
      1. Introduced by: Bertrand Meyer
      2. On: 2021-09-10
      3. Importance: serious
      4. Resolve before: start of any coding of the alarm management module.
      5. To resolve:
            Stakeholders: heating control engineers
            Documents: heating system manual (version 4, expected 2021-10-10).

It takes only minimal effort to produce such a sketch of what the missing part will look like, but doing so systematically is essential to the quality of requirements. It is also a matter of courtesy: giving the consumer of the requirements an idea of why something was left out and what you intend to do about it.

The TBD list — similar to such "metarequirements" elements (1.9.4) as a table of contents or table of figures at the beginning of a requirements document — can be generated automatically by the text-processing system. As a side benefit, it provides a useful indication of the state of completion of the requirements effort and its progress.

5.9 DOCUMENTING GOALS

The rules discussed so far in this chapter apply to all four PEGS. The Goals book has distinctive features (3.4, page 38). It addresses a broader audience, including high-level management and others who need to be informed of the project's overall scope and purpose but:

- May not directly participate in the project, other than to approve its launching and determine acceptance of its intermediate and final results.
- May not possess specific technical IT or subject-matter expertise.

The Goals book should be adapted to this audience and its needs. In particular:

- It should be short (thirty to sixty pages is typical).
- It should convey general ideas, not technical details.
- It should take the perspective of the enterprise, not the project, including benefits (the topic of its G.3 chapter) and limitations (G.3).
- It should emphasize clarity and readability, making graphical representations (5.5.2) particularly appropriate in many cases.

Emphasizing clarity does not mean sacrificing integrity. The picture given in the Goals book may be simplified, but should still be accurate. The book should in particular resist the temptation to gild the picture or over-promise. The backlash would inevitably come.

5.10 THE SEVEN SINS: A CLASSIC EXAMPLE

To conclude this discussion of how to write good requirements, we go back to a small example that has figured in several classic papers. You will find the references in the bibliography section of the present chapter (page 103).

The example's origin is an article on proofs of program correctness by a well-known computer scientist, Turing-Award winner Peter Naur. Two researchers on software testing (another approach to verification), John Goodenough and Susan Gerhart — G&G below — criticized the paper and stated in passing that part of the problem was a poor requirements specification; in their paper, they offered a replacement. A third paper, by the present author, critically analyzed their own specification. What follows is a thoroughly updated version of that analysis.

We will take up the problem again when discussing formal methods in chapter 9, providing in 9.5 a mathematical specification and a new English-language specification derived from it.

The problem under examination — splitting a text across lines — is very small, far from the requirements complexity of modern software systems. This simplicity is part of what makes the example fascinating: it serves as a microcosm of much of what can go wrong in requirements writing. It is almost scary: if there is so much potential for messing up in a small text-processing case, what about a real industrial project? The reassurance is that it is indeed possible to write good requirements, large or small, by following the principles of this Handbook. For a large example, see the Companion to this Handbook, which applies the principles to a significant industrial system.

A warning about the text-formatting example

This example is a simple problem. You may have the impression that the following discussion (and the further formal treatment in 9.5) belabors it far beyond its significance. If you feel that way, jump to the next chapter at the first sign of boredom. But do come back later. However small and seemingly obvious, the example is full of surprises and of lessons which apply to requirements of systems, all the way up to the very large, and are much more vividly highlighted on the very small.

5.10.1 A simple specification

The problem description in Naur's original program-proofs article was as follows:

The Naur specification

Given a text consisting of words separated by BLANKS or by NL (new line) characters, convert it to a line-by-line form in accordance with the following rules:

1   Line breaks must be made only where the given text has BLANK or NL;

2   Each line is filled as far as possible as long as

3   No line will contain more than M characters.

(In Naur's paper, M was called "MAXPOS". Other than this change meant for brevity, the Naur and G&G specifications in the present discussion are verbatim citations from the originals.)

The intent is clear: the program reformats a text by re-splitting it over lines filled as much as possible. With the example input on the left below, and $M = 9$, the output might be as on the right. (BLANK characters represented as "␣" for readability; NL shown by starting a new line.)

Input				Output (M = 9)								
1	5	10	15	1	2	3	4	5	6	7	8	9
T O ␣ ␣ B E ␣ ␣ ␣ ␣ O R ␣ ␣ N O T				T	O	␣	B	E	␣	O	R	
␣ ␣ ␣ ␣ T O ␣ ␣ ␣ ␣ ␣ ␣ ␣ ␣ ␣ ␣				N	O	T	␣	T	O	␣	B	E
␣ ␣ ␣ ␣ ␣ ␣ ␣ ␣ ␣ ␣ ␣ ␣ B E ␣												

With the understanding that it was not written as a model requirements text, but as a short problem description in an article devoted to another topic (program proofs), it is a useful exercise to assess this requirements specification, asking yourself for example:

- Does it clearly describe the problem?

- Is there always a solution?

- Can there be more than one solution?

- Does it say too little (ambiguity)? Too much (noise, overspecification)?

5.10.2 A detailed description

Goodenough and Gerhart criticized Naur's program-proving approach on a number of grounds and, interestingly for this discussion, mentioned that part of the problem was a poor specification. They provided their own replacement, which we will analyze.

The Goodenough-Gerhart specification

The program's input is a stream of characters whose end is signaled with a special end-of-text character, ET. There is exactly one ET character in each input stream. Characters are classified as:
- Break characters - BL (blank) and NL (new line);
- Nonbreak characters - all others except ET;
- the end-of-text indicator — ET.

A word is a nonempty sequence of nonbreak characters. A break is a sequence of one or more break characters. Thus, the input can be viewed as a sequence of words separated by breaks, with possibly leading and trailing breaks, and ending with ET.

The program's output should be the same sequence of words as in the input, with the exception that an oversize word (i.e. a word containing more than M characters, where M is a positive integer) should cause an error exit from the program (i.e. a variable, Alarm, should have the value TRUE). Up to the point of an error, the program's output should have the following properties:

1   A new line should start only between words and at the beginning of the output text, if any.
2   A break in the input is reduced to a single break character in the output.
3   As many words as possible should be placed on each line (i.e., between successive NL characters).
4   No line may contain more than M characters (words and BLs).

The text appears again on the next page, with some of its deficiencies — the "seven sins" — highlighted. Before turning (or scrolling) the page, though, it is useful to go through the text yourself and assess its quality. Did you find anything suspicious? You can compare your results with the following analysis.

The Goodenough-Gerhart (G&G) specification (annotated)

The program's input is a stream of characters whose end is signaled with a special *1*
end-of-text character, ET. There is exactly one ET character in each input stream. *2*
Characters are classified as: *3*

- Break characters - BL (blank) and NL (new line); *4*
- Nonbreak characters - all others except ET; *5*
- the end-of-text indicator — ET. *6*

A word is a nonempty sequence of nonbreak characters. A break is a sequence of *7*
one or more break characters. Thus, the input can be viewed as a sequence of words *8*
separated by breaks, with possibly leading and trailing breaks, and ending with ET. *9*

The program's output should be the same sequence of words as in the input, with the *10*
exception that an oversize word (i.e. a word containing more than M characters, where *11*
M is a positive integer) should cause an error exit from the program (i.e. a variable, *12*
Alarm, should have the value TRUE). Up to the point of an error, the program's output *13*
should have the following properties: *14*

1   A new line should start only between words and at the beginning of the output *15*
      text, if any. *16*

2   A break in the input is reduced to a single break character in the output. *17*

3   As many words as possible should be placed on each line (i.e., between *18*
      successive NL characters).
      19

4   No line may contain more than M characters (words and BLs). *20*

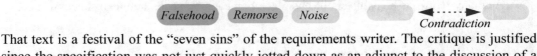

Overspecification   Ambiguity   Synonym

Falsehood   Remorse   Noise   Contradiction

That text is a festival of the "seven sins" of the requirements writer. The critique is justified since the specification was not just quickly jotted down as an adjunct to the discussion of a non-specification problem, but presented as a response to the bad quality of the original Naur problem statement. We take the problems in the order of the text, numbers in parentheses referring to its line numbers. For clarity, we represent a BLANK (space) character as ⌴.

(*1*) and (*10*) introduce a **contradiction**. The input is not a "sequence of words" (*10*) but a stream of characters. These are different kinds of entities: ['T', 'O', '⌴',   'B', 'E'] is a sequence of five elements (characters) whereas ["TO", "BE"] is a sequence of two elements (strings). The statement that *"The program's output should be the same sequence of words as in the input"* is interesting (less politely, it is a **falsehood**) since in fact **neither the input nor the output** is a sequence of words; they are both sequences of characters. True, (*8-9*) states that *"the input **can be viewed as** a sequence of words separated by breaks"* but this is only an explanation (noise, as will be seen below); saying that A "can be viewed as" B does not mean that A is B.

(*1*), (*2*), (*7*) and (*10*) introduce **synonyms**: "stream" and "sequence" mean exactly the same. "Sequence" is the better term, since it has a precise mathematical definition (see "Sequences", 9.2.6, page 166); "stream" is more vague. Requirements must use a single term for every notion (No-Synonym Principle, page 74: keep names and concepts in one-to-one correspondence).

The introduction of the ET character (*1-2, 6*) is gratuitous **overspecification**. True, the C programming language terminates strings with a special character, a "null", written \0; and in some file systems a sequential file has an end marker. Such conventions, however, are pure implementation matters. The ET character was not part of the original Naur specification; it is not necessary for understanding the problem (or for implementing a solution, since any programming language or library mechanism for reading files will make it possible to read characters until the end without having to know how end-of-file is marked internally); it seriously complicates the specification; and it leads to other problems.

One of these other problems comes out in the next sentence (*2*) after the introduction of ET. *"There is exactly one ET character in each input stream"* is pure **noise** since it has already been specified that ET is a *"special"* and *"end-of-text"* character. Clearly, since a sequential file has exactly one end, if ET is the end-of-character, there can only be one ET. The extra precautionary explanation wastes readers' time (or makes them raise unnecessary questions). The word *"special"* is itself noise: what makes a character "special"? Saying that ET is "end-of-text" is enough to mark it as special. See how overspecification, far from helping, creates an urge for *explanation* (5.4), which in a seemingly endless pursuit only causes new intellectual contortions.

Another **synonym** case is *"nonempty"* sequence of characters (*7*) versus *"one or more"* characters (*8*). The two mean the same thing but in requirements the change of phrasing can cause confusion. (No-Synonym Principle again.)

"Oversize word" (*11*) is **noise** since the concept is defined precisely next (same line) and the term "oversize" is not used in the rest of the specification. There was no need to introduce it.

"M *is a positive integer"* is **remorse**: M is a parameter of the problem and should have been introduced at the beginning, not after the concept has been used. The phrasing is also a case of **ambiguity**: we have to understand that M applies to the processing as a whole, rather than being defined in each case. In other words, the statement *"a word containing more than* M *characters, where* M *is a positive integer, should cause an error exit"* could be interpreted to mean that every word of length 2 or more causes an error exit, since such a word has the property that it is *"more than* M *characters, where* M *is a positive integer"* (take M = 1). Proposing such an interpretation is playing silly, of course, but only because we know about the problem domain (Environment): we all have at least an intuitive understanding of the kind of text processing involved. Consider now the case of a developer interpreting requirements specification for a domain in which he or she is not an expert: true confusions and misunderstandings can result. These problems are entirely avoidable if we take a systematic approach to describing the problem: define each element exactly once; rather than explaining, make the definition precise.

The whole idea of introducing (*12-13*) "*a variable, Alarm*" that "*should have the value TRUE*" is pure **overspecification**. It is not the business of a problem description to enjoin the programmers to use particular variables. Specify error cases and (at the appropriate level of detail) the processing for each of them.

The requirement that the program's output should have the required properties "up to the point of an error" (*13*) is a case of **ambiguity**: it does not determine whether an oversize word should be partially output or not. Assume M = 6 and the input

THAT␣IS␣THE␣QUESTION

so that the first two lines of the output can be

THAT
IS␣THE

What, however, is "the point of the error"? We can take it to be the beginning of the oversize word, in which case the output stops here; or the first offending letter, in which case we must output a third line with M characters:

QUESTI

With the text as given, either of these interpretations is as plausible as the other — in this case not even depending on familiarity with the problem domain. (Plain ambiguity: neither common sense nor text-processing expertise helps.) The situation is typical of many requirements documents which devote great care to unimportant matters, resulting in noise and overspecification, while remaining silent on important properties, which developers need to know.

"*A new line should start only between words and at the beginning of the output text*" (*15-16*) introduces **ambiguity**. The phrasing is infelicitous in any case: it is not that a new line "should" appear between words and at the beginning (otherwise there would be new-line characters between all words!); the text should have said that it "*may only*" appear there. But — worse — the sentence also suggests that it is OK to add a new-line character at the beginning of the text. The problem here is that the G&G specification does not define what it means by "*new line*", causing confusion since this term conflicts with a defined concept, the new line or NL *character* (*4*). The authors are relying on the reader's intuition of what a *line* is. When they write that a "*new line*" should "*start*" they are not just talking about the characters following an NL character, but also about the first line, usually not preceded by NL. This intuitive understanding, however, is not explicitly specified, and creates a contradiction with concepts that are.

Never make such an assumption in a requirements document; define all concepts (Glossary Principle, 6.4, page 107). It is particularly ironic here that, as we will shortly see, the authors do attempt a few lines down (*18-19*) to define (if not "*new line*") the notion of "*line*", and manage to get it wrong!

"*The output text, if any*" (*15-16*) is **remorse** (5.2.3). So far the reader has been led to assume that there would be an output. That seems like a matter of course: a text-formatting program takes some input and produces some output. We were told, unambiguously, that (*10*) "*The program's output should be*" a sequence of words. If it is (or "*should be*") something, it must exist. But now, 15 lines into a 20-line specification, comes the news that it might not. Why? Under what conditions? No clue. To the programmer trying to implement a solution, the mystery is not reassuring.

The requirement (*18*) that "*as many words as possible*" should be put "*on each line*" is a new case of **ambiguity**, but of a different nature from the preceding ones. With the input text

TO_BE_OR_NOT_TO_BE

and $M = 8$, all of the following candidate outputs satisfy the other conditions and have the same number of lines (3, the minimum possible):

1 2 3 4 5 6 7 8		1 2 3 4 5 6 7 8		1 2 3 4 5 6 7 8
T O _ B E _ O R		T O _ B E _ O R		T O _ B E
N O T _ T O		N O T		O R _ N O T
B E		T O _ B E		T O _ B E
(A)		(B)		(C)

This example shows that it is impossible to ensure that the output fits "*as many words as possible on each line*" for *all* lines: (A) and (B) fill up the first and second lines as much as possible, but not the last one; (B), the first and last but not the second one; (C), the second one but not the others. Seen that way, the specification is a case of **falsehood** rather than ambiguity. If we accept that it was really intended to mean "the number of lines should be the minimum possible", then it is not a falsehood, but we have to deal with the ambiguity: in such examples, which of the three variants does it define as acceptable?

The indication that the text should satisfy some properties "*up to the point of an error*" (*13*) seems to suggest that it was written under the assumption that processing would be purely *sequential*, filling each line as much as possible before proceeding to the next line. Under this interpretation, there is only one suitable output in the example: (A). Is also possible, however, that the authors intended to allow any output meeting the criteria; then (A), (B) and (C) are all acceptable results. A requirements specification allowing several solutions is called *non-deterministic*. If that was the intention, the text should have explicitly mentioned the non-determinism, a much more interesting property than the included noise and overspecification elements.

"*Each line (i.e., between successive NL characters)*" (*18-19*) is again **remorse**, defining in the penultimate line a concept already used before. It is also something worse: a **falsehood**. It is simply wrong that a line is always delimited by two new-line characters: consider the first and last lines, both of which are flanked by only one NL, respectively after and before. This wrong definition reflects absent-mindedness in the writing of the specification, but imagine again a problem domain where the programmer's intuitive understanding is of no help. Programmers may follow the definition and implement the wrong behavior.

The final statement in the text (*20*), "*no line may contain more than* M *characters (words and BLs*", contains yet another **falsehood**: a word is not a character! A word is a sequence of characters (*7*). There are several ways to express the intended property, but the best one is simply to remove the useless and ultimately damaging attempt at explanation: "*(words and BLs)*". Just stating "*no line may contain more than* M *characters*" is precise and definitive. We see here one more attempt at explanation that brings no good and causes harm.

It is indeed fascinating to see how the last two falsehoods, and many of the other deficiencies identified in the previous discussion, follow from worthy intentions gone sour. The attempt to explain "*word*" peters out as badly as the attempt to explain "*line*". This phenomenon is characteristic of requirements documents gone awry. Remember the Explanation Principle: specification beats explanation. *Say it once, say it well.*

5.10.3 More ambiguity!

At this point you might think that we have squeezed the text-formatting example more thoroughly than any single lemon in the entire world history of lemon-squeezing and split it more thinly than any single hair in the entire world history of hair-splitting. The analysis of the G&G specification cannot possibly have missed any flaw, however minute. And yet it did! A pretty important ambiguity at that. In fact, two ambiguities.

In all the preceding example solutions, lines start with a letter. Now assume (still for M = 8) that the input is ⎵TO⎵BE⎵OR⎵NOT⎵TO⎵BE, as earlier but with an added initial space (or several initial breaks). Then none of the previous solutions is correct any more, since they do not start with a space and hence, for that character, violate the condition that "*A break in the input is reduced to a single break character in the output*" (*17*). We may contract breaks (indeed we must), we may not remove them. A correct solution is:

```
⎵TO⎵BE
OR⎵NOT
TO⎵BE
```

The same phenomenon occurs if the text (ignoring the spurious "ET" business) *ends* with one or more break characters: they have to yield a trailing space.

There is neither contradiction nor falsehood here: this interpretation of the problem makes sense. It looks suspicious, however, since text formatting of the given style typically gets rid of ending and trailing breaks altogether. Formatted text does not generally start or end with spaces. The ambiguity comes very close to a contradiction in light of "*As many words as possible should be placed on each line (i.e., between successive NL characters)*" (*18-19*), already flagged for other problems. While not explicitly stating it, this phrasing strongly suggests that for inside lines the first and last word are directly flanked by NL characters, without any intervening space. If so, the property would presumably apply also to the first and last lines, although (as we have seen) the statement mistakenly did not take them into account.

By the way, what output shall we produce for an input made of break characters only: an empty text, or one consisting of a single space? Not the most poignant of all dilemmas, but in the requirements of more significant systems such ambiguities could have serious consequences.

We have reached the stage of making conjectures about the requirements authors' intent; that should never be the case with well-written requirements. It is possible, although unlikely, that the intent was indeed to preserve a leading or trailing break, but at the very least (if only because this convention is counter-intuitive) the specification should then have stated it explicitly, removing any doubt in the minds of readers and particularly of implementers.

5.10.4 Lessons from the example

In light of the preceding analysis it is interesting to compare the two specifications. G&G criticized the Naur specification (page 94) and explicitly presented the revision (page 95) as an improvement. Is it?

The original did have a serious flaw: the absence of any mention that the problem only has a solution if no word is longer than M. Other than the need to specify this condition (which is easy to add), it was simple and immediately understandable. In its effort to leave no stone unturned, the revised version entangles itself in contradiction after complication and ambiguity after incongruity. Every attempt at clarification results in added noise or worse, while leaving open some real questions, including:

- In the case of an oversize word, **how much** of the input text must we process?

- Do we discard a **leading or trailing break**, or do we keep it, and if so in what form (such as a single space)?

- Must the program fill lines as much as possible in the order of the input text (**sequential processing**), or is it possible to fill later lines more than earlier ones (for example to produce a more pleasing visual effect) as long as the total number of lines is minimum?

- More generally, can the problem admit more than one correct output (**non-determinism**)?

- Is there always **at least one** correct output?

The extra length of G&G as compared to Naur (a ratio of 4) seems hard to justify with so many questions left unanswered.

The lesson for requirements writers is clear: do not attempt explanation (except in the few places where it might be essential according to the list of 5.4); ruthlessly cut noise; spot and remove ambiguities; constantly aim for precision; and remember ("Requirements Questions Principle", page 22) that one of the key aims of a requirements specification is to uncover all important questions about the problem and answer them.

5.10.5 OK, but can we do better?

With the extensive criticism leveled so far at the G&G text, you are entitled to a switch from the negative to the positive. What would be a satisfactory version of this specification, immune to such criticism?

Such a replacement is indeed coming, but it will take advantage of a detour through the tools of mathematical reasoning, the key to precision. Chapter 9, devoted to formal methods, takes up the problem again in a section entirely devoted to it ("An example: text formatting, revisited", 9.5, page 171). It first develops a mathematical model; then, coming back to English with the benefit of that model ("Back from the picnic", 9.5.7, page 178), it proposes a new natural-language version, quite different from anything we saw in the present chapter. You are encouraged to analyze it — just as critically as this discussion did for the G&G version — for its adherence to quality factors for requirements, and its avoidance, or not, of the Seven Sins of the Specifier.

5-E EXERCISES

5-E.1 Addressing criticism

Sections 5.6.1, 5.6.2 and 5.6.3 provide three examples of proposed replacements for deficient phrasings of the requirements, then have some criticism of the replacements themselves. Using if necessary your intuitive understanding of the problem domain in each case, provide your own replacements addressing the criticism. Include a discussion of the issues involved and a justification for your rewrites.

5-E.2 Text formatting

Propose a better version of the text-formatting requirements of section 5.10. Submit it to critical analysis and compare it to the two given there. (Note: preferably do this exercise before reading chapter 9, which discusses the example further and proposes both a formal replacement and a non-formal one. You may want to go back to your answer after reading that chapter, and consider whether it needs updating in light of the concepts introduced there.)

5-E.3 Do not just format, justify

Adapt the specification that you obtained in exercise 5-E.2 to a variant of the problem in which output text is left- and right-justified through the possible addition of blank characters.

Evaluate how much you had to change, as a clue to the *modifiability* (4.11, page 65) of your original specification.

BIBLIOGRAPHICAL NOTES AND FURTHER READING

Anyone writing requirements and other technical texts should read and apply the precepts of the soon-centenary *Elements of Style* [Strunk-White].

The examples and criticism of bad specification elements are from [Wiegers-Beatty 2013], which presents more rules of requirements style.

A discussion of the Single Point of Maintenance rule (page 76) appears at [IfSQ 2016].

The network architecture diagram of page 80 is from [Wikipedia: SOA] and the diagram illustrating table notations on page 83 from [Wikipedia: OSI], both Wikipedia pages.

The "seven sins of the specifier" (5.2) are an updated version of those in [Meyer 1985]. That article also discussed the Naur [Naur 1969] and Goodenough-Gerhart [Goodenough-Gerhart 1977] specifications discussed at length in the present chapter.

[Bruel et al. 2021] is a survey of notations for requirements (5.5), particularly formal notations (5.5.3). It also includes a discussion of tools that use a restricted version of natural language (as mentioned at the end of 5.5.1).

David Parnas has promoted the systematic use of tabular specifications (5.5.4); see [Parnas 2001] (and a summary and assessment of the approach in [Bruel et al. 2021]).

The concept of "multirequirements", the combined use of multiple notations for requirements, is discussed in [Meyer 2013].

6

How to gather requirements

Who provides the source of requirements? How do you process their input? What are the pitfalls? This chapter describes the gentle art of obtaining requirements information from stakeholders and other sources, a process known as *requirements elicitation*.

6.1 PLANNING AND DOCUMENTING THE PROCESS

In the Standard Plan for requirements (chapter 3 of this Handbook), one of the chapters of the Project book (P.7, *Requirements process and report*) is devoted to documenting the requirements process itself, in particular the elicitation effort. It serves a dual role:

- It starts out as the overall plan for conducting the requirements process.
- Then, as elicitation proceeds, the requirements team updates it (in line with the "Requirements Evolution Principle", page 23) to record outcomes of the process and lessons learned.

While the effort devoted to this task must remain moderate (in line with the "Requirements Effort Principle", page 31, which reminds us that requirements are not an end in themselves), it is important to take advantage of chapter P.7 to record any difficulties encountered during elicitation, solutions that were found to overcome them, and any useful observations about the process and its results, including any perceived limitations or uncertainties, as this information may help the development team process the requirements.

6.2 THE ROLE OF STAKEHOLDERS

In a naïve view of requirements elicitation, you go to stakeholders (or, even more naïvely, "users") and they tell you what they want. Oh, the beauty of a simple world! Just figure: you meet Jill from accounting and Joan from sales, they explain their needs, you write everything down and pass it on to the developers. Then at the end of the month you get your paycheck as a business analyst, and at the end of the year they get the system of their dreams.

Except that if the world were that simple we would not need business analysts and a comprehensive requirements engineering process. A more balanced view involves not one force but three, pulling the project in different directions as illustrated on the next page:

- The **inductive** force (bottom-up): the wishes of the stakeholders.
- The **deductive** force (top-down): the project initiators' vision for a future system. Steve Jobs stated that "*People don't know what they want until you show it to them.*" (And Henry Ford, supposedly, "*If I had asked people what they wanted, they would have said faster horses*".)

© The Author(s), under exclusive license to Springer Nature Switzerland AG 2022
B. Meyer, *Handbook of Requirements and Business Analysis*, https://doi.org/10.1007/978-3-031-06739-6_6

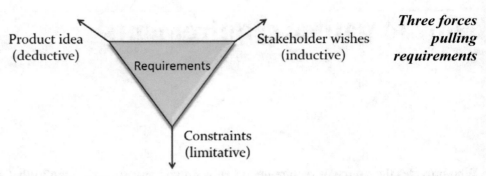

- The **limiting** force: the constraints of the environment, from laws of physics to legal regulations, companies' business rules, available budget, time constraints ("*we **must** release the system at the Consumer Electronics Show next January!*"), availability of qualified personnel. Both stakeholders' desires and innovators' ideas have to contend with this reality check.

We may view the inductive part as "*tell me!*" (what you, the stakeholder, want). The deductive part is "*show me!*" (what you, the IT person, could do for me, for example by demonstrating a prototype as discussed in 6.11 below). The **limiting** part is "*no you can't!*"

In practice, requirements will be a tradeoff between these three forces. The present chapter discusses the inductive part: finding out what stakeholders need.

6.3 SOURCES OTHER THAN STAKEHOLDERS

Information elicited from stakeholders, studied in the next sections, is not the sole source of requirements. Here are some others, which can all be important.

Potential requirements sources	
Source	Justification and comments
Preparatory discussions	A project is not born in a vacuum. Someone had the idea (or appropriated it). There were email exchanges, meetings supported by PowerPoint presentations and producing minutes, preliminary plans. The record of these discussions is often a precious source of information on the context and parameters of the project. (In line with the Requirements Repository principle of section 2.1.7, it is desirable, whenever you spot such an element, to record it in the repository.)
Product vision	This is the "deductive" force in the Three Forces diagram: the project initiators' idea of what the system should be. Do not neglect it: many projects result from the initiative of a project champion, for example a high-level executive; you cannot afford to ignore his or her agenda.
Legal contract	A project often proceeds from a legal contract, setting its organizational parameters. Some of its information is relevant for requirements.

Manual procedures	If a system will automate a previously manual process, it is important to study that process, not only through stakeholder interviews and workshops (discussed below) but also through existing documentation.
Previous system	Often a new system replaces an existing one ("*brownfield*" project) rather than starting from scratch or replacing manual processes ("*greenfield*"). The requirements for the new system should make use of the previous system's documentation and the experience of its users.
Competing systems	Maybe competitors already provide systems to address the same general goals; or you considered using an existing system, commercial or open-source, and decided to build your own instead. In both cases, the study of existing offerings provides a precious source of information.
Documents on the application area	Particularly for the Environment part (book E, see 3.5), existing documents may provide important information and reduce the need for stakeholder interviews. They are part of the "**limiting**" forces in the Three Forces diagram of page 106 and include regulatory documents specifying constraints that the project and system will have to observe.
Interfaced systems	"Interfaced" systems are those with which the future system will have interfaces. It is important to examine them since they form part of the environment and constrain the new system. They are also a *risk* factor, as studied in 6.11.7 below. (In return, examination of the interfaces might lead to requests to adapt these other systems, if feasible.)
Previous projects	Particularly for the project part of requirements (book P, see 3.7), the record of previous projects, in both the target and production organizations (1.1.3), provides valuable lessons: how successful were they? How far was the actual development time from original estimates? This information is important to assess the realism of project objectives by drawing the portrait of an organization that has historically been good — or not — at making realistic plans and executing them.

6.4 THE GLOSSARY

An important goal of requirements elicitation and more generally of the requirements effort is to document the terminology of the project, which in the Standard Plan of chapter 3 is at the very beginning (E.1) of the Environment book.

Glossary Principle

Requirements must contain (in the Environment book) a list of all the domain-specific concepts relevant to the project and the corresponding definitions, endorsed by the respective qualified stakeholders.

Note the reference to endorsement; the corresponding quality factor, "Endorsed", 4.14, page 68, is particularly relevant for the Glossary.

The principle states that the glossary must define "*all*" domain-specific concepts:

- Many technical domains — the Environment part of the four PEGS, on which all others depend per the rules given by the figure of page 37 — use words from ordinary language in a special technical sense, which can confuse outsiders, in particular developers.
- Even within a single field, it is not uncommon that different people, for example different SMEs, have a different understanding of the same concepts. The work of producing the glossary will bring such differences to light and force a resolution.

The next two subsections discuss these two challenges.

6.4.1 Clarify the terminology

The glossary will contain a definition for all technical terms and acronyms relevant to the project. Requirements engineers must be careful not to take terms for granted, even those that seem innocuous at first; they must obtain precise definitions from stakeholders and record them.

In this effort you should set aside your ego by not hesitating to ask elementary questions, even late in the process, and even when you have already asked them. When you start talking to domain experts, you may not feel like interrupting them at every sentence; after a while they will start assuming you have understood the basics. You may fear sounding silly if you ask elementary questions much later into the project. (As — in everyday life — when you were introduced to someone long ago, did not get the name or forgot it, have met the person regularly since, and are afraid to ask again.) While the cliché that "there are no stupid questions" may not hold everywhere, in this context it does. Timidity in requirements elicitation is not a virtue but professional malpractice.

You will actually look far less stupid by harping on basic questions, such as "*sorry if you explained already, but please tell me again what you mean by X*", than by not asking and then misunderstanding requirements.

6.4.2 Kidnapped words

A particular source of mistakes involves **kidnapped words**: terms from ordinary language that professionals in a field use in a specific technical meaning, which outsiders may miss.

As an example from the field of academia, if the term "PhD student" comes up in a discussion between academics and university administrators, everyone knows that the word "student" in it does not have its usual meaning. A "PhD student" is a junior scientific collaborator, more akin to employees than to "students" of other kinds. IT people building a management system for the university may lack this knowledge, and mistakenly think that "PhD student" is just one category of "student", along with "bachelor student" and "master student". Misunderstanding the word would be even worse with "postdoctoral students", as they are not students at all but aspiring assistant professors waiting for a faculty position to free up. Failure to recognize that a single term covers different concepts will lead to an inadequate system.

Every field has its share of words hijacked from ordinary language for a special meaning. Software is no exception: two programmers discussing the "*complexity*" of an algorithm are not pondering how hard it is to understand, but assessing its asymptotic time or space behavior mathematically through a "big-O" or "big-theta" approximation, as in "O ($n \log n$)". Another illustration is the use of the word "*reserve*" in an example of this Handbook (7.1, page 129) with a technical meaning specific to the insurance industry.

Kidnapped words are more likely to cause confusion than special technical terms, which immediately stand out. In the university example, a non-expert encountering the term "ECTS" will naturally ask what kind of animal that is (and will be rewarded with a lecture about the "European Credit Transfer System" and the "Bologna Agreement"). Because such technical terms obviously cry for a definition in the requirements documents — specifically, the Glossary — they are less treacherous than innocent-looking repurposed ordinary words.

6.4.3 Acronyms

While it is desirable to minimize the use of acronyms, which can render texts hard to understand, some will remain necessary; they must all appear in the glossary. A common mistake (frequent in particular among students told to include a glossary for their projects) is for the corresponding entries to include just the acronym's expansion. Good try, but not good enough! The expansion could be as obscure as the acronym itself — or more. Far more people can use HTML than can explain what in the world a "HyperText Markup Language" is. CMMI is a well-known framework for improving process quality in organizations, but "Capability Maturity Model Integration" does not mean much to the uninitiated.

Every glossary entry for an acronym must include both the official expansion of the name and a description of the concept. For example:

> *CMMI* (Capability Maturity Model Integration): a set of standardized goals, practices and qualification criteria for improving the development processes of organizations and assessing their level of maturity.

Acronym Principle

In glossary entries introducing acronyms, do not just expand: explain.

6.5 ASSESSING STAKEHOLDERS

Although it can be embarrassing to admit it — especially in their presence — not all stakeholders are created equal. There are obvious differences of authority: the higher up they are in the management chain, the more attention you need to pay to their views. More generally, we may distinguish two criteria for assessing how much time to spend with various stakeholders:

- Influence (both ways): how much will specific stakeholders *be affected* by the system, and how much can they *affect* it (as in the case of managers)?

- Availability: how much time are they willing and able to devote to helping with the requirements effort?

To keep things simple, we may define just two levels for each of these assessments, getting a **stakeholder map** with four quadrants:

The four-quadrant stakeholder map		
Availability ↘ **Influence** ↓	High	Low
High	**Key Stakeholders**	**Shadow Influencers**
Low	**Fellow Travelers**	**Observers**

The benefit of preparing a stakeholder map is to identify stakeholder-related risks early, and avoid serious later trouble. Of the four categories, two are *not* a particular source of concern:

- *Key Stakeholders* (high availability, high influence). They are typically easy to identify and make themselves heard, for a good reason — they are the ones primarily affected by the project or affecting it, and are your basic day-to-day requirements partners. Since they are so visible and obviously important, the project is unlikely to overlook their input.

  Examples of Key Stakeholders include: top management having decided to start the project and defined the vision; the "product owner" of an agile project; representatives of future users of the system, such as human resources personnel in a payroll project.

- *Observers* (low availability, low influence). They should be kept in the loop but they are unlikely to cause major problems.

  Examples of Observers may include: the legal department (unless the project is likely to cause major legal issues, or in a project addressing legal matters); technical writers.

The categories to watch for (this is where the stakeholder map can help) are the other two, highlighted in the table:

- **Fellow Travelers** (high availability, low influence). The risk here is to waste your time and resources on people who may themselves have lots of time on their hands and a willingness to express opinions and demands on many aspects of the system. Such stakeholders are involved but not committed. The risk for the requirements engineers is to devote too much time to them and consideration to their views, at the expense of more critical stakeholders.

- **Shadow Influencers** (low availability, high influence). An example may be system administrators, who will have a key role in deploying and managing the system, and whose input is needed to ensure that it will be deployable and manageable, particularly in the DevOps model of system construction (12.4.2). Like sysadmins everywhere, they may be running around extinguishing so many fires as not to find time for you unless you really insist. The risk here is high: missing out on the input of key people.

By drawing a stakeholder map, you can spot these two categories early and mitigate the corresponding risks to the project. (Do exert some diplomatic skills, as it may not always be a good idea to inform people they have been categorized as low-influence.)

6.6 MAKING BUSINESS ANALYSTS AND DOMAIN EXPERTS WORK TOGETHER

Before jumping into elicitation, we look at the human side. The first chapter explained ("Who produces requirements?", 1.10.2, page 16) the distinction between business analysts (requirements engineers) and Subject-Matter Experts. As noted then, these groups are usually distinct: few people are experts in both requirements engineering and a specific application domain. (The exception, as we saw, is a pure-software project such as a compiler.)

A good picture of the difficulties that arise when we bring the two groups together appears in a perceptive article from 1981 (!) by Laura Scharer. Although it is anecdotal, rather than based on a scientific study, anyone who has been involved in interactions between IT specialists and domain experts will recognize the stereotypes that often exist on both sides:

Stereotypes in business analysts' and domain experts' views of each other (according to Laura Scharer)	
How analysts see SMEs*	**How SMEs* see analysts**
Do not really know what they want.	Do not understand "the business".
Cannot articulate what they want.	Handle company politics awkwardly.
Have too many "needs" that are politically motivated.	Try to tell us how to do our jobs.
Want everything right now; cannot prioritize needs.	Cannot translate a system definition into a successful system. Say no all the time.
Want "me first", not company first.	Place too much emphasis on technicalities.
Refuse to take responsibility for the system.	Are always over budget.
Are unable to provide a definition for a system that will work.	Are always late.
Are not committed to system development projects.	Ask users for time and effort, even to the detriment of their primary duties.
Are unwilling to compromise.	Set unrealistic standards for requirements definition.
Cannot remain on schedule.	Are unable to respond quickly to legitimately changing needs.

*In the original article: "users" instead of "SMEs"

While exaggerated, the picture serves as a warning of the cultural divide that often exists at the start of projects. It can be useful, at the first meeting between the two sides in a new project — for example, a stakeholder workshop as discussed below — to show this list. You can find it in the form of PowerPoint and PDF slides on this Handbook's site, and use it to kick off the meeting in a lighthearted way while making each side aware of the other's possible prejudices.

6.7 BIASES, INTERVIEWS AND WORKSHOPS

The most common elicitation technique is the **stakeholder interview**: you identify a representative of a stakeholder category, for example a future user or an SME, prepare a list of questions, set up an individual meeting, and use the meeting to elicit answers to these questions.

While clearly useful, interviews have limitations: they can take considerable time, and the view they yield can be biased by the choice of interviewees. (How can we be sure that a particular accountant is representative of the views of the accounting department, and a particular engineer of those of the engineering team?) These two problems compound each other:

• Because interviews take time, you may have to limit the number of interviewees, and risk missing some important viewpoints, causing a **selection bias**.

• People who do have time may not be the most useful, causing **availability bias**. The true experts (the best "SMEs") are by nature busy: their expertise is in high demand. Scheduling an interview with them can be hard. Others will be readily available; but that very availability can raise the suspicions that they are "fellow travelers" in the sense of stakeholder maps (6.5). Large organizations sometimes include employees who have opinions on everything and are eager to share them, but (perhaps because they are past their highest-competence date) are not those most deeply involved with the actual business.

Selection and availability biases cannot be fully avoided, but a technique that helps is to conduct a **stakeholder workshop**. Instead of a single interviewee, a workshop involves a number of stakeholder representatives; it is particularly useful to invite members of groups whose views might differ — for example, sales and engineering — and who might not regularly discuss these differences with each other, or even be aware of them.

The elicitation process uses similar techniques, discussed next, for workshops as for interviews, but bringing together members of various groups is an effective way to discover their differences of views. The goal is to avoid making costly requirements mistakes simply because you listened to the wrong person, or to only some of the right persons.

Workshops and interviews are complementary. The best technique is, after identifying stakeholders and devising an elicitation plan, to:

• Start with a workshop (or several for a complex project) to help define the scope of the elicitation process, highlight key issues, detect possible conflicts, and identify stakeholders who deserve specific interviews.

• Continue with these specific interviews.

• Convene a final workshop or workshops to resolve open issues and conflicts.

The next sections explore specific interview techniques (6.8), specific workshop techniques (6.9), and techniques that apply to both settings (6.10).

6.8 CONDUCTING EFFECTIVE INTERVIEWS

Interviews should follow a well-defined process.

6.8.1 Setting up and conducting an interview

The following guidelines, successively addressing the "why", "when", "who", "what" and "how" of stakeholder interviews, will help you make the process successful.

Planning and executing a stakeholder interview	
Why?	*Pre-interview*: make sure the interviewer clearly knows why the person is being interviewed (specific role in the organization, specific knowledge, job potentially affected by the future system, possible later role in the project…).
	In-interview: keep the discussion in line with the defined goals.
When?	*Pre-interview*: set up a precise time and place (physical or electronic) as well as a duration.
	In-interview: stick to the schedule. (If it turns out the person has more to say, *and* that the extra information is useful to the project, schedule another interview). There is no universal rule for the interview's length, but most interviews should take an hour or two, with follow-up sessions if necessary.
	Post-interview: write an interview report summarizing the key take-aways from the discussion.
Who?	*Pre-interview*: establish knowledge of the interviewee's background.
	In-interview: keep in mind any specifics that might either reinforce or limit the interviewee's answers. (Example of the reinforcement case: the interviewee has an important decision role. Example of the limiting case: the interviewee is known to have a vested interest in specific solutions.)
What?	*Pre-interview*: Have a specific list of set questions, but keep generous time for unplanned questions (see "open-ended questions in 6.10.4 below).
	In-interview: keep enough time for both the set and open-ended parts.
How?	*Pre-interview*: identify any parameter that might increase or decrease the effectiveness of the interview.
	In-interview: apply the rules on good questions given below (6.10). Be prepared to adapt the prepared strategy if some of the parameters are not as expected.

The site for this Handbook includes a form that you can use to apply these guidelines when preparing for an interview, conducting it, and producing the interview report ("*post-interview*" part of the "When" entry).

6.8.2 Interview reports

The following rules apply to producing an interview report. (They are also applicable to reports of *workshops* as discussed next.)

Guidelines for interview and workshop reports
R1 The report should not be a detailed record of the discussion ("who said what", as in minutes of a meeting) but only a list of the **key lessons** learned from the interview.
R2 It should in general be doubly **ego-less**. On the interviewer side, it should not be influenced by personal views of the analyst conducting the interview. On the interviewee's side, it should state the category of personnel represented by interviewees rather than their identity. (Remember that "stakeholder", per the definition of 1.1.4, denotes not one person but a category of people in the organization.) An exception is the interview of a decision-maker whom it may be relevant to identify.

Applying the first of these guidelines requires a certain effort at abstracting and synthesizing the results. In line with the "Requirements Effort Principle", page 31, you should decide whether the effort is justified. If not, better a verbatim, minutes-like report than no report at all.

Beyond individual interview reports, the results of interviews should find their place — alongside workshop reports — in a global elicitation report, for which the Standard Plan reserves a specific chapter: P.7, "*Requirements process and report*" (see page 43). That chapter need not, however, include all individual reports, especially if the process has involved many interviews. To avoid the chapter becoming too long and tedious, you may group the reports of several interviews into a general summary.

6.9 CONDUCTING EFFECTIVE WORKSHOPS

A workshop is a session involving a number of stakeholder representatives; like an interview, it should be short, typically a few hours. If there are more things to discuss, it is better to set up follow-up sessions, with the benefit of reflection in-between, than a single long session.

6.9.1 Why workshops help

The advantages of workshops include the following.

Benefits of workshop	
Fairness	Workshops help reduce the two kinds of bias caused by interviews, as discussed in 6.7: selection bias and availability bias.
Cost	Workshops are generally less disruptive of people's work than multiple individual interviews, and require less setup work.

Effectiveness	Workshops make it possible to discover conflicting stakeholder views early, and reconcile contradictions before they have had the opportunity to affect the development process and the adequacy of the future system.
Prioritization	Workshops help set the relative priorities of stakeholder needs (as discussed below in "Get stakeholders to prioritize", 6.10.5, page 121).
Structure	Interviews take time and have to be scheduled individually. If you are relying on interviews only you might, just because of the vagaries of scheduling, meet some critical shareholders only late in the process, and hence get started on the wrong understanding. With workshops, you have less of a risk of missing key contributions.
Representativity	If well organized, workshops cut across organizational boundaries.
Teamwork	Workshops foster interaction and cooperation between management, developers, future users and other stakeholders.
Buy in	A good workshop will create a team spirit among stakeholders from various origins and helps make them feel the system will be theirs, not something imposed on them. Such involvement can be useful during the project, if it runs into difficulties or hostility and you need supporters; and after deployment, to ensure its adoption and success.
Change management	Workshops help manage user's expectations and their willingness to accept organizational changes resulting from the deployment of the future system.

6.9.2 When to run workshops

A workshop cannot have the depth of an individual interview and is particularly adapted to the identification and resolution of issues on which different stakeholders have complementary or contradictory perspectives. Hence the process suggested at the beginning of this discussion (page 112): start and end with one or more workshops, with interviews in-between. The initial workshops are more free-ranging, to make sure no important matter gets missed; the final ones are more focused, to make sure no important uncertainty remains unresolved. In other words, open at the start and close at the end.

6.9.3 Planning a workshop

To achieve the benefits listed above, workshops, whether towards the beginning or towards the end of elicitation, need to be carefully planned and executed. A workshop that turns into a free-for-all, where everyone tries to throw in an opinion and the most vociferous monopolize attention, will cause harm, not good. Use the following guidelines to prepare for the meeting.

Workshop preparation guidelines

W1 Define a list of issues to be addressed.

W2 Define a strict workshop schedule, with a set time devoted to each issue, plus time at the end for "any other items" that may have been missed in the list.

W3 Select participants carefully, by ensuring that each important category is represented, and to the extent possible that no one person or group will dominate the others.

W4 Try to obtain from each key participant the name of an alternate, who may be available if the primary participant has a conflict at the last minute.

W5 Using a calendar tool such as Doodle, set a time that suits most intended participants.

W6 Circulate the list and the schedule with enough lead time (typically, two or three weeks) for the future participants to react by adding points that have been forgotten. (In anticipation of this possibility, leave some slack in the original schedule.)

W7 If the meeting is to be onsite, make sure the chosen room is suitable. Do not neglect details such as room setup: classroom-style is inadequate; to promote cooperative discussion use instead a circular arrangement or, better yet, a U-shaped table organization, which makes it possible to project slides that everyone will see. Have an ample provision of whiteboards, post-it notes and other tools of fruitful solution-oriented meetings.

W8 If the meeting is virtual, use an adequate tool and ask participants to turn on their cameras (visual interaction helps, and there is nothing worse for participants who have their webcams on to be confronted by others who just appear as black squares).

W9 Hybrid meetings — with some participants onsite and others remote — are tricky. Check the quality of the connection and projection to ensure a seamless experience between the two groups. Often the onsite participants are poorly heard and not individually visible to the remote ones (only as a group, with a single camera and a so-so microphone in the meeting room); this situation is frustrating and should be corrected by the addition of specific cameras and high-quality multidirectional microphones specifically intended for meeting rooms.

W10 (For the benefit of the requirements team, not necessarily for distribution to the participants) make sure to have an explicit list of the essential questions, typically a small number, that the workshop must absolutely answer.

6.9.4 Running a workshop

During the workshop, enforce the announced schedule, which will include (as noted above) an open-ended "other items" part. Your focus should be dual:

• Making sure all announced issues are resolved.

• Remaining on the lookout for issues that the elicitation effort has missed so far, including "obvious" elements that are in fact obvious to everyone but the requirements team, and often turn out, once identified, to be not so obvious after all, or to be obvious to different stakeholders in different ways (as will be discussed shortly: "Uncover the unsaid", page 118).

Run an orderly meeting, making sure that every category gets its day in court, regardless of being represented by someone shy or someone assertive. Do not hesitate to cut off discussions if they get started on either:

- Issues that (however interesting) are not important for the system's development.

- Issues that are relevant, but require a detailed discussion, of interest to some participants only and taking too much time. Once such an issue is identified and threatens to take up too much of the rest of the meeting, stop the discussion and move the details to either individual stakeholder interviews or a small separate workshop with the directly involved participants.

6.9.5 After the workshop

After every workshop, the organizer should produce a report and circulate it to all the participants, for information and possible correction. Good workshop reports should follow the earlier general advice ("Guidelines for interview and workshop reports", page 114). In addition:

- The emphasis is on issues and solutions, not on the conversation itself. This is the reason why the document is a "workshop report", not "workshop minutes". It is not important to record what was said; the goal is to report what was decided and what remains to be resolved.

- Accordingly, the summary of discussion results should be egoless. It is generally not productive to record that it was Jill from accounting who mentioned the need for the system to produce documents for auditors. Do report, in as precise a form as possible, the audit-related requirements that the meeting has identified. You may find it useful to attribute them to the accounting department (not a person), but such a comment is mostly useful to indicate which persons or groups should be consulted for further action.

- An important component of the report is indeed the identification of further elicitation actions that may be required. Here you can list individuals — having attended the workshop or not — who were recognized as having the potential answer to remaining questions.

- Devote particular attention to contentious issues. Specify the resolution if it was made during the meeting; if not, define the subsequent decision process. In either case, explain what the conflict was about, so that developers wondering about a certain decision (or approached by stakeholders disagreeing with a decision) will have a clear idea of the issue and how it was resolved during the workshop. Tricky requirements issues should be resolved by the requirements and not turn into tricky design and implementation issues.

Workshop reports should become part of the requirements documents (they serve as one of the inputs to chapter P.7 of the Standard Plan, "Requirements process and report", see page 35). They will provide precious insights to the development team.

6.10 ASKING THE RIGHT QUESTIONS

The following rules are equally applicable to stakeholder interviews and workshops.

6.10.1 Uncover the unsaid

One of the challenges of the elicitation process is to bring to light information that is known to stakeholders but so deeply ingrained that they do not even think of mentioning it. The development team may not be privy to such implicit information, which can be essential to the project's success. "Kidnapped words" (6.4.2) are an example, but the problem is more general.

Members of any professional specialty share knowledge that is obvious to them (and hence not usually stated explicitly in their discussions and documents), but not to outsiders. Anyone who has ever been the only non-MD in a dinner conversation between medical doctors will recognize the phenomenon. Members of any organization typically have their own common knowledge: elements of information which they may consider so obvious as not to deserve an explanation or even just an explicit mention of their existence. Becky Winant provides a good example from her experience of requirements elicitation:

> *One analyst did not include in his requirements document the database that fed his system. I asked him why.*
>
> *He said, "**Everyone knows it's there. It's obvious.**"*
>
> *Words to be wary of!*
>
> *It turned out that the database was scheduled for redesign.*

6.10.2 Cover all PEGS

A common mistake in requirements elicitation is to ask questions only about the system part ("*what do you want the system to do?*"). "System" or S is only one of the four PEGS of requirements. Elicitation should address all four PEGS:

> **Elicitation Coverage Principle**
>
> In soliciting requirements input from stakeholders, cover all four PEGS: Project, Environment, Goals and System.

Some of the questions should address the **Project**: while in the abstract it might be tempting to define the system regardless of development constraints, it is important to identify such constraints and any organizational characteristics that will affect the development.

Other questions should address the **Environment**: elicitation must list all environment properties, which are particularly prone to phenomenon of the "unsaid" discussed above. Many business rules and legal constraints, for example, are obvious to professionals in a given area; they may not think of stating them in a requirements discussion. It is the task of the analyst to push hard enough to obtain all relevant properties. In particular, when stakeholders evoke a specific rule, prod them until you have ascertained whether it is an environment-imposed property or a system functionality decision ("Distinguishing system and environment", 1.1.2, page 2).

Yet other questions should address the **Goals**: particularly when talking to high-level executives and other decision-making stakeholders, analysts should strive to get a clear idea of the business benefits that the target organization is expecting from the system.

You should, of course, also include questions on the **System**, but without confusing the roles of requirements engineers and other stakeholders, as discussed now.

6.10.3 Do not confuse roles

In asking questions about the system (either prior to its development or, in a more agile view, while it is being developed), remember that it is not the task of non-IT stakeholders to define its precise functionality. As noted at the beginning of this chapter (6.2), requirements elicitation is inductive: its aim is to collect information from the future beneficiaries of the system (and to ensure that they indeed will be beneficiaries, not victims). Defining the system's functions is part of the *deductive* component and is not the goal of requirements elicitation.

Non-IT stakeholders often *will* make suggestions, and are welcome to; people in the business can come up with excellent ideas that may escape the technical experts. These suggestions, however, are no substitute for proper requirement engineering:

- Stakeholders are typically influenced by the systems they know, whereas you may be looking for more innovative solutions.
- Stakeholders may also not be fully aware of the third, "limitative" force in the Three Forces diagram of page 106: the technical, financial and other constraints.

Take all stakeholder suggestions into account, but be ready to abstract and adapt them.

6.10.4 Ask effective questions

Good questions for stakeholder interviews and workshops satisfy the following criteria (due in particular to Winant and Derby, see the bibliographical section):

- They seek **useful answers**. A question is relevant if answers will help build the system.
- They are **egoless**. As an interviewer, you are in the service of the project and should not let your own background and personality interfere with the elicitation process. While an overbearing attitude can be damaging, the more serious risk is the reverse: being afraid to ask questions (for example about accounting rules, if that is the project's area) for fear of looking stupid. Put your pride aside and ask all questions that can help clarify the properties of the project, environment, goals and system.
- They make **no assumptions**. You should not prejudge the answer. Be ready for surprises.

Example questions that refrain from making assumptions are *context-free* questions, such as:

- *"Where do you expect this to be used?"*
- *"What is it worth to you to solve this problem?"*
- *"When do you do this?"*
- *"How might it be different?"*

Meta-questions (meaning questions about the questions) can help you escape a restrictive interview or workshop framework and discover the "unsaid" elements:

- *Are the questions I have asked so far relevant?*

- *Is there anything else I should be asking you?*

- *Whom else should I be interviewing on this topic?*

More question types, from suggestions by Derby and (separately) Wiegers and Beatty:

Open-ended	What?	*What happens when...?* *What happens next?* *What factors are involved?* *What is behind that?* *What else?* *What else could...?*
	How?	*How do you use the product to ...?* *How do people decide which option to select?* *How did that happen?*
	Why? (see below)	*Why do you...?* *Why **don't** you...?* *Are there any other reasons?*
	Could...?	*Could you see a way to use the product to solve this problem?* *Could you conceive of an example in which you would use the product this way?* *Could you see a way to use the product to solve this problem?*
Closed	Specific	*Do you have any problem with function X of the current system?* (Follow-up with specifics, e.g. *"Can you recreate the problem?"*)
Multiple-choice (useful to set priorities, see 6.10.5)		*Which would you prefer, A, B, or C?* *If you had to choose one, would you choose, X, Y, or Z?*
More question styles		*Would you ever need to...?* *Does anyone ever...?* *Where do you get...?* *Can you show me?* *Can you give me an example?*

To avoid irritating stakeholders with "why"-style questions, Derby suggests rephrasing them in "how" or "what" style: *How did this come to be? What was the thinking behind that decision?*

6.10.5 Get stakeholders to prioritize

The process of gathering wishes from stakeholders can suffer from the kid-outside-a-candy-store phenomenon. I want everything, of course!

The risk is not indigestion, but the reverse: not getting anything at all.

Projects hit hurdles. Budgets get cut. Schedules get shortened. Milestones get pushed back. Competitors release products, forcing an acceleration of your development. In such circumstances, the project will have no choice but to sacrifice some of the announced functionality (or hopefully transfer it to a future release). From being just unpleasant, this decision can turn catastrophic if the choice of which elements of functionality to keep and which to drop, made in the heat of the moment, turns out to be wrong.

The better solution — reflected in one of the quality attributes for requirements, "Prioritized", 4.13, page 67 — is to make the choice in advance. Ask stakeholders, when they describe their wishes, to prioritize them. As with other elicitation decisions discussed in this chapter, the final prioritization decisions will rest with the requirements team (which may need to arbitrate between priorities argued by different groups), but the process starts with stakeholders.

A simple form of prioritization distinguishes just three levels, defined by the consequence of the project missing the functionality:

- Critical (show-stopper): the system cannot ship.
- Important: the system can ship, but will be seriously hampered.
- Nice-to-have: some users may be disappointed by the absence of the functionality.

A risk of this approach is criticality inflation: interviewees may be tempted to stuff everything into the first category or reluctantly into the second one, for fear that anything in the third will automatically be dropped at implementation time.

In reality, development teams do not necessarily reason this way: for each feature, they look at both its importance to the project and its assessed development effort; features that are easy to implement ("low-hanging fruit"), even if just nice-to-have, have a good chance of making it into the product.

To counter criticality inflation, a useful practice is the **virtual budget**. Given a list of desirable features, you ask interviewees to put an economic value on each. You give them a theoretical budget of 100 dollars (or whatever your currency is) and ask them to allocate it to the features, with a minimum of (for example) $2 or $5 depending on the number of features. This technique is a good way to force stakeholders to discuss how essential the various units of functionality are, relative to each other. (One of the tools in this Handbook's web site allows you to play the virtual budgeting game interactively.)

Whatever technique you decide to use, prioritize. You will almost certainly have to choose between features. The process will be much more efficient and professional if, instead of making that choice in a panic, with deadlines looming (or past) and executives screaming, you have planned for it early on, calmly evaluating the merits.

6.11 PROTOTYPES: TELL OR SHOW?

The three-forces diagram from the beginning of this chapter (6.2, page 106) includes the deductive part of requirements: along with the inductive force, determined by stakeholder needs, and under the constraints of the limitative force, there always exists a deductive force, resulting from the project originators' vision for the system. It pro-

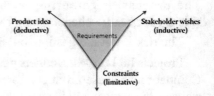

ceeds from an application of the "show me" (instead of "tell me") approach. Sometimes, especially for innovative systems, it can be useful to take "show me" one step further by presenting stakeholders with an actual program, a *prototype*, illustrating some aspect of the system.

6.11.1 What is a prototype?

A prototype provides an alternative, or a complement, to the classical question to stakeholders, "*what would you like?*", with its risk of either silence or a rambling discussion ranging across the trivial, the irrelevant and the infeasible. With a prototype, you demonstrate to stakeholders an actual program simulating some aspect of that system — or let them run it themselves — in the hope of getting useful responses, positive and negative. The question becomes: "*is this what you would like?*". A requirements prototype has the following characteristics:

- It is a program illustrating possible choices for some of the future system's properties.
- In both size and development effort, it is much smaller (often by several orders of magnitude) than that system.
- It is often parameterized, making it possible to try out some of the choices and discover their consequences. Such interactive feedback can be more effective than an abstract discussion.
- It is not designed to be part of the future delivery of the system and will normally be discarded once it has fulfilled its role.

Three kinds of prototype possessing these properties are:

- Throwaway prototypes (6.11.3), providing a first version to be discarded.
- UI prototypes (6.11.4), supporting experimentation with variants of the user interface.
- Feasibility prototypes (6.11.5), exploring the practicality of certain features.

6.11.2 Incremental prototypes

Before considering actual prototypes in the sense defined above, we note that the term "prototype" is sometimes used to denote something else: successive versions of a system produced in an iterative, incremental mode. This usage is misleading and is mentioned here only to avoid confusion. A prototype, as noted, is not designed for inclusion in the system under development. As a result, it is subject to looser constraints of quality. An incremental delivery is a first step towards the actual system and is subject to the same rules and standards.

The software industry has massively moved to incremental development, whose variants will be examined in detail in chapter 12. Such a discussion does not belong here, since an incremental release is not a prototype.

6.11.3 Throwaway prototypes

"Prototype" is sometimes used in the sense of a first version of a system meant to be discarded after yielding some lessons.

This concept is central in particular to the "Spiral" lifecycle model studied in a later chapter ("Rescuing the Spiral model", 12.2, page 212); we will see that a risk associated with this technique is the pressure to ship a prototype not intended for that purpose.

6.11.4 UI prototypes

The "show rather than tell" approach is particularly interesting for requirements affecting the user interface (UI) part of the system. Thereby lie both one of the major attractions of prototypes and one of their major limitations:

- Attraction: the best UI principles and UI experts are no substitute for the unfettered reactions of future users given the opportunity to play with a live version of the UI (even if, as any UI prototype, it is just a Potemkin façade with no meaningful processing behind it).

- Limitation: user interfaces are almost never the most difficult part in the construction of modern software systems. More precisely, while a bad UI can be catastrophic, it is much easier to correct than mistakes affecting deeper aspects of the requirements. A poorly scheduled project (Project mistake), a missed critical environment constraint (Environment mistake), a misunderstanding regarding the organization's needs (Goals mistake) and a wrong definition of a major system function (System mistake) may delay the project significantly or yield a flawed result. In comparison, a UI flaw is usually something that you can fix, even late in the process.

6.11.5 Feasibility prototypes

The frequent focus on UI prototypes distracts from a form of prototype which can be particularly useful for requirements: feasibility prototypes, intended to test whether certain functions required by the implementation will be doable at all.

Feasibility prototypes are particularly useful in connection with two intentionally adjacent chapters of the Project book in the Standard Plan: P.5, Required Technology Elements, and P.6, Risks and Mitigation Analysis. Any project depends on outside technology elements (identified in P.5), including APIs (interfaces to existing software). One of the biggest threats to software development — specifically, to the *predictability* and *controllability* of software development — is the sudden realization that a piece of the technology considered to be necessary for the realization of the system is not up to expectations.

There are many reasons to devote special attention to external technology elements:

- For hardware devices, supply-chain issues can arise.
- Open-source community software developments are attractive, but they are dependent on the goodwill of developers who may abruptly decide to move their interest elsewhere.
- Commercial products carry their own risks. While small companies can often be trusted (as they care about retaining individual customers), large software companies make policy

decisions based on their own perceived long-term interests and have been known to drop entire lines of products without a blink, hanging entire classes of users out to dry.

- More generally, the software industry is a highly dynamic environment with quick obsolescence. Products that are not continuously maintained can quickly become unusable. It is easy for a project member to state, on the basis of a successful earlier experience, that the project does not need (for example) to develop its own multilanguage-support solution since product X will support it; by the time the project needs it, product X may no longer be available, or up to date, or applicable to the project's specific circumstances.

- A particular source of obsolescence is the phenomenon familiarly known as *dependency hell*. Many open-source products in particular rely on other products, which have their own dependencies; but each element in the chain continues to evolve on its own, and it may turn out that version *n* of product A only works with version *m* or greater of B which is no longer supported, or supported on iOS but not Android while the project needs both platforms.

Such a case struck the author (in a software project) during the writing of this Handbook. The project involved an attempt to update a graphical interface from the GTK graphical framework, adequate for many years but now marked as obsolete, from the GTK 2 level to GTK 3. While GTK 2 was not being supported anymore on major platforms, GTK 3 turned out to be lacking in key capabilities. The result was a more than half-year release delay and several person-years of effort devoted solely to *restoring functionality that used to work*. Such unexpected roadblocks are a potential major threat to any project.

While no project is entirely immune from the risk of a required technology that fails to live up to expectations, protection measures are available. The first step is to pay attention to the two Standard Plan chapters cited above:

- Filling in P.5, Required Technology Elements, implies identifying all the existing systems including among others APIs, operating systems, tools, databases and hardware on which the new system is expected to rely.

- Filling in P.6, Risks and Mitigation Analysis, involves assessing the readiness of these systems for the needs of the development.

Feasibility prototypes step in when this assessment cannot just rely on opinion, documentation, or the experience of prior usage. Run tests of the expected functionality on a small scale, to discover any flawed or missing feature which could severely impair the project if it would only hit it when needed for real.

Feasibility Prototype Principle

To avoid major project risks (chapter P.6 of the Standard Plan), the requirements effort should identify project-critical elements of needed technology (P.5) and, in case of any doubt about their actual capabilities, develop and run feasibility prototypes to asses their readiness and adequacy for the project.

6.11.6 Limitations of prototypes

All prototypes, including those not specifically intended to get feedback on the user interface, suffer from the risk of undue focus on superficial interface matters. Even if you have designed the prototype to elicit input on non-UI matters, the UI is what the stakeholders see when presented with it, prompting comments that may detract from deeper issues. "*I have to click too many times to get to the product list*": maybe such a reaction is representative of a badly conceived functionality, but it may just as well be a trivial UI detail that can be corrected later.

Another risk with prototypes is that they get hijacked to become the real system. A prototype can be dangerously successful: an impressive demo leads stakeholders (most frighteningly, executives) to believe that the system is just around the corner. The pressure then builds up to expand the prototype to become the system. There is nothing wrong with this view if instead of a prototype the demo showed the result of one of the *iterations* in an explicit incremental development process (which, as noted above, is sometimes also called a prototype, but is a different kind of beast). If it is a requirements prototype, however, it is usually not suitable for transformation into an actual system:

- A prototype is designed to illustrate and evaluate some aspects of the system, for example the UI. It may be weak on other equally (or more) critical aspects, such as data management.

- To make sure it quickly produces visible results, a prototype almost invariably sacrifices some of the factors of software quality. For example, it may ignore efficiency concerns, which do not matter for small demos but prevent the design from scaling up. In such a case an impressive demo may be deceptive: perhaps the prototype successfully addressed the easy issues and skirted the difficult ones, such as choices of architecture and algorithms. You must always identify the prototype as such and avoid raising unwarranted expectations.

The following advice expresses some of the preceding observations on prototypes:.

Prototype Principle

- When used with the appropriate caution, prototypes are an important tool in the requirements elicitation process.
- Distinguish requirements prototypes from incremental system versions obtained in iterative development.
- Always present a requirements prototype as such, identifying the system properties that it is intended to assess, and avoiding any confusion with the actual system and any misplaced expectation.

6.11.7 Risk assessment and mitigation

The discussion of feasibility prototypes brings to the forefront the key issue of risk analysis. While a full discussion involves project management issues beyond the scope of this requirements Handbook, the requirements effort has among its responsibilities to provide risk and mitigation information. Possible problems with a needed technology, as discussed in 6.11.5 above, are an example of a risk that can be identified at the requirements stage.

There are many other examples, such as the sudden unavailability of key personnel (a developer leaving the company or falling ill), the disturbance caused by the unexpected release of a competing product, and a change of the environment (as may arise from new regulations) affecting the assumptions made so far.

The following principle guides risk analysis:

Risk Principle

The analysis of any identified risk (particularly in P.6, Risks and Mitigation Analysis) must include the following elements:

R1 Identification of the risk.
R2 Assessment of the likelihood that it will materialize.
R3 Assessment of the damage to the project (cost, delays, …).
R4 Description of the mitigation strategy or strategies if any.
R5 Assessment of the cost of the retained mitigation strategy or strategies.

It is not enough in risk analysis to stop at R1, identification. You should also have some idea of the probability of its occurrence (R2) and the resulting damage (R3). (Risk analysis techniques often use as a key indicator the *product* of these two quantities.) The project should explore the possible mitigation actions (R4) early; since any such action implies an extra cost (otherwise, it would have been chosen in the original strategy), you must also assess that cost (R5).

6-E EXERCISES

6-E.1 Throwaway prototypes and second-system effect

A classic book on software project management, [Brooks 1975-1995], advocated throwaway prototypes through a colorful slogan: "*Plan to throw one away; you will anyhow*" (discussed further in "Rescuing the Spiral model", 12.2, page 212). The same book — based on Brooks's experience as operating system architect for IBM's OS 360 and some of its successors — also presents another concept, the "*Second-system effect*". This phrase covers the following observation about a typical career progression for a technology innovator:

- In your first serious project, you have convinced a few people to let you go ahead with your ideas, but — perhaps because they are not 100% sure you will succeed, and want to hedge their bet — you are severely constrained in personnel and financial resources. In addition, you are working under a tight schedule. These limitations force you to make considerable sacrifices in your ideal list of features.

- That first project is successful. Basking in that success, for your second project you are given (by superiors in a large company such as IBM, or investors in your own new venture) far more resources and latitude. As a result you "throw in the kitchen sink": you now have the freedom to include all the brilliant ideas that you had suppressed in your first, penurious effort. The result is product bloat and creeping featurism, defeating feasibility (4.6) and ending in project failure. Maybe the limitations and constraints that you kept cursing during your first project were in fact key ingredients of its success; removing them causes unbridled complexity and defeat.

Discuss how these two considerations from the same book — the advice to use throwaway prototyping, and the description of the second-system effect — relate to each other. Are they compatible? Are they contradictory?

(If you consult Brooks's work, you will note that in the book's second edition he states that he now considers the first edition's "*Plan to throw one away*" advice to have been misguided. You may factor this analysis into your discussion.)

6-E.2 A glossary for web-based sales

The glossary in the example requirements document at [Bair 2005] is a placeholder (with only one entry). Complete it by providing definitions for other concepts pertaining to the example.

6-E.3 A glossary for text formatting

Produce a glossary for the Naur-G&G example of the previous chapter ("The seven sins: a classic example", 5.10, page 93). After reading its formal treatment in a later chapter ("An example: text formatting, revisited", 9.5, page 171), update the glossary as (and if) needed.

6-E.4 A workshop plan

Produce a requirements workshop plan, following the guidelines of section 6.9.3, for the example requirements document of exercise 6-E.2.

BIBLIOGRAPHICAL NOTES AND FURTHER READING

The Henry Ford quip about horses and cars is not attested but is in character. Steve Jobs's comment about customers is cited in his standard biography [Isaacson 2011].

[Christel-Kang 1992] provides a good summary of elicitation issues.

A complement to the figure showing the three forces pulling requirements, page 106, is Van Lamsweerde's illustration of influences on and from requirements in the project lifecycle (top of next page).

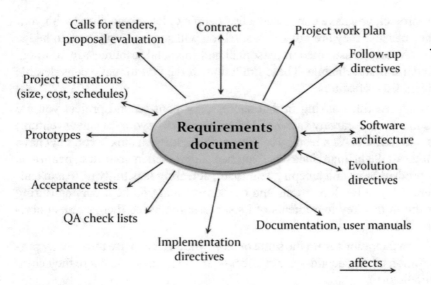

Calls for tenders, proposal evaluation

Contract

Project work plan

Follow-up directives

Influences on and from requirements (after [Van Lamsweerde 2008])

Project estimations (size, cost, schedules)

Requirements document

Software architecture

Prototypes

Evolution directives

Acceptance tests

QA check lists

Documentation, user manuals

Implementation directives

affects

Stakeholder maps (6.5) have their own dedicated site: [Stakeholder maps].

The analyst-SME culture-clash table of page 111 is from [Scharer 1981]. In the literature it is sometimes cited in variously modified forms, but the version shown is the original from the article, with no change other than the replacement of "*users*" with "*SMEs*".

The example of important but unstated requirement properties on page 118 ("*everyone knows it's there*") is from Becky Winant in [Winant 2002], also the source for many of the example interview and workshop questions in 6.10.4. Additional sources are [Derby 2010] (from which the list of question types on page 120 is taken) and [Wiegers-Beatty 2013].

The list of advantages of workshops in 6.11 is inspired by [Young 2002]. Another insightful discussion of workshops is [Gottesdiener 2002].

Fred Brooks's original *Mythical Man-Month* [Brooks 1975-1995] advocated throwaway prototypes (6.11.3); the second edition backpedaled on this advice (see exercise 6-E.1 above).

A variant of the concept of feasibility prototype (6.11.5) is the notion of **tracer code**, introduced by David Thomas and Andrew Hunt in [Thomas-Hunt 2019]. Inspired by "tracer bullets", which help improve the precision of artillery by illuminating the trajectory from end to end, tracer code is an implementation of some functionality all the way through, bringing potential problems and solutions to light. Unlike prototypes, whose natural fate is to be discarded after providing some information, tracer code will normally remain in some form in the final product.

7

Scenarios: use cases, user stories

In the System book — and occasionally in the Goals and Environment books — you must describe behaviors (1.6.1). One way is to present typical usage scenarios; for example, in an insurance system, how the system will process a claim, as seen from the viewpoint of a claims agent.

Requirements engineering methods use three kinds of scenario:

- A **use case** is a complete run through the system, as in this example.
- A **user story** is of a much smaller scope: one unit of interaction, for example logging into the system. User stories play a particularly important role in the definition of requirements in agile methods such as Scrum.
- A **use case slice** is a combination of the previous two notions.

Section 7.1 describes use cases, 7.2 presents user stories. Section 7.4 discusses the relevance and limitations of these techniques for requirements analysis, in preparation of a comparison with object-oriented requirements in chapter 8.

7.1 USE CASES

Several use case formalisms exist. The most widely publicized ones are graphical, using figurines to represent actors of the process. It is convenient to use a tabular and textual notation due to Cockburn (see bibliographical notes). The following example, describing the handling of a claim by an insurance company, is from the same source. (The "*Comment*" parts are not by Cockburn but added here as explanations.)

Use case: process insurance loss claim	
Name	Process_loss_claim *Comment: this use case is about processing a "claim", that is to say a request for payment following a loss event for a customer.*
Scope	Insurance company operations
Level	Business summary
Primary actor	Claims adjuster *Comment: a "claims adjuster" is a representative of the insurance company in charge of assessing insurance claims.*
Context of use	Claims adjuster handles claim.

© The Author(s), under exclusive license to Springer Nature Switzerland AG 2022
B. Meyer, *Handbook of Requirements and Business Analysis*, https://doi.org/10.1007/978-3-031-06739-6_7

Preconditions	A loss has occurred.
	Comment: necessary condition for the use case to proceed.
Trigger	A claim is reported to the insurance company.
	Comment: event causing the use case to proceed.
Main success scenario	1. A reporting party who is aware of the event registers a loss to the insurance company.
	2. A clerk receives and assigns the claim to a claims agent.
	3. The assigned claims adjuster:
	• 3.1 Conducts an investigation.
	• 3.2 Evaluates damages.
	• 3.3 Sets reserves.
	Comment: a "reserve" in the insurance business is an accounting provision made upon receipt of a claim (particularly a large one), based on an estimate of the possible cost to the company, prior to the final assessment which may take days, weeks or more. Provisioning such an estimate in the meantime avoids a disruptive financial surprise at the end of the process in case it does lead to the determination that the company must pay up.
	• 3.4 Negotiates the claim.
	• 3.5 Resolves the claim and closes it.
Success guarantee	The claim is resolved and closed.
Extensions	A. Submitted data is incomplete:
	• A.1 Insurance company requests missing information.
	• A.2 Claimant supplies missing information.
	A.2.1 Claimant does not supply information by deadline:
	A.2.1.1 Adjuster closes claim.
	B. Claimant does not own a valid policy:
	• B.1 Insurance company declines claim, notifies claimant, updates claim, closes claim.
Stakeholders and interests	*Comment: this section describes the various actors in the process — people and organizations.*
	• Insurance company divisions which sell insurance company policies.
	• Insurance company customers who have purchased policies.
	• Department of Insurance who sets market conduct.
	• Claimants who have loss as a result of act of an insured.
	• Insurance company Claims Division.
	• Future customers.

The core component (highlighted) is the **main success scenario**, giving the sequence of steps of an instance of the use case. Such scenarios have strong similarities to algorithms or programs:

- Their steps can be decomposed into sub-steps: here step 3 itself consists of a sequence of sub-steps, as does a subroutine (also called subprogram, method, function) in programming.

- Although the example does not illustrate it, a scenario can include conditional steps (two sub-scenarios, of which one will be chosen based on the outcome of a certain condition).

Unlike an algorithm or program, however, a use case (and more generally a scenario, such as a user story as reviewed next) is not meant to be carried out by a computer: instead, it describes the interaction between a human actor and the system.

The **level** entry characterizes the level of abstraction. A use case can describe a process at many levels, from the highest (a bird's eye view of an overall business process, meant to be complemented by further use cases for the details) down to the detailed descriptions of the system's actual operation.

A **precondition** is a limiting condition governing the use case's applicability. A **trigger** is an event that sets off the use case. Note the difference: the precondition is a logical condition which should hold if the use case is to be executed, but does not by itself cause such an execution. Only the trigger does. In the example, the precondition is that a loss has occurred; the trigger is that the loss has been reported. Beyond their application to use cases, preconditions are a general requirements concept, also known as an "assumption" and discussed in 1.7.

The **success guarantee** characterizes the state resulting from a successful execution of the use case, per the "main success scenario". In the terminology of mathematical software verification, from which the term "precondition" is borrowed, it would be called a "postcondition". Like preconditions, postconditions (success guarantees) are a general concept of requirements, which we encountered in 1.7. We may also relate success guarantees to a testing concept, "oracle", which denotes the condition that a successful test must ensure.

Extensions describe departures from the main success scenario. They serve two purposes:

- An extension can specify an alternate path for cases in which the main success scenario hits a condition that prevents it from proceeding — such as, in the example, a claimant who does not have an applicable insurance policy.

- Extensions also support *reuse* of elements common to several use cases. It is good practice to divide a set of related use cases into a base use case (covering common elements) and extensions. For example, in a further development of the claim-processing use case, variants for accident, loss and robbery might have both common elements and specific details. Rather than writing three separate use cases with significant repetition, you can write one base claim-processing use case, then extensions covering the specifics of each variant.

The use case lists, towards the beginning, the **main actor** responsible for carrying out instances of the scenario. It concludes with a list of **stakeholders**: other groups of people who may be affected. We saw how important it is for requirements in general to include consideration of all possibly affected stakeholders ("Categories of stakeholders", 1.10.1, page 13).

7.2 USER STORIES

A use case is a complete path taken by an actor through the system. A user story is also a usage scenario for actors interacting with the system, but much more limited in scope and complexity.

User stories play an important role for requirements in *agile methods*, a set of development methods which promote incremental program construction. Two of the best-known agile methods are XP (Extreme Programming), which introduced user stories, and Scrum, today the most widely used. In agile methods, the basic development iteration involves a developer picking the next item from a list of functions to be implemented, implementing it, and moving on to the next one. For such a scheme to work, each such function has to be small; a use case in the above style is not adequate because it describes a collection of related functions rather than a unit of functionality. For this reason, agile methods generally rely on a finer-grain unit: the user story.

The standard format for a user story consists of three elements:

- A <u>role</u>, denoting the main actor of a use case (remember "Special case: role", page 11).
- A desired <u>function</u> — part of the system's behavior ("Behavior", page 8).
- A business <u>purpose</u> (a goal in the general requirements terminology: "Goal", page 6).

For example:

> As a <u>claims agent</u>, I want prompt <u>claim processing</u>, so as to <u>achieve customer satisfaction</u>.

A standard set of quality criteria for user stories goes by the acronym INVEST:

The INVEST criteria for user stories	
Criterion	**Explanation**
Independent	Each user story should be describable on its own.
Negotiable	A user story is not a cast-in-stone specification imposed by a business analyst, but a proposal intended for discussion with stakeholders and, particularly, with the programmer who implements it and may find reasons to suggest changes.
Valuable	The functionality captured by a user story should bring the organization a demonstrable business benefit.
Estimable	The user story should be described precisely enough to allow at least a rough estimate of the effort required to implement it.
Small	Unlike use cases, user stories capture small units of functionality, typically implementable in a few person-days or at most weeks.
Testable	Every user story should lend itself to the design of one or more tests assessing whether a candidate implementation meets it. In keeping with other principles of agile development, particularly XP, the agile advice is to write these tests immediately after writing the user story, before starting the implementation.

7.3 EPICS AND USE CASE SLICES

User stories and use cases lie at opposite ends of the size and complexity range for scenarios:

- A user story describes a small and focused scenario, which a programmer can typically implement in a few days.

- A use case covers an entire path of interaction with the system, all the way to obtaining a meaningful result. It may involve a considerable amount of system functionality.

Compare, in a system supporting an e-commerce platform, *"validate seller login"* and *"enable seller to enter a new range of products"*.

A need also exists for scenarios at levels of granularity in-between these extremes. To address it, one may start from either end: gather user stories into larger units; or decompose use cases into smaller units. These two ideas lead to *epics* and *use case slices*.

The first approach starts from the user story side, towards larger granularity. An epic is a collection of user stories, all directed towards a common goal (in the general requirements sense of this term, the "G" in PEGS). A typical epic for an e-commerce platform could be *"decrease the percentage of fraudulent sellers by 20%"*, involving many user stories.

The second approach starts from the use case side, towards finer granularity. "Use Case 2.0", the revision (introduced around 2006) of the original use case methodology from the 1990s, includes the notion of use case slice. In the words of the concept's originators (see the bibliographical notes), a use case slice consists of *"one or more stories selected from a use case to form a work item that is of clear value to the customer"*. The use case slice *"acts as a place-holder for all the work required to complete the implementation of the selected stories"*. Consider (in the e-commerce example) a sophisticated use case describing the process of registering a new seller on the e-commerce site. It may be interesting to extract from it a use case slice describing all the paths through the use case that have relevance to issues of security and fraud-prevention.

The term *scenario* covers use cases, user stories, epics, use case slices and any other technique that specifies system behavior by describing paths of interaction with the system. The discussion of scenarios, in the following section and in the next chapter, will mostly take use cases and user stories as examples but applies just as well to all other variants.

7.4 THE BENEFITS OF SCENARIOS FOR REQUIREMENTS

Scenarios — in particular use cases and user stories — describe units of behavior. They can help requirements in two different ways:

- As an **elicitation tool**. Chapter 6 emphasized how important it is to use a diversity of techniques to ensure that stakeholders express their needs. Scenarios, which express snapshots of system behavior in a form that speaks directly to future users, can be easier to obtain from them than more abstract specifications.

- As a **verification tool**. Both use cases and user stories describe scenarios of possible use that have been identified as essential: whatever else the system does, it must support these scenarios. Put another way, they are *system-level tests*. What a test case is to a single program element, a use case or user story is a test of the entire system or a subsystem.

To cover these two roles, the Standard Plan of requirements reserves not just one but two chapters to scenarios:

- G.5 in the Project book, for the principal high-level scenarios, of interest to all stakeholders and directly connected to the Goals.

- S.4 in the System book, for detailed scenarios (use cases or, depending on the project's choice, user stories) exercising specific functions of the system.

References to these scenarios can also occur in the verification plan (S.6).

7.5 THE LIMITATIONS OF SCENARIOS FOR REQUIREMENTS

Use cases and user stories cannot by themselves define requirements. Several reasons make them insufficient for that purpose.

Note first that scenarios only apply — out of the four PEGS — to the System and to the Goals. They bring nothing to the specification of the Project and Environment.

For the description of system properties (behaviors), the most important limitation is that a scenario only describes one case (or a set of related cases if we take advantage of conditional branching and extensions). Typically, it describes the most desirable case (*"main success scenario"* as illustrated in 7.1) and some variants (*"extensions"*). Those cases, however, are the easy part.

If software development could focus on the simple, straightforward cases, it would be a cakewalk. Much of the difficulty of software and particularly of software requirements comes from the myriad of variants that any significant system must be prepared to handle. Even in a basic case such as insurance-claim processing in 7.1, any attempt to specify things seriously leads to an explosion of cases, which no scenario-based technique can handle. Consider this part of the "extension" (extracted from the complete text on page 130):

Extensions	B. Claimant does not own a valid policy:
	• B.1 Insurance company declines claim, notifies claimant, updates claim, closes claim.

There will inevitably be cases of the company mistakenly declaring that the claimant does not own a policy and then correcting the mistake (for example, the renewal was in the mail). There has to be a scheme for that case, such as reopening the claim. As another example, the "main success scenario" includes the following:

Main success scenario	[Extract only, from the full scenario on page 130] 3. The assigned claims adjuster: • 3.1 Conducts an investigation. • 3.2 Evaluates damages. • 3.3 Sets reserves. • 3.4 Negotiates the claim. • 3.5 Resolves the claim and closes it.

It will inevitably occur in practice that some customer, during the "negotiates the claim" step, contests the result of the earlier "evaluates damages" step as too low, or the adverse party's insurer contests it as too high. Then step 3.2 needs to be reopened after 3.4, causing what in programming would be called a loop.

One can add "extensions" covering such situations, or write new use cases to address them, Scaling up such a strategy is, however, hopeless: for any non-trivial system there are so many combinations that it is impossible to describe them all, or even a small subset. Requirements must provide a description of the system (and other PEGS components) at a more abstract level.

The difference between scenarios and requirements is a generalization of the difference between a test and a specification. We could attempt to specify an integer function by stating that it yields 0 for the argument 0, 1 for 1, 4 for 2, 9 for 3 and 16 for 4. That would not be a specification, however, just a set of tests. It says nothing about the function's result for 5, 6, or one million. (You may try, for fun, to use a curve-fitting program, easy to find on the Web, to see which functions — besides "square" — match these tests.) A true specification is: "$f(n) = n^2$ for every integer n." It captures all possible cases, not just a few out of a myriad or infinity.

The influence of scenario-based specifications can be seen in many Web applications which work well for users whose needs exactly fit one of the planned schemes but let you down as soon as your need is in any way special. A serious requirements effort cannot stop at identifying the most common cases; it must define general behaviors.

7.6 THE ROLE OF USE CASES AND USER STORIES IN REQUIREMENTS

The consequences of the preceding discussion are clear. Scenarios are not suitable by themselves as requirements. Combined with other techniques, however, they can play an important part in the requirements effort, in two ways:

• As **a requirements elicitation tool.** Identifying user stories and use cases helps identify key components and behaviors of the system.

• As a **requirements verification tool**. While scenarios can only cover a very small subset of the possible paths through the system — a drop in the ocean — they can cover some of the *most important* paths. In this role they address an important form of completeness: the system's ability to handle the scenarios of most importance to key stakeholders. The notion of scenario completeness (11.3) will address this concern.

Useful requirements demand more abstract descriptions of behavior. Modern object-oriented requirements analysis, studied in the next chapter, provides a better approach.

The following principle summarizes this assessment:

> **Scenario Principle**
>
> Take advantage of use cases, user stories, use case slices, tests and other forms of scenarios as tools for elicitation and verification of requirements.
>
> Do not use them as a substitute for actual requirements specifications.

7-E EXERCISES

7-E.1 Scenarios for graphical manipulation

Numerous interactive systems make it possible to produce figures, typically as part of a text, and perform various manipulations of them (move, rotate, group, …). Typical examples in the Microsoft world are Word and PowerPoint. Using any such systems with which you are familiar as a user, and assuming that you were instead in the designer's seat, write the fundamental use cases and user stories for the figure-related capability. Define any epics or use case slices that may be deduced from them.

7-E.2 User stories from a use case

From the insurance-related use case of this chapter (first presented in 7.1), derive user stories.

BIBLIOGRAPHICAL NOTES AND FURTHER READING

The book that originally popularized use cases was [Jacobson 1992], which covers a broader spectrum of software engineering techniques and remains an important reference. A shorter but effective exposition of use case techniques is [Cockburn 2001]. The example in section 7.1 is based (with permission) on its use cases 19 and 21 (themselves credited by Cockburn to the Fireman's Fund insurance company).

[Glinz 2000], a classic paper on the suitability of UML for requirements, contains an in-depth critical analysis of the limitations of use cases, which also provides important insights (for anyone working with use cases anyway) on how to use them effectively.

A discussion of requirements, [Meyer 2012a], takes seriously the idea of using a curve-fitting tool to find functions matching the first few values of the square function (page 135), leading to a few unexpected solutions.

On user stories, a good reference is a book about requirements in agile methods: [Leffingwell 2011]. On agile methods in general see [Meyer 2014]. The INVEST set of criteria for user stories (7.2) appears in [Wake 2003-2017], from which the explanations on page 132 are taken in part.

[Jacobson-Spence-Kerr 2016] is the reference on use case slices and more generally on Use Case 2.0.

8

Object-oriented requirements

There are two fundamental ways to describe a system (of any kind, software or not): procedural and object-oriented (OO). This distinction is just as applicable to requirements as it is to software design, to programming and to many other software and non-software tasks.

For software design and programming, object-oriented techniques have achieved widespread use thanks to their ability to enhance the *extendibility* (ease of change) of systems, the *reusability* of their components in other systems, and their *reliability* (correctness, robustness, security). These qualities are desirable for requirements as well.

This chapter explains object-oriented requirements and their relation to other specification techniques such as use cases.

8.1 Two kinds of system architecture

Any description of a non-trivial system needs to be structured into parts, called *units* or *modules*. The distinction between procedural and OO reflects the two possible criteria for choosing units. Think of these criteria as "**what the system does**" and "**what it does it to**":

- You can define each unit to cover an elementary or complex *operation* performed by the system. For example, a payroll program has the operation "produce the monthly payroll". This is the **procedural** style. (See the bibliographical section about terminology.)

- You can define each unit to cover a kind of *thing* handled by the system. We say "objects" (or sometimes "data") rather than "things". For example, a payroll system works with such objects as paychecks, salary scales, employee records… This is the **object-oriented** style.

To describe a system, you need to account for both aspects, operations and objects, so the question can never be to choose one and exclude the other. The question is which of the two viewpoints to choose for *structuring* the description into manageable chunks. Does a module represent a unit of functionality or a unit of data? Each answer selects one of the two criteria for such units, but the other side remains:

- In procedural decomposition, every element of data gets attached to operations, and passed around (in the form of arguments, or shared data structures) between operations.

- In OO decomposition (or "object technology"), every operation gets attached to one data type, through the notion of class as discussed next.

In either case, both operations and data types remain. The difference lies in which of the two gets to define the modular structure of a system.

© The Author(s), under exclusive license to Springer Nature Switzerland AG 2022
B. Meyer, *Handbook of Requirements and Business Analysis*, https://doi.org/10.1007/978-3-031-06739-6_8

8.2 THE NOTION OF CLASS

The central concept in the object-oriented approach results from the preceding observations. A class is a module (unit of decomposition of a system's description) based on the specification of a certain type of objects; it comes complete with all operations applicable to these objects. (This is how "*every operation gets attached to an object type*" as stated in the previous section.)

Definition: class

In object-oriented approaches to system modeling and structuring, a class is a system unit specifying a type of object with the associated operations and their properties.

In presentations of OO programming, you may have seen "class" defined as "*an encapsulation of data fields and functions*" (perhaps with "method" for "function"). While acceptable for OO *programs*, this presentation is too low-level for a general definition, as the distinction between "fields" and "functions" only matters for implementation. More abstractly, in particular for requirements, we characterize data types through **operations**. For example a class describing the concept of customer in an insurance-claim-processing system has various operations:

- **Queries**, providing information about the customer: name, address, policy number, bank account information (for reimbursement)…

- **Commands**, to update the corresponding objects: record a new claim from this customer, reject a claim, update account information, update address…

When it comes to implementation, some of the queries may be implemented as fields in the data structure representing a customer, and others as functions to be computed, for example by retrieving information from the database; but that is solely an implementation matter. From a more abstract perspective, the relevant distinction is between queries and commands:

- A query asks something, as in "*what is this customer's policy number?*".

- A command does something, as in "*record this policy number for this customer*".

Although "object" gave the OO approach its name, "class" is the fundamental notion. The two should not be confused:

- An object is a data structure.

- During its operation, a system works with objects; typically many of them, but not of arbitrary form: objects are of given *object types*. Example object types in an insurance system are *AGENT*, *CUSTOMER*, *INSURANCE_CLAIM*, *POLICY*…. We say that the corresponding objects are **instances** of their respective types.

- What characterizes an object type is that all its instances are susceptible to the same operations. In OO modeling, we define an object type through these operations and their properties. For example, we define the object type *CUSTOMER* through the applicable operations (queries and commands): *name*, *policy_number*, *record_policy_number* and so on.

- "Class" is another name for "object type".

8.3 RELATIONS BETWEEN CLASSES AND THE NOTION OF DEFERRED CLASS

Part of the appeal of the object-oriented model is the simplicity of OO system descriptions, relying on classes as just defined and only two relations between them: client and inheritance.

A class C is a client of another S (and S a "supplier" of C) simply if operations on instances of C can use instances of S. For example, operations on an insurance claim (see the use case presented on page 130, which the present chapter will refine further) involve, among other objects, an insurance company, a clerk and a claim handler. In an OO model the class representing insurance claims will be a client of the classes representing the other three concepts.

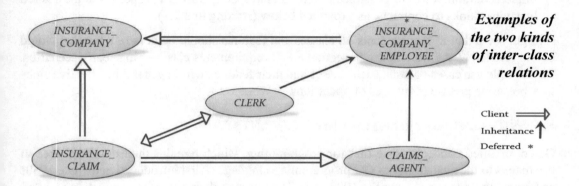

Examples of the two kinds of inter-class relations

A class inherits from (is an "heir" or "subclass" of) another if it represents a specialized or extended version of the other's concept. For example clerks and claims agents both belong to the general category of insurance company employees, which can be represented by another class *INSURANCE_COMPANY_EMPLOYEE* with the two inheritance links shown in the figure. This class will be a client of *INSURANCE_COMPANY*. "Client" and "inherits from" are the two relations that can exist between classes, represented by different kinds of arrow in the figure and playing distinct roles.

The "descendants" of a class are all the classes that inherit from it directly or indirectly (including by convention the class itself). The other way around we talk of "ancestor" classes.

Note that there can be cycles in the client relation (in the example, *INSURANCE_CLAIM* and *CLERK* are clients of each other), and a class can directly be a client of itself, but the inheritance relation admits no cycles. This rule does not preclude *multiple* inheritance, whereby a class inherits from two or more others, as long as the relation remains acyclic.

In an OO program, most of the features (commands and queries) of a class are **effective**, meaning that the class text provides, for each of them, an algorithm for its implementation. A class whose features are all effective is itself called an effective class. In some cases, and particularly for requirements, it is useful to define features without providing an implementation. Features that are specified but not implemented are called **deferred**; and a non-effective class (one that has at least one deferred feature) is a deferred class. (Alternative terms: "implemented" or "concrete" for effective, and "abstract" for deferred.) *INSURANCE_COMPA-NY_EMPLOYEE* in the example should most likely (as marked) be a deferred class since it describes a general concept. Deferred classes are used in particular for the following purposes:

- In programming, a deferred class may have alternative implementations (also known as "*effectings*") in descendant classes.

- In requirements, declaring classes and features deferred enables you to specify that some functionality must exist while staying away from any consideration of implementation and hence from the risk of *overspecification* (discussed in 4.7.3, page 59). Even without an implementation, it will be possible in such cases to specify *abstract* properties of the desired behavior thanks to contracts, as explained below (starting in 8.7.1).

It might seem that in requirements *all* classes and features should be deferred, but that would be too restrictive. As we will see in section 8.8.1, requirements classes can specify scenarios, for example use cases or tests; such classes and their features will in general be effective since they prescribe precise sequences of operations.

8.4 WHY OBJECT-ORIENTED REQUIREMENTS?

Object-oriented concepts arose first for programming, which remains their dominant area of use thanks to the availability of OO programming languages (first introduced in the late 1960s and reaching wide usage from the 1990s on). The range of their potential application is, however, much broader. Broad enough in fact to encompass all tasks of software construction, from requirements to design, implementation of course ("programming" in a strict sense), and even verification. Of direct interest in this Handbook is the application to requirements.

The reason for this wide applicability is that object technology is more than a programming technique: a *modeling* technique, providing powerful conceptual tools to describe systems and reason about them. These systems can be software systems, but do not have to; even in the software case, OO modeling provides benefits outside of implementation.

Discussing a system as a set of object types (classes) characterized by the applicable operations yields a number of benefits, which have been widely recognized in the programming world but can apply to requirements as well. They include the following:

- **Stability through the evolution of the software**. This is probably the most powerful argument. As needs evolve and system usage brings feedback from the field, changes will occur; but they should as much as possible affect individual modules, not the *decomposition* into modules. We do not want to be rethinking the architecture time and again. With this criterion in mind one may note that functions (operations) come and go, but the main object types remain more stable in the face of evolution. Adding new operations to a class does not affect the architecture; but in a functional decomposition, adding a new type of object can require updating many functions. Hence the higher resilience of an architecture based on object types rather than functional (procedural) blocks.

- **Information hiding**. To deal with large system descriptions, it is essential to limit the knowledge that each unit needs to possess about others to use their services. Functions offer a first form of information hiding: you may call a function through its name and list of arguments, without knowing the implementation. With classes, you may in addition declare, as part of the specification of a class, that some of the properties are for internal use only, within the class, and not accessible outside. We call them "secret". The main purpose is the same as in the previous point: limiting the effect of changes (since information hiding ensures that changes will in many cases affect secret properties only, and hence that their consequences will be limited to the corresponding class).

- **Reuse**. If we are trying to apply the results of one project to another, reusing individual operations will generally not suffice. Operations such as "record an insurance claim", "process an insurance claim", "dismiss an insurance claim" and others are closely connected. The notion of an *insurance claim* — as a class which includes all these operations — is a more realistic unit of reuse.

- **Classification**. As in any scientific or technical endeavor, descriptions of large systems need to organize the concepts in hierarchies, to take advantage of commonality. The corresponding OO technique, inheritance, makes it possible to describe new classes as extensions or specializations of existing ones, without repeating common properties. Along with information hiding, inheritance is a key tool in harnessing system complexity.

- **Modeling power**. OO concepts can yield system descriptions that are clear and intuitive, since the notions of object, class and inheritance are easy to grasp. Some classes have immediately tangible counterparts in the system environment, as in the examples of insurance-related classes in the preceding section. They are called "Environment classes", Concrete and Abstract, in the classification presented later in this chapter ("The seven kinds of class", 8.8, page 154). Even classes of other categories, which do not just cover "objects" in the ordinary non-technical sense of the world, capture clearly defined concepts.

- **Abstraction**. Deferred classes and features, introduced in the preceding section, make it possible to specify the presence of certain types of objects and of certain operations on them without giving implementation details (but with abstract behavioral properties through contracts). This powerful requirements technique is a hallmark of object-oriented modeling.

OO programming techniques offer other important benefits; in particular, *polymorphism* and *dynamic binding* yield a flexible programming style and further support the goals of ease of change and reuse. These techniques are available at the level of programming and generally not directly relevant to requirements.

The advantages listed above are, however, as applicable to requirements, and as fruitfully, as they are for design and implementation.

8.5 AN OO NOTATION

How do we express object-oriented implementations, designs, and (the case of direct relevance to this Handbook) requirements? Many object-oriented languages exist, including:

- C++, not just an OO language but more generally a modernization of C, itself a systems programming language widely used since the 1970s to write low-level code, to which C++ adds notions of class and inheritance. "Low-level" is not here a pejorative term, but indicates that C and C++ retain features close to the hardware and operating system, enabling programmers to retain tight control over execution-time behavior. Another OO extension for C is Objective-C, which achieved widespread use thanks to its former role in Apple's MacOS platforms.

- Java, which removed from C++ the compatibility with C to ensure closer conformance to OO principles, and C#, initially close to Java but then extended in its own directions.

- Eiffel, which was devised from the start as a pure-OO notation for requirements and design as well as implementation.

Examples of OO requirements in this chapter and some subsequent ones will use Eiffel as it most directly reflects the concepts of OO modeling with no dependency on earlier notations such as C. Readers can easily transpose the examples to other OO notations they may know, such as Java.

One of the reasons for using this notation is that it is largely self-explanatory. The following example, sketching one of the classes of the preceding example, suffices for our later discussions (when extended with the "contract" mechanism introduced below). Lines starting with "--" are comments; those marked "Note" have been added for the benefit of the present discussion (as distinct from other comments, which are a normal part of the class texts).

```
class CLAIM_AGENT inherit
   INSURANCE_COMPANY_EMPLOYEE
feature
   handled: LIST [INSURANCE_CLAIM]
            -- The claims handled by this claim agent.
            -- Note 1: This feature is a query.
            -- Note 2: The presence of this feature makes CLAIM_AGENT a client class
            --         of INSURANCE_CLAIM, as shown in the figure of page 139.
```

> *process* (*c*: *INSURANCE_CLAIM*)
>   -- Handle claim represented by *c*.
>   -- Note 3: This feature is a command.
>   -- Note 4: The presence of the argument *c* also makes the class a client of
>   --   *INSURANCE_CLAIM*.
>   -- Note 5: The next line expresses that the feature is deferred.
>   **deferred**
>   **end**
> … More features (queries and commands) may be included here …
> **end**

8.6 AVOIDING PREMATURE ORDERING

Beyond the factors explained in the preceding section, an important reason behind the success of OO techniques has to do with the avoidance of premature *time-ordering decisions*. While it is possible for an OO specification to express a time-ordered scenario such as a use case, object technology also supports a more general and abstract specification style, based on *contracts*.

8.6.1 The limitations of sequential ordering

Like the procedural style in programming, the time-ordered style of use cases in requirements forces us to specify the order of execution of operations, as in the following extract from the example of chapter 7:

Use case: process insurance loss claim	
Name, scope, level, primary actor, context of use, preconditions, triggers	(See the rest of the example on page 130.)
Main success scenario	1. A reporting party who is aware of the event registers a loss to the insurance company.
	2. A clerk receives and assigns claim to a claims agent.
	3. The assigned claims adjuster:
	•3.1 Conducts an investigation.
	•3.2 Evaluates damages.
	•3.3 Sets reserves.
	•3.4 Negotiates the claim.
	•3.5 Resolves the claim and closes it.
Success guarantee, extensions, stakeholders, interests	(See section 7.1 and the rest of the present section.)

Note how the use case defines a strict order for the steps. Forcing such an ordering specification at the level of requirements is often a premature decision. In reality, the order of the steps is not cast in stone. Using a preset ordering is convenient to describe *desirable* scenarios, or more generally the *expected* ones. But what happens is not always what we desire or expect.

To specify scenarios that depart from the standard ones, we saw that it is possible to use **extensions**. The example of section 7.1, page 129 included two extensions:

Reproduced from "Extensions" on page 130

Extensions	A. Submitted data is incomplete:
	•A.1 Insurance company requests missing information
	•A.2 Claimant supplies missing information
	A.2.1 Claimant does not supply information by deadline:
	A.2.1.1 Adjuster closes claim
	B. Claimant does not own a valid policy:
	•B.1 Insurance company declines claim, notifies claimant, updates claim, closes claim.

Many other extensions may be necessary. For example, steps 3.4 and 3.5 of the "main success scenario" (page 130) specify that the adjuster "*negotiates the claim*" and "*resolves and closes*" it; but — in addition to the questions already raised in 7.5 — what if the customer still disagrees after the "negotiation"? What if the customer does not receive the compensation and complains? Should the claim not remain open until the customer has been paid?

Writing ever more use-case "extensions" to cover all such situations is not a workable solution; the explosion of special cases will soon be intractable. This phenomenon limits the usefulness of use cases as a specification technique. In practice, it is possible to write use cases to cover the most common scenarios, but they are only a small subset of the possible ones, in the same way that, in programming, tests can only cover a minute subset of possible inputs.

Constraints between the operations do exist. But instead of *timing* constraints it is often more general and effective to model them as *logical* constraints.

8.6.2 A detour through stacks

Before returning to the insurance-claim requirements, it is illuminating to contrast the two styles, time-oriented and logical, on a well-known computer science example.

A "stack" in computer science is a data structure that stores objects to support retrieval in a "last-in, first-out" (LIFO) regimen. Think of a stack of plates, where you can deposit one plate at a time, at the top, and retrieve one plate at a time, also at the top. We may call the two

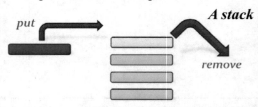

operations *put* and *remove*. Both are commands (often known under the alternative names *push* and *pop*). We will also use an integer query *count* giving the number of elements.

Assume we wanted to specify the behavior of a stack through use cases. Possible use cases (all starting with an empty stack) are:

```
put
put ; put
put ; put ; put        -- etc.: any number of successive put (our stacks are not bounded)
put ; remove
put ; put ; remove
put ; put ; remove ; remove
put ; put ; remove ; remove ; put ; remove
```

and so on *ad libitum* (or *ad nauseam*).

We should also find a way to specify that the system does **not** support such use cases as

```
remove ; put
```

or even just

```
remove
```

since it is not possible to remove an element from an empty stack. More generally the LIFO discipline implies that we cannot remove more than we have put.(Such illegal usage sequences are sometimes called "misuse cases".)

We may write as many such use cases as we like — some expressing normal sequences of operations, others describing erroneous cases — without capturing the fundamental rule that at any stage the number of *put* so far has to be no less than the number of *remove*.

Expressing the fundamental LIFO stack rule in this form would already be an improvement on specification through use cases. But we can actually do better by stating the *logical* constraints associated with the stack operations. The two basic concepts are:

- Precondition: a condition that must initially hold for an operation to be possible.

- Postcondition: a condition that will hold as a result of an operation.

The respective keywords are **require** and **ensure**. We can express the logical rules in a class specifying the behavior of stacks:

```
class STACK feature
    put (x: INTEGER)                              -- We assume stacks of integers for simplicity.
            -- Push x on top of stack.
        deferred
        ensure
            count = old count + 1
        end
    remove
            -- Pop an element from top of stack.
        require
            count > 0
        deferred
        ensure
            count = old count − 1
        end
    count: INTEGER
            -- Number of items in stack.
    invariant           -- See explanation of class invariants on the next page.
        count ≥ 0
end
```

The self-explanatory notation **old** e in a postcondition denotes the value of an expression e prior to execution of the operation.

This specification expresses the key properties: the query *count* gives the number of elements; a push operation is always applicable and results in a stack with one more element; a pop operation is applicable only to a stack with at least one element and yields a stack with one fewer element. (A more complete version would also have a query *item* giving the top stack element, and add to the postcondition of *put* the property *item* = x. It could support stacks of elements of any type, not just integers. It could also express that stacks are bounded, forcing *put* to have a precondition. See the exercises at the end of this chapter. The simplified version above is sufficient for the present discussion.)

The specification states what can be done with stacks (and what cannot) at a sufficiently high level of abstraction to capture all possible use cases. It enables us to keep track of the value of *count* in the successive steps of a use case; it tells us for example that the use case

put ; *put* ; *remove* ; *remove* ; *put* ; *remove*

must be supported (successive values of *count* are 0, 1, 2, 1, 0, 1, 0), but not the following:

> *put* ; *put* ; *remove* ; *remove* ; *remove*

since prior to the last step *count* will be 0, violating the precondition of *remove*.

The precondition and postcondition of an operation govern its interaction with the rest of the world and are correspondingly called its **contract**. A class as a whole also has a contract, consisting of the contracts of all its operations (its features) plus a possible "class invariant" describing a general property of the instances, preserved by all commands. Here, for example, both *put* and *remove* preserve the invariant property *count* $\geq$ 0.

Stacks are a data structure used in programming, not a case of industrial requirements. Beyond this example, however, the analysis yields general conclusions for requirements:

- Use cases only describe *specific* instances of behavior.
- An OO model with contracts yields a more abstract and hence more *general* specification.

As discussed below (8.7.3, 8.7.5), use cases will remain useful as a complement.

8.7 LOGICAL CONSTRAINTS VERSUS PREMATURE ORDERING

As the stack example illustrated, object-oriented specifications stay away from premature time-order decisions by focusing on object types (classes) and their operations (queries and commands), without making an early commitment to the order of executing these operations.

8.7.1 A contract-based specification

Here again is the essence of "main success scenario" in the insurance example (the original with more details was on page 130).

> 1. A reporting party who is aware of the event registers a loss to the insurance company.
>
> 2. A clerk receives and assigns claim to a claims agent.
>
> 3. The assigned claims adjuster:
>   - 3.1 Conducts an investigation.
>   - 3.2 Evaluates damages.
>   - 3.3 Sets reserves.
>   - 3.4 Negotiates the claim.
>   - 3.5 Resolves the claim and closes it.

(Note about the example's Environment: as noted on page 130, a *reserve* in the insurance business is a monetary amount that an insurer, when receiving a claim, sets aside as a financial provision estimating the financial liability that may eventually result from the claim. Reserves are important as an accounting precaution for difficult cases that may cause a prolonged analysis, or even litigation, and incur a high cost which will only be known at the end of the process.)

As a specification, this scenario is trying to express a few useful things; for example, you must set reserves before starting to negotiate the claim. But it expresses them in the form of a strict sequence of operations, a *temporal* constraint which does not cover the wide range of legitimate scenarios. As in the stack example, describing a few such scenarios is useful as part of requirements elicitation, but to specify the resulting requirements it is more effective to state the *logical* constraints. Here is a sketch of how the class *INSURANCE_CLAIM* could specify them in the form of contracts.

```
class INSURANCE_CLAIM feature
        -- Boolean queries (all with default value False):
    is_investigated, is_evaluated, is_reserved, is_agreed, is_imposed, is_resolved: BOOLEAN
    investigate
            -- Conduct investigation on validity of claim. Set is_investigated.
        deferred
        ensure
            is_investigated
        end
    evaluate
            -- Assess monetary amount of damages.
        require
            is_investigated
        deferred
        ensure
            is_evaluated
            -- Note: is_investigated still holds (see the invariant at the end of the class text).
        end
    set_reserve
            -- Assess monetary amount of damages. Set is_reserved.
        require
            is_investigated
            -- Note: we do not require is_evaluated.
        deferred
        ensure
            is_reserved
        end
```

negotiate
            -- Assess monetary amount of damages. Set *is_agreed* only if negotiation
            -- leads to an agreement with the claim originator.
    require
        is_reserved
        is_evaluated
    deferred
    ensure
        is_reserved
        -- See the invariant for *is_evaluated* and *is_investigated*.
    end
impose (*amount*: *INTEGER*)
            -- Determine amount of claim if negotiation fails. Set *is_imposed*.
    require
        not *is_agreed*
        is_reserved
    deferred
    ensure
        is_imposed
    end
resolve
            -- Finalize handling of claim. Set *is_resolved*.
    require
        is_agreed **or** *is_imposed*
    deferred
    require
        is_resolved
    end
invariant   -- "⇒" is logical implication.
        is_evaluated ⇒ *is_investigated*
        is_reserved ⇒ *is_evaluated*
        is_resolved ⇒ *is_agreed* **or** *is_imposed*
        is_agreed ⇒ *is_evaluated*
        is_imposed ⇒ *is_evaluated*
        is_imposed ⇒ **not** *is_agreed* -- Hence, by laws of logic, *is_agreed* ⇒ **not** *is_imposed*
end

Notice the interplay between the preconditions, postconditions and class invariant, and the various boolean-valued queries they involve (*is_investigated*, *is_evaluated*, *is_reserved*…). You can specify a strict order of operations o_1, o_2…, as in a use case, by having a sequence of assertions p_i such that operation o_i has the contract clauses **require** p_i and **ensure** p_{i+1}; but assertions also enable you to specify a much broader range of allowable orderings as all acceptable.

The class specification as given is only a first cut and leaves many aspects untouched. It will be important in practice, for example, to include a query *payment* describing the amount to be paid for the claim; then *impose* has the postcondition *payment = amount*, and *negotiate* sets a certain amount for *payment*. Such aspects are not hard to complete but have been left out above to keep the example short. (Remember that the Companion to this Handbook has many practical specification examples.) The following subsections describe the key points to be learned from the example as it stands.

Even in this simplified form, the specification includes a few concepts that the original use case left unspecified, in particular the notion of imposing a payment (through the command *impose*) if negotiation fails. Using a logical style typically uncovers such important questions and provides a framework for answering them, helping to achieve one of the principal goals of requirements engineering ("Requirements Questions Principle", page 22).

8.7.2 Logical constraints are more general than sequential orderings

The specific sequence of actions described in the use case ("main success scenario") is compatible with the logical constraints: you can check that in the sequence

---

                    -- The following is the "main success scenario", already reproduced on page 147.

investigate

evaluate

set_reserve

negotiate

resolve

---

the postcondition of each step implies the precondition of the next one (the first has no precondition). In other words, the temporal specification satisfies the logical one. But you can also see that prescribing this order is a case of overspecification (as defined in 4.7.3, page 59): other orderings also satisfy the logical specification. It may be possible for example — subject to confirmation by Subject-Matter Experts — to change the order of *evaluate* and *set_reserve*, or to perform these two operations in parallel.

The specification does cover the fundamental sequencing constraints; for example, the pre- and postcondition combinations imply that investigation must come before evaluation and resolution must be preceded by either negotiation or imposition. But they avoid the non-essential constraints which, in the use case, were only an artifact of the sequential style of specification, not a true feature of the problem.

The logical style is also more conducive to conducting a fruitful dialogue with domain experts and stakeholders:

- With a focus on use cases, the typical question from a requirements engineer (business analyst) is "*do you do A before doing B?*" Often the answer will be contorted, as in "*usually yes, but only if C, oh and sometimes we might start with B if D holds, or we might work on A and B in parallel…*", leading to vagueness and to more complicated requirements specifications.

- With logic-based specifications, the two fundamental question types are: "*what conditions do you need before doing B?*" and "*does doing A ensure condition C?*". They force stakeholders to assess their own practices and specify precisely the relations between operations of interest.

8.7.3 What use for scenarios?

Use cases and more generally scenarios, while more restrictive than logical specifications, remain important as complements to specifications. They serve as both input and output to more abstract requirements specifications (such as OO specifications with contracts):

- As **input** to requirements: initially at least, stakeholders and Subject-Matter Experts often find it intuitive to describe typical system interactions, and their own activities, in the form of scenarios. Collecting such scenarios is an invaluable requirements elicitation technique. The requirements engineer must remember that any such scenario is just one example walk through the system, and must *abstract* from these examples to derive general logical rules.

- As **output** from requirements: from an OO specification with its contracts, the requirements engineers can produce valid use cases. "Valid" means that the operation at every step satisfies the applicable precondition, as a consequence of the previous steps' postconditions and of the class invariant. The requirements engineers can then submit these use cases to the SMEs and through them to stakeholders to confirm that they make sense, update the logical conditions if they do not (to rule out bad use cases), and check the results they are expected to produce.

8.7.4 Where do scenarios fit?

While many teams will prefer to write scenarios (for the purposes just described) in natural language, it is possible to go one step further and, in an object-oriented approach to requirements, gather scenarios in classes.

We will see later in this chapter (section 8.8) that an OO requirements specification includes classes of several kinds. One of the categories (see 8.8.1) is expressly intended for scenarios. A *scenario class* will include a number of routines, each typically representing a use case or user story. Such routines are expressed in the notation of an object-oriented programming language, as convenient and expressive here, to describe processes of interaction with a system, as it is for its traditional use of describing programs.

A scenario routine will use these mechanisms to express a use case or user story in terms of the features of other (non-scenario) classes of the OO specification. Scenario classes, taking advantage of OO structuring mechanisms, particularly inheritance, can provide groupings at different levels, as introduced in 7.3: epics and use case slices.

Scenario classes are examples of **specification drivers**. Classes in the other categories describe types from the environment, the project or the system (its design or its implementation). A specification-driver class, for its part, specifies patterns of *exercising* the mechanisms provided by such classes. Besides scenario classes, another example of a specification driver is a *test* driver, which triggers features of implementation classes and checks the outcomes through test oracles. Specification drivers generalize this notion to any class whose purpose is to exercise features of a given set of classes. They serve various purposes, in particular for software verification; scenario classes are a particularly useful application of the idea.

8.7.5 Different roles for different techniques

The preceding discussions suggests that a complementarity exists not only between scenarios (such as use cases) and OO specifications but also between the *roles* involved. Let us now review this human aspect.

Scenarios, while not appropriate as requirements specifications, are a productive tool in the dialog with Subject-Matter Experts and other non-IT-specialist stakeholders since they reflect the intuition of how one will work with the system. Using them alongside OO specifications (both as inputs to them and outputs from them) leads to a productive distribution of tasks represented by the following figure.

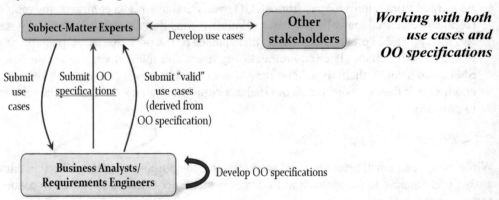

Working with both use cases and OO specifications

This scheme is subject to variation; in particular, depending on matters specific to each project and discussed elsewhere in this Handbook:

- All stakeholders might qualify as Subject-Matter Experts; then the top-right box goes away.

- Even if "other stakeholders" exists as a distinct category, there is no universal rule forcing BAs (business analysts) to go through designated SMEs only to obtain information from stakeholders. Each project sets its own policy on this matter.

The diagram, covering the general case, shows the use of scenarios and OO specifications by various categories of requirements builders. One possible complaint against logic-based specifications is that they are not to everyone's taste. In reality, anyone can learn to use them (the underlying concepts are very simple), but the focus on logical reasoning is one of the reasons for having a separate category of requirements engineers or business analysts. These requirements experts should fully master the corresponding techniques. The distribution of tasks then becomes clear, as already outlined above:

- SMEs and other stakeholders may prefer, at least initially, to reason in terms of scenarios.

- It is the task of BAs to abstract these specific cases into general specifications, using the techniques of object-oriented requirements and contracts.

- A constant back-and-forth takes place; in particular, BAs show the consequences of their OO modeling to the other two groups, to check that their understanding is correct.

Many specialists of non-IT areas will (as experience shows) naturally take to the OO style and the associated logical mechanisms. But even if they do not, the BAs should.

It is in fact paradoxical to encounter resistance to such methods based on the argument that "*it is too hard for our people*". The basic justification for having requirements experts, be they called business analysts or requirements engineers, is precisely that they master techniques unique to the engineering of requirements. If requirements were all about listing individual scenarios — "*the user can do this and then that, the system will respond by this and then that*" — there would hardly be a need for a separate profession. Good requirements analysis is about abstracting from special cases to general specifications. The best path is to abstract from scenarios to contracted classes.

8.7.6 Towards formal methods and abstract data types

The intrusion of logic into the descriptions — see for example the invariant of class *INSURANCE_CLAIM* on page 149 — is a first step towards making use of mathematical techniques in requirements. Simple mathematics, based on elementary logic, but mathematics all the same.

The general application of mathematical techniques to reasoning about software is known as *formal methods* and goes beyond this first step. Chapter 9 is devoted to formal methods and followed by a discussion in chapter 10 of a particular formal notion, *abstract data type*, the mathematical counterpart to the software notion at the core of object technology: class.

8.7.7 "But it's design!"

Although at this stage you should have no doubt about the suitability of object-oriented principles for requirements, it is still useful (if only for discussions you may have with colleagues steeped in more traditional approaches) to dispel a common misunderstanding: that such specifications as illustrated in the preceding example, based on classes and contracts (plus inheritance to organize the classes into hierarchies), are premature designs or even — heaven forbid! — premature implementations. If so, they would be subject to the reproach of "overspecification" (4.7.3, page 59).

Of course they are not. In the present discussion, classes are modeling tools at the requirements level. OO modeling means that you describe elements (from the Project, Environment,
Goals or System) through types of objects and the applicable operations. These classes are
purely descriptive; they need not contain any inkling of future design decisions.

The "*but it's premature design!*" reaction is ironic when used to advocate use cases, which
present a clear risk of premature design since they specify ordered sequences of operations,
leading to the temptation of writing programs along those same ordering patterns.

8.7.8 Towards seamlessness

While free from design and implementation considerations, the classes written for requirements purposes are still classes and can be expressed in an object-oriented language that also
supports design and implementation classes. The benefit here is to avoid harmful changes of
concepts and notations when going through successive steps of the software lifecycle.

This approach is known as seamless development and discussed in more detail in connection with the place of requirements in the software lifecycle (see "Seamless development",
12.6, page 218). One of its beneficial consequences is **reversibility**: having everything
expressed in a single notation makes it easier to update the requirements at any stage in the
project, even deep into design, implementation or verification, in line with the Requirements
Evolution Principle ("The evolution of requirements", 2.1.4, page 23).

Without having seen yet the full discussion of seamlessness, we may take advantage of the
preceding discussion to analyze the diverse nature of classes that appear in requirements and
at other stages of software development. This analysis leads us, in the next section, to an
important classification of the various kinds of class.

8.8 THE SEVEN KINDS OF CLASS

A seamless OO approach unifies the development process. At all stages — requirements,
design, implementation... — the general development pattern consists of:

- Producing classes.

- Equipping them with operations ("features"), which determine client-supplier relations.

- Organizing them in inheritance hierarchies.

Classes at different levels typically describe objects of a different nature, explained below with
(for a change) examples from a railway control system. The variety of these uses of classes
highlights the versatility of this central construct of object technology and justifies its use as
the unifying concept of seamless software development.

8.8.1 Requirements classes

The following three categories cover pure-requirements classes (independent from design and implementation choices). They are relevant for most projects.

Kind of requirements class	Specifies	Relevant book in Standard Plan	Example
Concrete Environment	Type of material objects from environment	Environment (E.1, E.2)	*RAILROAD_ CROSSING*
Abstract Environment	Type of conceptual objects from environment	Environment (E.1, E.2, E.3, E.4, E.5, E.6)	*RAILROAD_CROSSING _CONTROL,* *LINE_SCHEDULE*
Scenario	Use case, user story, use case slice, test case	Goal (G.5) System (S.4, S.6)	*TRIP_BOOKING*

A **Concrete Environment** class describes tangible objects from the environment, such as a (physical) railroad crossing. It should pertain to a concept defined in chapter E.2 (components) of the Environment book. When you choose a name for such a class, always consult the glossary (E.1, see 6.4) to use terminology that is consistent with the requirements.

An **Abstract Environment** class similarly describes "objects" of the environment, but they are intangible objects, designed as part of a human *model* of how the environment works. An example of such an object — an instance of an abstract environment class *SCHEDULE* — is the schedule of a certain line, say the Zurich-Paris TGV connection. It specifies which connections are available between these cities on given dates. It is not something that you can see or touch but is a fundamental concept of the environment. (You may be able to see and touch a printed schedule, but the actual object of interest is the abstract schedule, not a specific physical representation of it.) Abstract environment classes may pertain to concepts from the following chapters of the Environment book: E.2 (components), E.3 to E.6 (constraints, assumptions, effects, invariants). Like concrete environment classes, they must be named in conformity to the glossary (E.1).

A **scenario class** is a description of a relevant sequence of interactions with the system. Examples include use cases and user stories, such as the process for booking a train journey; another example is a test case, describing a sequence of actions to exercise functions of the system. Scenario classes may be related to:

• A high-level use case specified in the Goals book (chapter G.5).

• A detailed use case or user story specified in the System book (chapter S.4).

• A test scenario, also from the System book (chapter S.6).

8.8.2 Design and implementation classes

Some classes reflect design and implementation choices. They pertain to the system part of requirements and are relevant for all projects.

Kind of design or implementation class	Specifies	Relevant book in Standard Plan	Examples
Design	Type of objects used to implement a design choice, particularly a design pattern	System	*STATE, VISITOR*
Implementation	Type of objects used for implementation	System	*STATION_LIST*

A **Design class** provides a mechanism reflecting a certain design choice. (Or "architectural" choice; for this discussion there is no significant difference between the terms "design" and "architecture".) The examples given correspond to standard "design patterns": State and Visitor.

An **Implementation** class is an element of the object-oriented implementation of the system. In the code of a large system, most of the classes will typically be implementation classes.

8.8.3 Goals and project classes

Beyond the description of the system and environment, you may use classes describing elements of the goals (other than scenarios, covered in 8.8.1) and the project itself:

Kind of goal or project class	Specifies	Relevant book in Standard Plan	Examples
Goal	Type of objects describing project goals	System	*PASSENGER_SATI SFACTION_INDEX*
Project	Type of objects describing tasks and other project components	System	*MILESTONE, TEST_PLAN*

While every OO project will use classes of the other five categories, these two only arise for a project that also uses OO modeling to describe elements of the project itself and its goals.

8.8.4 Permissible relations between classes

Possible relations between classes of the seven categories, compatible with the allowable mutual references between the four PEGS books ("Possible references between the books", page 37), are as follows, with the arrows covering both of the relations (client and inheritance) through which a class can refer to another in an OO framework:

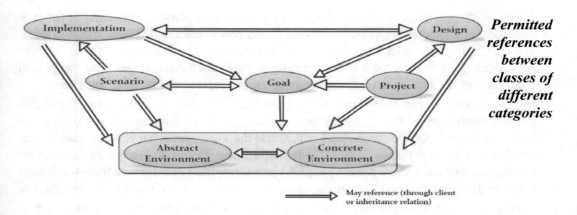

Permitted references between classes of different categories

(In addition, a class may reference another of the same category, as an implementation class inheriting from another implementation class; the diagram omits the corresponding self-links.)

Where the diagram goes beyond the earlier general discussion of mutual references is that with seamless development everything is expressed in the same notation and on the basis of the concept of class, common to all levels of description. In particular:

- Environment classes, Abstract and Concrete, may refer to each other; for example a *RAIL-ROAD_CROSSING* (concrete) is controlled by a *RAILROAD_CROSSING_CONTROLLER* (abstract), implying that the two classes reference each other.

- Environment classes do not depend on any others; but classes from all other categories may reference them. Because in such cases the other classes may refer to both Abstract and Concrete Environment classes, the diagram bundles these two categories together.

- Scenario classes typically describe specific schedulings of system operations: use cases, user stories, test cases with their test scripts and oracles. As a consequence, they involve references to the Implementation classes that such scenarios will exercise, and may also involve operations from Design classes.

- Scenario classes will often, in addition, specify a scenario's effect on the Environment, abstract and concrete, particularly for a test case that includes oracles specifying expected environment changes.

- Implementation classes need to describe the effects of operations on the Environment. This should not be the case with Design classes as they describe architectural choices, valid independently of the particular system (for example a *VISITOR* or *COMMAND* class in the corresponding design patterns).

- Correspondingly, Project classes should not reference Implementation classes (as it is improper for project plans and other project documents to refer to details of the implementation), but they may refer to Design classes. For example, the description of a project task may indicate that it is devoted to constructing or verifying a certain high-level component ("cluster") of the system, such as the database engine, represented by a Design class.

- Implementation classes implement designs, but Design classes may also reference implementations; this property reflects the porous nature of the distinction between design and implementation in OO development. For example the Visitor pattern involves a mutual relation between general visitor classes (Design) and others specific to the system (Implementation). Similarly, the MVC pattern (Model-View-Controller) may involve mutual relations between the Controller and View parts, hence between Design and Implementation classes.

- All classes except Environment ones may refer to Goal classes (if present). Such references are encouraged since they enhance *traceability* by helping to relate various parts of the system and the requirements themselves to business goals. (Remember the discussion of the corresponding requirements quality factor: "Traceable", 4.8, page 61. Also note that the definition of another quality factor, "Justified", 4.2, page 49, states that a requirement is justified if it helps reach a goal or satisfy a constraint.)

- The relationship to Goals is particularly important for Scenario classes. In this case references can also exist in the reverse direction, Goal class to Scenario class, since goals may include high-level use cases (chapter G.5 of the Standard Plan).

- As already implied by the general specification of possible references between the requirements books on page 37, no classes of other categories will refer to Project classes. Project classes themselves may refer to Goal and Environment classes.

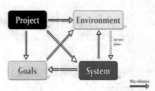

8.9 GOING OBJECT-ORIENTED

This chapter has presented a review of object technology, taking the focus away from its programming-oriented elements (such as polymorphism and dynamic binding) and instead highlighting general OO abstraction mechanisms, particularly apt to benefit requirements.

Object-oriented requirements concepts complement and reinforce all the other techniques in this Handbook. OO principles are principally (for requirements as for other applications) a structuring discipline, which provides the best known solution for organizing the requirements of large, complex systems into coherent structures. Requirements artifacts such as scenarios (use cases, user stories) and tests have a natural place in such a structure.

Integrating these ideas in a standard requirements process is not hard and can help achieve the benefits of extendibility and reusability, as desirable for requirements as they are for other tasks of system development. While the Companion to this Handbook presents more detailed examples, the ideas presented in this chapter (and complemented in the next two chapters by the discussion of formal methods and abstract data types) suffice to let you apply object-oriented principles to the production of effective requirements in your own projects.

8-E EXERCISES

8-E.1 Bounded stacks

Adapt the stack class of 8.6.2 to specify that stacks are of a maximum size, *capacity*. (*Hints*: the features of the class must now include *capacity*; *put* now needs a precondition.)

8-E.2 Queues

A queue is a structure with the same overall interface as stacks — *put*, *remove* and *item* operations, with the same signatures, although not the same contracts — following a FIFO discipline (first-in, first-out) instead of the stacks' LIFO. Write a class *QUEUE* describing queues of integers. You may assume, as in the original stack class, that queues are unbounded (the solution to the preceding exercise will apply if you need to add a requirement of maximum capacity) (*Hint*: start from the model of class *STACK* and adapt the contracts — preconditions, postconditions — to reflect the FIFO rather than LIFO behavior.)

8-E.3 Scenarios as routines

Write the insurance-claim use case example (7.1 and rest of chapter 7) in the form of a routine. Since such a routine would go into a scenario class (8.7.4), you may specify the elements of that class needed by the use case and related ones.

8-E.4 Class model

The draft requirements document in [Bair 2005] has an empty "Class Model" section. Using the concepts of the present chapter, write the key requirements classes for the corresponding system. (The requirements, not the implementation!) For each class, state the category (from the seven in section 8.8) to which it belongs. You do not need to write the scenario classes, covering use cases, in detail, only to sketch them. see the next exercise.

8-E.5 Scenario class

Write one or more scenario classes covering the use cases in the example requirements document from [Bair 2005].

BIBLIOGRAPHICAL NOTES AND FURTHER READING

A general discussion of object technology, focused OO design programming with elements of OO requirements, is "*Object-Oriented Software Construction*", 2nd edition [Meyer 1997].

About the word "procedural" used as an antonym to "object-oriented": either of the terms "functional" and "operational" would in principle be more apposite, since non-OO approaches base modules on "functions" or "operations" (rather than object types, the basis of OO decomposition). In software, however, both of these terms are also used with other meanings:

- "Functional programming", practiced in "functional languages", denotes a form of programming that shuns operations that can change the state (particularly repeated assignments to variables), relying instead on functions in the strict mathematical sense. We will see an example of this style in the specification of abstract data types (see the explanations in "Functional and imperative styles", 10.8.2, page 199).

- "Operational" specifications use an algorithmic style (almost the opposite of "functional").

Since both terms are preempted by these existing meanings, "procedural" has come to be the accepted term for non-OO or pre-OO.

Misuse cases (page 145) have applications in security, to specify patterns of attack against which one should protect a system. See [Alexander 2003].

On specification drivers (8.7.4) see [Naumchev-Meyer 2016].

The classic reference on design patterns (8.8.2) is [Gamma et al. 1994].

9

Benefiting from formal methods

"Formal", in software engineering, means precise and rigorous. In other words: *mathematical*, since mathematics is the language of precision and rigor.

Formal notations are not a panacea. Some things are best expressed in natural language, for example love letters — which fall beyond the scope of this Handbook — and, closer to our topic, many parts of requirements. A formal model is, however, appropriate for some delicate parts of requirements, particularly where misunderstandings could have serious consequences, and whenever you need to obtain firm answers to questions about the project, system, environment and goals. This chapter explains how a mathematical approach can help requirements.

9.1 THOSE RESTLESS SWISS!

Let us start with a trifling example which provides an exotic illustration of the role of formal expression. A newsletter sent sometime in 2019 by a Swiss phone company to its customers, intended to provide them with (unsolicited) practical advice, started:

> *Dear customer, do you know that* 10.7% *of Swiss people relocate every year*?

Reading this, the customer might be forgiven for wondering, at least for a few moments: does the population of Switzerland really include a nomadic tribe of some 940,000 people (10.7% of the Confederation's inhabitants) who every year move to a new abode?

Maybe not. Maybe we are not talking about the *same* 940,000 people. Probably, what the authors meant was: every year, there is a different group of 940,000 people who move.

Wait: they do not have to be *all* different. It is entirely possible and even likely that on occasion *some* people move one year and then again the year after.

A completely satisfactory phrasing, in English, of what the author (probably) intended to say will appear below (9.3.4). But if we really want to guarantee precision and remove any ambiguity, English or another natural language is not our best tool. We need mathematics.

Mathematics, not natural language, indeed provides the standard notation for expressing properties precisely. To state that addition is commutative, we could in principle say

> *"If given two numbers you first compute the result of adding the second to the first, and then compute the result of adding the first to the second, you will always, whatever the numbers are, get the same result from both computations."*

We could. (Until about the 16th century this was more or less what people did.) On the other hand, "for all a and b, $a + b = b + a$" is clearer and simpler. Even better, using the standard

© The Author(s), under exclusive license to Springer Nature Switzerland AG 2022
B. Meyer, *Handbook of Requirements and Business Analysis*, https://doi.org/10.1007/978-3-031-06739-6_9

notation $\forall$ to express "for all", and specifying which set of numbers we are talking about, for example real numbers R:

$\forall a, b\colon R \mid a + b = b + a$

Clear, no-fuss and definitive.

Software requirements too can benefit from the same virtues of precision, conciseness and clarity that have made mathematics the universal language of science. Requirements are in fact especially in need of these qualities and of the concepts of this chapter. If a few recipients of a newsletter misunderstand a fun fact about residency habits, not much harm will result. If a developer misunderstands a detail of a mission-critical system, the consequence could be an industrial accident or severe financial damage.

9.2 BASIC MATH FOR REQUIREMENTS

The mere mention of mathematics sends some people running for cover. We will see later (9.4) who may and should be exposed to formal notations for requirements. But the reluctance is largely groundless. Most applications to requirements only need simple, high-school-level math. Here are the basic concepts. They take up only a few pages, you know many of them already, and they will take you quite far.

9.2.1 Logic and sets

A **boolean formula** states a property that has value T (true) or F (false). It is made of *boolean variables*, each also with value T or F, and operators $\neg$ ("not"), $\wedge$ ("and"), $\vee$ ("or"), $\Rightarrow$ ("implies"). $\neg a$ has value T if and only if a has value F; $a \wedge b$ has value T if and only if both a and b do; $a \vee b$ has value F if and only if both a and b do; $a \Rightarrow b$ is the same as $(\neg a) \vee b$.

We deal with **sets** of objects. A set can be defined by "extension", through the list of its elements in braces, as in $\{0, 1, 2\}$, or by "comprehension", starting from an existing set A: if p is a boolean-valued formula, $\{x\colon A \mid p\,(x)\}$ is the subset of A containing all elements, if any, for which p has value T.

Predicate expressions on sets use *quantifiers* $\forall$ ("for all") and $\exists$ ("there exists"): $\forall\, x\colon A \mid p\,(x)$ is true if and only if $p\,(x)$ is true for *all* elements x of A if any; $\exists\, x\colon A \mid p\,(x)$ if and only if it is true for *at least one* element of A. (For empty A, they are respectively true and false.)

Given a set A, any object x either is a **member** of A or not, a boolean property written $x \in A$ and its negation $x \notin A$. If B is also a set, $A \subseteq B$ ("subset") expresses that any member of A is also a member of B. Equivalently: $B \supseteq A$ ("superset"). These properties hold if A and B are the same; $A \subset B$ as well as $B \supset A$ ("strict" subset and superset) hold if $A \subseteq B$ but B has at least one member not in A. $\varnothing$ is the empty set: $x \notin \varnothing$ for any x, and $\varnothing \subseteq A$ for any A. Element order, in a definition by extension, is irrelevant: $\{0, 1, 2\}$ and $\{2, 0, 1\}$ are the same set. All that characterizes a set A is membership: whether $x \in A$ for any given x — here, in both cases, if and only if x is 0, 1 or 2.

The number of elements of a finite set A is called its **cardinal**; we write it $\overline{A}$ (another common notation is $|A|$). For example, $\overline{\{0, 1, 2\}}$ is 3.

9.2.2 Operations on sets

Operations are applicable to sets. Intersection: $A \cap B$ contains elements that appear in both A and B. Union: $A \cup B$ has those appearing in either or both. Difference: $A - B$ (sometimes written $A \setminus B$) has those in A but not in B. Note that $A \cup B = (A \cap B) \cup (A - B) \cup (B - A)$.

$P(A)$ (note the special "P", which stands for "parts" or "powerset") is the set of all subsets of A. For example $P(\{0, 1, 2\})$ is $\{\varnothing, \{0\}, \{1\}, \{2\}, \{0, 1\}, \{0, 2\}, \{1, 2\}, \{0, 1, 2\}\}$, a set of 8 sets. If A is a finite set and $\overline{A}$ (its cardinal) is n, then $\overline{P(A)} = 2^n$. (In the example that powerset cardinal is 2^3, or 8.)

$A \times B$ ("Cartesian product") is the set of all pairs $[x, y]$ such that $x \in A$ and $y \in B$. For example $\{1, 2\} \times \{0, 1, 2\}$ is a set of six pairs: $\{[1, 0], [1, 1], [1, 2], [2, 0], [2, 1], [2, 2]\}$.

9.2.3 Relations

A **relation** (short for "binary relation") over A and B is an element of $P(A \times B)$, meaning a set of pairs with first element in A and second in B. For example we may define a relation "$\leq$" over the set $\{0, 1, 2\}$ and itself, expressing that a number is less than equal to another, as $\{[0, 0], [0, 1], [0, 2], [1, 1], [1, 2], [2, 2]\}$. Another example over that same set is the relation *successor*, which pairs every number with the next number (if it has one in this set): $\{[0, 1], [1, 2]\}$.

A relation r over sets A and B has a **domain** and a **range**, subsets of A and B respectively:

- **domain** r is the set of elements a for which r has at least one pair $[a, y]$ for some y.

- **range** r is the set of elements b for which r has at least one pair $[x, b]$ for some x.

In the examples: **domain** "$\leq$" = **range** "$\leq$" = $\{0, 1, 2\}$; **domain** *successor* = $\{0, 1\}$; **range** *successor* = $\{1, 2\}$.

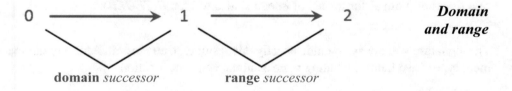

Domain and range

domain *successor*   range *successor*

Special relations over A and A itself for a given set A include the identity, $id[A]$, made of all pairs $[a, a]$ for all elements a of A, and the empty relation $\varnothing$ (with no pairs).

Since relations are sets, they are amenable to set operations. For example we may define a relation *sibling* as *sister* $\cup$ *brother*, the union of two relations; it contains all the pairs that appear in either or both of these relations.

9.2.4 Functions

A relation over A and B is a **function** if for any x in A it contains at most one pair with x as its first element. *successor* is a function but "$\leq$" is not because, among others, it has both $[2, 2]$ and $[2, 3]$.

A function is **total** over A if it has one pair (not just "at most one") starting with any given element of A. *successor* over $\{0, 1, 2\}$ is not total (it is **partial**) because it includes no pair starting with 2. If instead of $\{0, 1, 2\}$ we consider the full infinite set of natural integers, $\mathbb{N}$, then *successor* is a total function, since every integer n has exactly one successor $n + 1$.

The following notations denote the various sets of relations and functions (each but the last a superset of the next one):

- $A \leftrightarrow B$ is the set of relations over A and B.
- $A \nrightarrow B$ is the set of (possibly partial) functions from A to B.
- $A \rightarrow B$ is the set of total functions from A to B.

Another way of saying that a function f in $A \nrightarrow B$ is total (in other words, that it is also in $A \rightarrow B$) is that **domain** $f = A$ (rather than just **domain** $f \subseteq A$ as always).

A total function f in $A \rightarrow B$ defines, for every $a \in A$, a *unique* element b of B such that $[a, b] \in f$. We write that element $f(a)$. For a partial function we may also use this parenthesis notation, but only with a proof that $a \in$ **domain** f, a property known as the **precondition** of f.

In the $f(a)$ notation, a is an **argument** of the function, and $f(a)$ is the **result** of applying the function. When the source set A is a cartesian product such as $X \times Y$, we may write the function application as $f(x, y)$ (for $x \in X$ and $y \in Y$), an abbreviation for $f([x, y])$, and say that f takes two arguments. We also accept a function with no arguments, which always gives the same result (it is a *constant* function). That result is written just f as an abbreviation for $f()$.

For the sets to which the arguments and result belong, we also use the word **type**. The **signature** of a function is the specification of the types of its arguments and result. The following example, for the multiplication function over integers, illustrates how to specify the signature of a function (with $\mathbb{Z}$ for the set of integers, also written *INTEGER*):

   times: $\mathbb{Z} \times \mathbb{Z} \rightarrow \mathbb{Z}$

The signature will always include exactly one result type and may include any number of argument types (two here), including none as in the constant function

   zero: $\rightarrow \mathbb{Z}$

whose result is written *zero* (), or just *zero* without parentheses. (The intent in this example is that this fixed result will be 0.) These concepts and notations also apply to partial functions, with $\nrightarrow$ instead of $\rightarrow$.

We can generalize the parenthesis notation to a relation: if r is a relation over A and B and X a subset of A, then $r(X)$ is the set of all b such that r has a pair $[x, b]$ for some x in X. $r(X)$ is called the **image** of x by r. Note that $r(A)$ is **range** r. For a single element, we can use $r(\{x\})$.

9.2.5 Powers and closures

If *r* and *s* are relations — of any kind, including the special cases of partial and total functions — respectively over *A* and *B* and over *B* and *C*, their **composition**, written *r* ; *s*, is the relation formed of all pairs [*a*, *c*] such that there is a pair [*a*, *b*] in *r* and a pair [*b*, *c*] in *s*, for some *b*. For example, over people, the composition *daughter* ; *sibling* is *niece*:

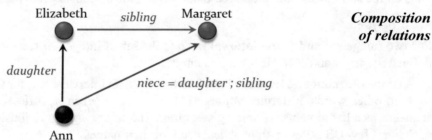

Composition of relations

The composition of two functions is itself a function; for example if *f* is a function in $A \to B$ and *g* is a function in $B \to C$, then *f* ; *g* is a function in $A \to B$. If we call this function *h*, the value of *h* (*a*) for any *a* in *A* is *g* (*f*(*a*)). (Another frequently used notation for *f* ; *g* is *g* ∘ *f*, but the semicolon notation is more convenient for formal specifications since it lists the operands in the order of their application to arguments.)

If *r* is a relation over *A* and itself (that is to say, *r* ∈ , then the **powers** of *r* are: r^0, the same as *id* [*A*]; then r^1, the same as *r*; next, r^2, defined as *r* ; *r*, meaning *r* composed with itself (for example, over people, $parent^2 = grandparent$). Next, r^3 is defined as *r* ; r^2 or equivalently r^2 ; *r* (for example, $parent^3 = great\_grandparent$); and so on. The figure below shows a relation *parent* between some members of a family (solid black arrows), and its second power $parent^2$ (dotted red arrows). It also shows $parent^0$, the identity relation, represented by the self-links.

Powers of a relation

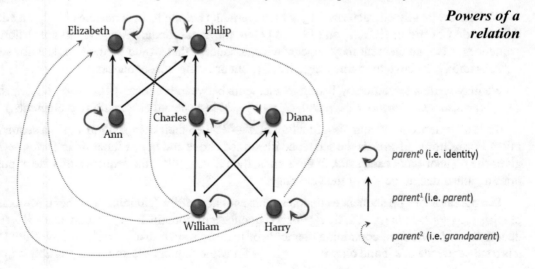

The union of all of these powers, $r^0 \cup r^1 \cup r^2 \cup \ldots$, written r^*, is the **reflexive transitive closure** of r. If we omit r^0 (the identity relation) we get the **transitive closure** r^+, non-reflexive. For example the transitive closure of the relation *parent* over people is *ancestor* (including *parent*, *grandparent*, *great_grandparent* and so on). The reflexive closure additionally includes each person among the person's ancestors. In the preceding figure, the transitive closure contains all the solid black and dotted red links; adding the self-links gives the reflexive version.

9.2.6 Sequences

For two integers a and b, the **interval** $a..b$ is the set of integers n such that $a \le n \le b$. It is defined for any a and b, but if $b > a$ it is empty.

A (finite) **sequence** s over A is a total function from an interval $1..n$, for some integer $n \ge 0$, to A. In other words, it defines values $s(1)$, $s(2)$, ... $s(n)$ in A, reflecting the notion of a sequence as a list of values in some given order. The following figure illustrates the sequence of the first few US states in alphabetical order of their names.

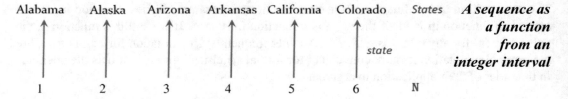

A sequence as a function from an integer interval

The value of n, the sequence's length (6 in the example), is written $s.count$. If it is 0, the sequence is empty. A^* is the set of sequences over A (a subset of $\mathbb{N} \nrightarrow A$). The sequence in the figure above is an element of *States**, if States is the set of US states.

Since a sequence is a function, **range** s is the set of its values (a subset of A); **domain** s is the set of valid indexes, an interval of the form $1..n$.

While a set is only characterized by which elements belong to it, sequences imply an additional notion of order: $[0, 1, 2]$ and $[2, 0, 1]$ have the same range, $\{0, 1, 2\}$, but are different sequences. Also, an element may appear twice, a concept that would be meaningless for sets: $[1, 2, 2]$ and $[1, 2]$ have the same range, $\{1, 2\}$, but are different sequences.

We may write a sequence by listing its elements between brackets: [*Alabama, Alaska, Arizona, Arkansas, California, Colorado*]. (A pair $[a, b]$ is a special case, with two elements.)

If s is a sequence in A^* and f is a function in $A \to B$, then their composition $s ; f$ is a sequence in B^*. For example, if *state* is the sequence illustrated above and *pop*, a function in *States* $\to \mathbb{N}$, gives the population of each state, in thousands, then *state* ; *pop* is the sequence of state populations as illustrated at the top of the next page.

The operator "+" on sequences denotes their **concatenation** (chaining together); for example, $[0, 1, 2] + [2, 1]$ is $[0, 1, 2, 2, 1]$. For a sequence s of domain $1..n$, we may use $s(i..j)$ to denote the **subsequence** containing elements of indexes k such that $i \le k \le j$, if any. Note that u is a subsequence of s if and only if $s = t + u + v$ for some sequences t and v, all possibly empty.

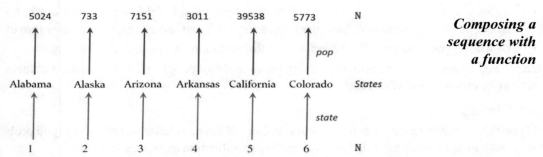

*Composing a
sequence with
a function*

Special cases, for *s* of length $n \geq 1$: *s.tail* is *s* $(2..n)$ and *s.head* is *s* $(1..n{-}1)$. *SUBSEQ* (s) denotes the set of all subsequences of *s*. For $n = 1$, the head and tail are empty.

If *s* can be written as $t + u$, then *t* is a **prefix** and *u* a **suffix** of *s* (so that an empty sequence is both a prefix and a suffix of any string, the head is a prefix, and the tail is a suffix).

9.3   THE RELOCATING POPULATION, CLARIFIED

The muddled relocation-statistics anecdote of the beginning of this chapter provides an inconsequential but telling example of how to use the preceding notations to remove ambiguities — or better yet, avoid them in the first place.

9.3.1 Naming components of a specification

The ambiguous English phrase was "*10.7% of Swiss people relocate every year*". To obtain a formal version, the first step is to give names to relevant sets, quantities and properties.

It is good practice to give upper-case names to sets. Let *SWISS* be the set of Swiss people and *YEAR* the set of years.

Let *Mover_count*, an integer, denote the number of "movers" in a year (10.7% of the Swiss population, meaning 940,321 as of September 1st, 2022.)

Let *p.is_relocating* (y) express the boolean property that person *p* relocates in year *y*.

9.3.2 Interpretation 1

With these notations, a possible interpretation of the ambiguous English sentence is:

F1	$\{s: SWISS \mid (\forall\, y: YEAR \mid s.is\_relocating\,(y))\}$ = *Mover_count*

If you are not used to formal reasoning, the following decomposition will help you make sense of this formula:

- Given a person *s*, then $\forall\, y: YEAR \mid s.is\_relocating\,(y))$ is a predicate expression, with value true or false. The value is true if and only if for all years *y* ("$\forall\, y: YEAR$") the property that s relocated during year *y* ("*s.is_relocating* (y)") holds.
- Then $\{s: SWISS \mid (\forall\, y: YEAR \mid s.is\_relocating\,(y))\}$ is the set of Swiss people (formally: the subset of the set *SWISS* of all Swiss people) such that the preceding predicate expression (they move every year) has value true.

- $\overline{\{s: SWISS \mid (\forall\, y: YEAR \mid s.is\_relocating\,(y))\}}$ is the cardinal of this set; in other words, the number of Swiss people who have the interesting habit that, every single year, they move!
- The whole specified property, F1, expresses that this number is equal to *Mover_count*.

Expressed informally: there is an interesting group of Swiss people, close to a million of them, who keep moving year after year.

9.3.3 Interpretation 2

If you think interpretation F1 is not what the authors of the newsletter wanted to say, you probably have in mind what the following competing specification expresses formally:

$$F2 \quad \forall\, y: YEAR \quad \mid \quad \overline{\{s: SWISS \mid s.is\_moving\,(y)\}} = Mover\_count$$

where (continuing to explain every element individually and slowly for full clarity):

- Given a year y, $\{s: SWISS \mid s.is\_moving\,(y)\}$ is the set of Swiss people who move during y.
- Then $\overline{\{s: SWISS \mid s.is\_moving\,(y)\}}$ is the cardinal of that set, meaning the *number* of Swiss people who move during y.
- Again assuming y is given, $(\overline{\{s: SWISS \mid s.is\_moving\,(y)\}} = Mover\_count)$, a boolean property, has value true if during that year that number is equal to 10.7% of the population.
- The full specification, F2, is obtained by putting "$\forall\, y: YEAR$" in front of this property, to express that it must be true for *every* year y.

Expressed informally: every year, out of the Swiss population, close to a million people move. (The specification does not say they are the same every year — as F1 did — but also does not say they are all different. We can indeed assume that there is no such obligation: there may be the odd person who moves both in year y and in year $y + 1$. Exercise 9-E.3 asks you to change specification F2 to say that the movers are all different from year to year.)

9.3.4 Back to English: the formal picnic

To dispel ambiguities during the requirements process, there is no substitute for a detour through mathematics as just illustrated, known as a **"formal picnic"**.

The idea of the formal picnic is that after you have (so to speak) done the math, you may want to write a natural-language version; you may in fact be required to provide it for the benefit of non-mathematically-inclined stakeholders. That version can and should be informed by the mathematical excursion. You will not write the same kind of English before and after having taken the trouble to produce a formal version.

Here the (ambiguous) original was

> E1 10.7% of Swiss people relocate every year.

If we look at F1, a mathematical equality, and want to state it in English, we may come up with:

> PN1 *The Swiss population includes people who relocate every year. They make up* 10.7% *of the population.*

Similarly, the version written mathematically as F2 yields:

> PN2 *Every year, the Swiss population includes people who relocate. They make up* 10.7% *of the population in that year.*

It is possible to make these statements a little shorter, but not by much if we want to retain clarity and precision (try it!).

Undertaking a formal picnic is an excellent way to improve *natural-language* specifications. Apart from its other benefits, a detour through a mathematical description can give you an excellent start to produce a better English (or other) description. The style of such back-from-the-picnic specifications tends to be markedly different from what most requirements writers would write otherwise; sometimes surprising in its dryness, but precise, more likely to avoid the typical "seven sins" (5.2.1) — particularly noise, overspecification, contradiction and ambiguity — and of direct use to implementation (without, however, prescribing any particular implementation). We will see a slightly larger example in the last section of this chapter (a rework of the text-formatting example of chapter 5).

The English versions above, PN1 and PN2, do not use mathematical terminology. We could follow the mathematical style more faithfully in English, reformulating F1 as (instead of PN1):

PN'1 *The Swiss population includes **a set of** people who relocate every year. **The size of that set is** 10.7% of the population.*

and similarly for the second interpretation. If you have a non-mathematical stakeholder constituency, the previous PN forms, avoiding mathematical terminology, are usually just as good. Whether the final English version uses math terms is not critical; what matters is that, whatever their phrasing, they benefit from the formal picnic in precision and rigor, reflecting the underlying formal specification work.

The formal picnic is an important tool of requirements engineering, which the following principle-style advice summarizes:

> **Advice: Formal Picnic**
> Use formal specifications to formulate or reformulate the corresponding natural-language specification with better precision, rigor and correctness.

9.4 WHO WRITES FORMAL SPECIFICATIONS?

The use of formal methods for requirements is not without controversy. There is no reason for emotional discussions; relying on mathematics is an essential condition of engineering in other fields, and the math needed for formally expressing most software requirements is in fact more elementary than the kind routinely used in (for example) electrical or mechanical engineering. Still, the arguments are still heard that "*we cannot explain this to our stakeholders*" and "*our programmers just do not have the appropriate background*". Neither holds:

- Non-programming stakeholders are often experts in their own discipline, sometimes at a high level of education, and it does not take long to teach them the basic conventions as explained earlier in this chapter. They will make the effort if informed of the benefit: getting enough precision to avoid costly and dangerous misunderstandings with the IT team, which would prevent them from getting what they want from the final product.

- For those who for any reason do not want to take the mathematical step, back-to-English versions, in the *formal picnic* style, are easy to produce, and will combine some of the best features of formal and informal approaches.

- As to the programmers who allegedly cannot take to formal reasoning, the argument is brittle. Would you accept it in another engineering area? ("*My electrical contractor never quite got the laws of electricity. After I build your house a circuit might blow up here or there, perhaps setting the place on fire on occasion. But you know how it is: I cannot demand too much from my people, they are overstretched intellectually. I hope you sympathize.*")

Any programmer who has learned the notion of conditional instruction (if-then-else) — that is to say, any programmer — can learn boolean formulae, predicate calculus and formal reasoning.

It is true that some programmers are more hands-on and less into abstract thinking. But any serious project needs people on both sides. After all, the IT industry is no longer in its infancy, when anyone who could write some code, *any* code, was in high demand. If your team cannot learn the basics of formal reasoning, the question is whether it is the right team for your project.

In several areas of IT, objections to formalism disappeared long ago, because there was no choice. In 1994-1995 Intel, the world's leading source of chips, was hit with a major bug causing wrong results in some special cases of division on its flagship Pentium processor. The bug caused an official write-off of close to half a billion dollars, and even more importantly a radical change in the way the hardware industry designs chips: from then on formal methods, particularly a technique known as "model-checking", have become a standard part of the process.

The case was typical of when no excuses stand against formal reasoning. After all, the Pentium bug only causes a small error in rare cases of division. (In 4.195.835 over 3.145.727, the discrepancy starts at the 4th digit after the decimal point: 1.3337... instead of the correct 1.3338...) But if you are providing chips to the world, the digits have to satisfy the specification. No one can say "who cares?": while the division might update the score of a player in a video game, it might just as well compute the dose of radiation to be applied to a cancer patient.

In software proper, a similar evolution has occurred in areas of mission-critical and particularly *life-critical* systems, such as transportation systems (controlling trains, planes or cars, including self-driving vehicles) and medical systems. An entire segment of the industry specializes in producing correct systems — *formally verified* systems — for such areas. Clearly, if a malfunctioning system can kill someone, arguments of the above kind ("*I cannot traumatize my poor team into using mathematical techniques*!") are not going to carry much weight.

Education plays an important role. Even in good universities, it is common that a majority of students going through a computer science or software engineering curriculum never get exposed to formal methods. (An interview question used by the author — as a reader of this Handbook, you get the benefit of a warning! —, "*Explain transitive closure*", elicits depressingly frequent silence even from graduates of good schools.) Even universities that conduct research in this area often offer formal methods only as an advanced, specialized course, which students do not connect with the practice of software development, itself taught with little mathematical basis. Formal methods should be presented as what they are: not an esoteric, specialized, difficult subject, not a replacement for classical forms of requirements, and not a panacea, but one useful tool that every IT expert must master.

This is also the lesson that you must retain as a reader of this Handbook: practice formal reasoning as illustrated in examples throughout the text, and learn to use it when elements of your requirements require precision.

9.5 AN EXAMPLE: TEXT FORMATTING, REVISITED

The text-processing problem of an earlier chapter ("The seven sins: a classic example", 5.10, page 93) provides a good example of where the precision of formal reasoning can help.

The task was to reformat a text to fill lines as much as possible with given maximum length M. We saw an attempt to express a fully detailed specification in natural language, to what incredible extremes it takes the description of this elementary problem, and how it ultimately fails anyway. The formal definition will be much simpler. In fact, when introduced below (S1, page 175), it fits on one line: if *in* is the input, a correct output *out* is a member of the set

$$\mu \, u: recast \, (\{in\}) \mid True, \, u.count \mid maxline \, (u) \leq M, \, new\_lines \, (u)$$

where μ denotes the minimum of a set under a given measure and *recast* yields all variants of a text with superfluous separators (spaces, new-lines) removed. The following discussion builds up this specification and examines its lessons for the requirements process.

9.5.1 Defining a framework

The general idea of the formal specification is simple: consider a text *in* (for "input") made of "letters" and "separator" characters (space and newline, called "break characters" in the original). We say that another text *out* is a "**recast**" of *in* if it differs from *in*, if at all, by replacing consecutive sequences of separators by a single separator, and removing separators at the very beginning or very end. (For example *out* below, with spaces represented as "␣", is a recast of *in*.) Then from *in* we want to produce a recast *out* of *in*, such that lines in *out* have length M at most, and (among all such *out*) the number of lines is minimal. That is all!

in	*out* 1 2 3 4 5	
␣␣ABC␣␣D␣␣EFG␣	ABC␣D	***A text and one of***
HI	EFG	***its recasts***
␣␣␣␣␣␣␣␣␣	HI␣J	***(M = 5)***
J␣KLM␣N␣␣OPQRS␣	KLM␣N	
T␣UV	OPQRS	
WXYZ␣␣␣␣␣␣	T␣UV	
	WXYZ	

In this example, *out* satisfies the condition with M = 5.

The formal specification uses the following sets (the symbol $\triangleq$ means "is defined as"):

CHARACTER $\triangleq$ *LETTER* $\cup$ *SEPARATOR*

SEPARATOR $\triangleq$ {*space*, *new_line*}   -- A fuller version could have others, e.g. Tab

TEXT $\triangleq$ *CHARACTER**   -- Possibly empty sequences of characters

BREAK $\triangleq$ *SEPARATOR*$^+$ -- Non-empty sequences of separators

LETTER is a set of characters; we need not know what they are as long as there is at least one (expressed as *LETTER* $\neq \varnothing$) and they are distinct from separators (*LETTER* $\cap$ *SEPARATOR* = $\varnothing$). Note the difference between a "separator" (single space or new-line) and a "break" (one or more of those).

The relation *recast*, stating that a text is a recast of another in the above sense, is *recast*1 *, the reflexive transitive closure of a simpler relation *recast*1. (Remember that the reflexive transitive closure, defined in 9.2.5, is the relation applied any number of times, including zero.) The relation *recast*1 exists between two strings *in* and *out* if *out* differs from *in* by the removal of a break at the very beginning or end or its replacement by a single separator. Formally:

Definition of *recast*1 (*in*, *out*: *TEXT*) (a boolean property)

$\exists\, b$: *BREAK* | -- *out* differs from *in* in one of three ways:

  in = *b* + *out* $\vee$ -- [L] Removal of a leading break

  in = *out* + *b* $\vee$ -- [T] Removal of a trailing break

  $\exists\, s$: *SEPARATOR*, *x*, *y*: *TEXT* |

    (*in* = *x* + *b* + *y* $\wedge$ *out* = *x* + [*s*] + *y*) -- [R] Replacement of a break by a single separator

---

For a pair [*in*, *out*] in the relation *recast*1, *out* is a version of *in* simplified in some way: [L] and [T] remove a spurious break, [R] collapses any number of consecutive separators into one. *Some* way, not all possible ways: other spurious breaks and consecutive separators may remain. This is where the power and beauty of reflexive transitive closure strike: *recast*, defined as *recast*1 *, gives us all possible variants of *in*, including those without *any* useless separators.

Also note that s in [R], a separator in *out* replacing a break *b* in *in*, can be **any** separator, independent of which separators make up *b*. So *recast*1 and as a consequence *recast* also give us all the variants of *in* obtained by replacing a space with a new-line and conversely. One of those will be (as formalized next, 9.5.3) the desired output: a text *out* "recast" from *in*, with no leading or trailing separators, no consecutive separators, a maximum line length of M, and the minimum possible overall number of lines.

9.5.2 The distinctive nature of requirements

We are not done with the formal specification, but the elements given so far already illustrate the striking difference of approach between requirements and programming. You will probably have noted the unexpected direction in which the specification works: it states how *in* may follow from *out* (by the addition of various substrings: *b*, *x* and [*s*]). That is not how programmers work: they write programs that produce the output from the input, not the other way around! It is actually possible to deduce a program from the given specification; essentially, generate many possible *out* texts and see which ones match *in* through one of the specified schemes. As a solution to the text-formatting problem, such a program would be horrendously inefficient. (At least, it sounds horrendous. Exercise 9-E.12 asks you to try that approach anyway, if only for fun.) Such concerns are irrelevant here, except to reinforce the distinction between requirements and programs. At the requirements level, all that matters is to describe the problem fully, precisely and correctly.

A formal specification does not just formalize: it makes it possible to deduce precise properties of the System (and the other three PEGS, not involved in this example), the way a mathematical theory yields theorems. For example, the following (assuming that [*in*, *out*] is a pair in *recast*) is a theorem about the requirements:

T1	$out.count \leq in.count$

To prove T1, it suffices to note that transformations [L] and [R] reduce the size of *in*, and [S] either reduces it too (by replacing consecutive separators with just one) or keeps it constant (by replacing a one-separator break with one separator, the same or another).

If we fancy implementing the specification literally, as mentioned above, T1 is good news: the computation might (or not) be horrendous, but it will not be infinite. If we take care of applying [R], in the case of a single-separator break, only to replace it with a ***different*** separator (otherwise [R] is useless since it changes nothing), each application of *recast*1 will either reduce the length or produce a different text of the same length, so the process will terminate.

9.5.3 Text formatting as minimization

From all the texts in *recast* ({*in*}), we need to find those with line lengths of at most M, and minimum number of lines. Let us use the notation

> M1 $\mu\, x: A \mid c\,(x) \mid m\,(x)$

for the subset of a set A consisting of elements, if any, that satisfy condition c and have minimal value for a numerical measure m. The letter μ, "mu", stands for "minimum". As an example with strings, the value of $\mu\, x:$ {"as", "you", "like", "it", "01", "012"} | *is_alphabetical* $(x)\mid x.count$ is {"as", "it"} since among applicable elements ("01" and "012" are not alphabetical) "as" and "it" have the minimum length, 2. We can also use several conditions and measures, as in

> M2 $\mu\, x: A \mid c1\,(x),\, m1\,(x) \mid c2\,(y),\, m2\,(y)$

which applies the condition $c1$ and minimizes $m1$, then applies $c2$ and minimizes $m2$. The order matters: reversing it may yield a different result. This variant M2 can be defined simply, by double application of the basic form, as:

> $\mu\, y: (\mu\, x: A \mid c1\,(x) \mid m1\,(x)) \mid c2\,(y) \mid m2\,(y)$

A measure we will be minimizing is, for an output text *out*, its number of new-line characters, defined as

> M3 $new\_lines\,(out) \triangleq \overline{\{x: \mathbf{range}\ out \mid x = new\_line\}}$

In English: the number of *new_line* characters in *out*. (What we really want to minimize is the number of *lines*, but since it is *new_lines* (*out*) + 1 we can for simplicity minimize *new_lines* instead.) We also, straightforwardly, define the largest word length of a text:

> M4 $maxword\,(in) \triangleq max\,(s.count \mid s \in SUBSEQ\,(in)\ \wedge\ \mathbf{range}\ s \subseteq LETTER)$

In English: the maximum length of a subsequence s of *in* made only of letters (without separators). We use *max* (*S*), *for* a set S of non-negative integers, to denote the highest value in S or, if S is empty, zero. Similarly, the largest line length:

> M5 $maxline\,(in) \triangleq max\,(s.count \mid s \in SUBSEQ\,(in)\ \wedge\ new\_line \notin \mathbf{range}\ s)$

In English: the maximum length of a subsequence s of *in* not containing a *new_line*. Given the definition of *CHARACTER* we could equivalently define *maxline* (*in*) as

> M6 $max\,(s.count \mid s \in SUBSEQ\,(in)\ \wedge\ \mathbf{range}\ s \subseteq (LETTER \cup \{space\}))$

The following properties complement T1:

	More properties of any texts *in* **and** *out* **such that** [*in*, *out*] **is in** *recast*	
T2	*maxword* (*out*) ≤ *maxline* (*out*)	-- where *WORDS* (*in*) and *breaks* (*in*) are
T3	*WORDS* (*out*) = *WORDS* (*in*)	-- respectively the sequences of words
T4	*breaks* (*out*).*count* ≥ *breaks* (*in*).*count* − 2	-- and breaks in *in*, see exercise 9-E.6.

T2 follows directly from comparing M4 and M6. For T3, we note that the three transformations [L], [R] and [S] in the definition of *recast*1 (page 172) affect separators only and hence have no influence on the words of *in*. For T4, we note that these transformations can only change the number of breaks by removing a heading break, a trailing break, or both.

9.5.4 The specification

With these definitions the requirements express themselves naturally. We need to produce, for any element *in* of *TEXT* satisfying *maxword* (*in*) ≤ M, a "recast" version *out* with a minimum number of separators, whose lines are at most M long, and having a minimum number of lines. Formally, we are looking for an element *out* belonging to the following set:

S1	μ *u*: *recast* ({*in*})	True, *u*.*count*	*maxline* (*u*) ≤ M, *new_lines* (*u*)

This formula (together with the definitions of *recast*, *maxline* and *lines*) is the specification of the Naur-G&G problem.

Understanding its meaning should be straightforward by now. Stated in operational style ("*we do this then that…*", even though the specification itself is not operational and should not be):

- We take all the strings *u* "recast" from *in*, meaning with leading and trailing breaks possibly removed, multi-separator breaks possibly reduced to single separators, and separators possibly exchanged (new-line for space or conversely). Remember (page 164) that for a relation *r* over *A* and *B* and a subset *X* of *A*, *r* (*A*) is the image of *A* by *r* (the set of elements associated by *r* with elements of *A*); here we are taking the image by the relation *recast* of a set {*in*} containing a single element.

- From those, we only retain the ones of minimum length (in other words, those minimizing the value of *u*.*count*). Since the transformations ([L], [R] and [S] on page 172) involved in *recast*1 only affect breaks, these texts are also the ones with a minimum number of separators.

- From those, we only retain the ones with all line lengths less than or equal to M.

- From those, we only retain the ones with minimum number of lines (or new-lines).

9.5.5 Analyzing the specification

The S1 formula exhibits a number of the representative properties of formal requirements.

First, it is based only on simple mathematical concepts and properties, typically taught in high school or undergraduate classes. There is really nothing to justify the reputation of difficulty of formal approaches.

Next, as already discussed (9.5.2), this form of specification drastically differs from a program in not prescribing any particular computational process. A program built naïvely along that definition would generate all the "recasts" of a text — by removing or replacing break characters one by one to compute *recast*1, then using an iterative or recursive scheme to compute the reflexive transitive closure — and would be outrageously inefficient.

This specification is, in addition, **non-deterministic** (as defined on page 99).The μ operator used in S1 does not yield a specific element of a given set but a subset of it, made of all elements minimizing a certain measure (and satisfying a certain condition). There may be two or more. Did you notice that the solution given to the example on page 172 was not the only possible one? Solution *other* is just as correct as the original *out* given there (and repeated here):

in		*out*			*other*			
1 5 10 13		1 2 3 4 5			1 2 3 4 5			
␣ ␣ A B C ␣ ␣ D ␣ ␣ E F G		A B C ␣ D			A B C			
		E F G ␣ ␣			D ␣ E F G			
[*Rest as on page 172*]		[*Rest as on page 172*]			[*Rest as on page 172*]			

Two competing recasts (for** M = 5**)

In a programmer's view of the problem, the natural approach is to process lines sequentially; in fact, to process the full text sequentially, reading it character by character. But there is no justification for that approach at the requirements level. (Some text-processing systems indeed balance spacing over entire paragraphs, to provide a more eye-pleasing effect.)

We have noted before that a key benefit of a formal specification is its readiness to **answer precise questions** about the problem and solutions. The following properties were unclear from either of the original specifications (as you can check by going back to pages 94 and 95):

Questions about the text-formatting problem

T5   Can there be more than one solution for a given input?

T6   Can the output text start or end with a break?

T7   What happens with an input text made of separators only (i.e. of a single non-empty break)?

For T5, as just discussed, the answer in the formal specification is a clear yes. For T6, the answer is no in this version. As for T7, the original specification could be construed, although not conclusively, to yield a one-space output; the formal specification yields an empty output.

All these properties can be proved formally, in the style of preceding proofs for T1 to T4; see exercise 9-E.7.

9.5.6 Proving requirements properties

The goal of mathematics is not to specify properties in a precise and rigorous way. That effort of specification (while useful by itself) is only a means towards the real goal of mathematics: to **prove** properties of the systems being specified, also known as *theorems*. The laws of logic, which are also the laws of mathematical reasoning, make proofs possible.

We have already seen some such properties: T1 to T7. Now we should prove the key property of the requirements. (Emphasis on: property of the *requirements*; not a property of a particular implementation. If a property has been proved for the requirements, it will apply to any specific implementation, but the other way around an implementation will have many specific properties beyond those of the requirements.) That key question is: **when do we have solutions?**

First we note an auxiliary theorem, the "minimization lemma", applicable to the minimization operator μ. It states that if A is finite the value of the expression $\mu\, x: A \mid c\,(x) \mid m\,(x)$ is always defined, and that it is non-empty if and only if at least one element of A satisfies c. (Note the importance of A being finite: $\mu\, n: INTEGER \mid$ True $\mid n$ is not defined since the infinite set *INTEGER* of all integers, positive, zero or negative, has no minimum.) The lemma is obvious but still deserves a rigorous proof (exercise 9-E.5).

With this lemma we can prove the main property of the text-processing specification:

Feasibility theorem
T8   A solution exists if for an input text *in* and only if *maxword* (*in*) $\leq$ M.

Let us prove the theorem, handling the two parts ("if" and "only if") separately. It is clear from S1 that a solution exists if and only if the set $\mu\, u: recast\,(\{in\}) \mid maxline\,(u) \leq M \mid new\_lines\,(u)$ has at least one element.

First assume that *maxword* (*in*) $\leq$ M; it suffices to show that the subset *SL* (for "small lines") of *recast* ($\{in\}$) made of elements *u* satisfying *maxline* (*u*) $\leq$ M is not empty; we will know then by the minimization lemma that a solution (a minimum based on that subset) exists. To prove that *SL* is not empty, we show that it includes a particular element, the text *owpl* (for "one word per line"). We obtain *owpl* as follows: start from *in*; remove any heading or trailing separators; replace any consecutive separators by a single new-line; replace any remaining space by a single new-line; repeat as long as any of these operations is applicable. They are all possible under the relation *recast*1, so applying them repetitively yields an element *owpl* of *recast* ($\{in\}$) (since *recast* is the reflexive transitive closure of *recast*1). By the property T3, page 175, *maxword* (*owpl*) = *maxword* (*in*). Now *owpl* has the property that each word appears on a single line; as a consequence, *maxword* (*owpl*) and *maxline* (*owpl*) are the same. Since we assume that *maxword* (*in*) $\leq$ M, it follows that *maxline* (*owpl*) $\leq$ M and hence that *owpl* is an element of *SL*.

The other way around, assume that a solution *out* exists. Then *maxword* (*out*) = *maxword* (*in*) again by T3. Also, *maxword* (*out*) $\leq$ *maxline* (*out*) by T2, page 175. Because *out* is a solution, *maxline* (*out*) $\leq$ M. As a consequence, *maxword* (*in*) $\leq$ M.

9.5.7 Back from the picnic

We saw earlier in this chapter (9.3.4) that a formal specification, in addition to its other benefits, can serve to produce, by going back from mathematics to natural language, a better informal requirements specification. Let us apply this "back from the for-  mal picnic" approach by re-couching the preceding specification in English. The idea is to follow the mathematical definitions faithfully, but express them in terms from everyday language.

Reformatting a text over lines

Definitions

1 A *text* is a sequence of *characters*, each of which is a *letter* or one of two *separators*: *space* and *new-line*.

2 Its *largest word length* is its maximum number of consecutive <u>letters</u>.

3 Its *largest line length* is its maximum number of consecutive <u>characters</u> other than <u>new-line</u>.

4 It is a *recast* of another if it is obtainable from it by zero or more of: removal of a heading or trailing <u>separator</u>; replacement of two consecutive <u>separators</u> by a single <u>separator</u>.

Input

5 A positive integer M.

6 A <u>text</u> of <u>largest word length</u> M.

Output

7 Among minimum-length <u>recasts</u> of the <u>input text</u>, one with <u>largest line length</u> M and minimum number of <u>new-lines</u>.

Feasibility and error handling

8 If there is more than one such possible <u>output</u>, any of them shall be deemed satisfactory.

9 Under the given conditions, there is at least one such <u>output</u>. If the <u>input text</u>'s <u>largest word length</u> is greater than M, there is none. Error handling for this case is specified separately.

The length of this specification is about three times that of the original Naur version; some of the added length follows from its more explicit style, with its four sections ("**Definitions**" and so on). Even so, it remains shorter than the G&G version, but without its noise, and with significantly more information (resolving the ambiguities).

It is also a good idea to add picnic versions of some of the formal properties (the "T" properties, T1 to T8). T5 to T7 were already expressed in non-mathematical English but we can do the same for those given formally so far (T1 to T4, pages 173 and 175, and T8, page 177):

Properties of a solution

T1	The length of the output text is at most equal to the length of the input text.
T2	[etc.: restate T2, T3, T4 and T8 in English, see exercise 9-E.8]

Such supplementary information is a form of *explanation* (remember "Binding and explanatory text", 5.4, page 77), but is neither noise nor overspecification and, because it has been proved mathematically, adds important information to the specification, reassuring the reader — in particular, the implementer — about the answers to key questions.

9.5.8 Error handling

The specification as given has a precondition: the text is assumed to have a maximum word length of M (condition 6 in the picnic version of the preceding page).

As long as everything is explicit, it is all right for a specification to include preconditions: not all problems have a solution. If you are specifying a function approximating the real square root of a real number, you have to assume that the number is not negative, since there is no solution if it is. If the input comes from a human user or another system, you may have to specify error handling (clause 9 above).

In other cases, you may want to specify partial processing for incorrect input. Such was the case for the G&G requirements, which stated (line 13 on page 96) that the output should satisfy specified properties "*up to the point of an error*". We saw in the discussion back then that this mention was overspecification (it demanded a program variable with a specific name), as well as ambiguous: does the output stop before the first oversize word or the first overflowing letter in that word? Let us accept the challenge, however, as a test of the expressive power of formal modeling and adaptability of the specification we have obtained. To resolve the ambiguity, we agree to output as many characters as possible, that is to say, include the beginning — the first M letters — of the first offending word (see exercise 9-E.14 for the other interpretation).

The adaptation is easy. Remember (9.2.6) that a prefix of a sequence s is a sequence t such that $s = t + u$ for some sequence u. Let *Prefixes* (s) be the set of all prefixes of s (which as special cases includes the empty sequence as well as s itself). Then instead of the original

$$\mu\ u\colon recast\ (\{in\})\ |\ \text{True},\ u.count\ |\ maxline\ (u) \leq M,\ new\_lines\ (u)$$

we define the set to which the solution *out* must belong as the following (changes highlighted):

S2 $\mu\ u\colon recast\ (P)\ |\ \text{True},\ u.count\ |\ maxline\ (u) \leq M,\ new\_lines\ (u)$
            where $P = \{\mu\ v\colon Prefixes\ (\{in\})\ |\ maxword\ (v) \leq M\ |\ -v.count\}$

The only difference is that instead of the recasts of *in* we work with the recasts of P, its longest prefix with no word of length greater than M. (Since P is the result of maximizing the length $v.count$, the formula uses the μ operator to minimize $-v.count$. Alternatively, one can define a maximization operator.) P is actually a set, but it is not hard to prove that P consists of at most one element; see exercise 9-E.13, which also requests the proof that, unlike with theorem T8 in the previous case, there is now always a solution. (In other words: T8 left open the possibility that the *set* of solutions could empty; with the present revision you have to prove that it is never empty, although it might consist of just the empty *text* as its single element.)

For completeness it is useful to see how to adapt the picnic (back-to-English) version to this new variant (changes highlighted, with the now useless and removed conditions crossed out):

Reformatting a text over lines (version with no precondition)

Definitions

    -- No change to definitions 1 to 4 from page 180, not repeated here.

Input

5   A positive integer M.

6   A text ~~of largest word length~~ M.   -- No more condition on the output text.

Output

7   Among minimum-length recasts of the longest initial segment of the input text having largest word length no greater than M, one with largest line length M and minimum number of new-lines.

Feasibility and error handling

8   If there is more than one such possible output, any of them shall be deemed satisfactory.

9   ~~Under the given conditions, There is at least one such output. If the input text's largest word length is greater than M, there is none. Error handling for this case is specified separately.~~

9.6 FORMAL REQUIREMENTS LANGUAGES

How do we express formal requirements? A number of "formal specification languages" exist for that purpose. Some of the best-known ones are Z, B, Alloy, TLA+ and Promela.

You already know a formal specification language: the notations introduced at the beginning of this chapter and used in the examples constitute one, without a name and without grand pretensions. It is, of course, nothing else than classical mathematical notation, with a few specific choices, such as using a colon and a bar in quantified expression $\forall\, x: A \mid p\,(x)$ (in preference to "$\in$" and "." which sometimes appear instead). As this example indicates, there does not exist a single language that could be called "*the* notation of mathematics"; while the most important conventions and rules, refined over centuries, are used by everyone, each author can introduce minor variants, typically for adaptation to a specific problem domain.

Formal specification languages, on the other hand, define fixed conventions of syntax and semantics, in the manner of programming languages. Relying on an explicitly defined notation promises several advantages:

Potential benefits of using an expressly defined language for formal specification	
A1	Precisely specified semantics.
A2	Facilitated exchange with specifiers and implementers.
A3	Mechanisms for structuring specifications, in particular large ones.
A4	Mechanisms for reuse of specification elements.
A5	Possibility of using tools, in particular verification tools.

The first point, precise meaning, should apply to any formal notation. A2 is an obvious benefit: with a precisely defined language, everyone — including requirements engineers and developers — is on the same page.

The next three benefits are also significant.

Mathematical notation as practiced by mathematicians is not intended for large specifications (A3). Intricate and sophisticated ones, yes, but not large by the standard of what large means in software engineering. A typical mathematical article or chapter is — as illustrated by some of the sections in this chapter, for example the introduction of text-processing concepts in 9.5.3 — an interspersed succession of formulae ("formal" by definition) and bits of natural language (non-formal, even if written with an eye on precision): announcements of what is coming, explanations, justifications, plus organizational elements such as section headers ("metarequirements" as defined in 1.9.4). Except in recapitulation sections, or in reference publications listing results only, it is not common for mathematical texts to contain long sections of purely formal text. There are no standard conventions for dividing large texts into smaller ones and expressing unambiguous references between the parts.

The indisputable champions here are not mathematical texts but *programming* languages, which must support specifications that are both large and precise, and have developed the corresponding solutions: modular structures with information hiding (separating specification, visible to the outside world, from implementation, internal only); functional abstraction mechanisms (routines); data abstraction mechanisms (classes); naming schemes making it possible to reuse the same names in different modules and to refer to names from other modules (through proper qualification); parameterization mechanisms (known as genericity) to make a module applicable to different types of objects; classification mechanisms (known as inheritance) to capture commonality between different modules and avoid repetition; type systems. Traditional mathematical notation has almost none of this. (The exception is the last of the mentioned mechanisms, typing, which was originally a theory developed as part of mathematical logic, although that theory has in return benefited from programming language advances). A formal specification language can provide some of these structuring techniques, applied not to programs but to specifications.

For reuse (A4), another area of little concern in traditional mathematical notation, specifically designed specification languages can provide useful mechanisms, again taking advantage of the example of programming languages.

Finally, one of the strongest reasons for using formal specification languages is the possibility of processing them through tools (A5). Basic tools can perform such tasks as syntax checking and configuration management, but the most useful tools address *verification*. As illustrated repeatedly in the text-formatting example of the previous section, formal specifications make it possible to express and prove important properties of a system. Such proofs are increasingly handled by automatic verification systems.

A particularly important class of formal verification systems addresses the needs of cyber-physical systems and other systems for which the model must address sequences of events happening over time. Some of the formal specification languages mentioned at the beginning of this section, Alloy and Promela, use "temporal logic" to model this aspect. Temporal logic includes mechanisms to reason about possibly infinite sequences of events, such as may occur in the life of a long-running system. In addition to the usual expressions of logic and formal modeling such as those of this chapter, it supports temporal expressions, including:

- $G\ p$ ("Globally p"), true if p holds in the current state and all later ones.

- $p\ U\ q$ ("p Until q"), true if q holds in the current state or a later one, and p holds in all the states (if any) before it.

For references on temporal logic, see the bibliographical section of this chapter, which also includes — as its first item — a detailed survey of formal notations for requirements.

9.7 EXPRESSING FORMAL REQUIREMENTS IN A PROGRAMMING LANGUAGE

As noted in the preceding discussion (points A3 in particular), programming languages offer many of the right foundations for formal specifications: they are precisely defined in terms of both syntax and semantics, offer carefully devised mechanisms for scaling up, and benefit from sophisticated tools and in fact entire IDEs (interactive/integrated development environments). Could they be suitable — as an alternative to specially designed formal specification languages — for requirements?

The answer would seem to be "no" if we consider that programming languages are meant for another purpose: specifying computations to be carried out by a computer. Where requirements call for descriptive techniques, programming languages are rich with prescriptive mechanisms — such as assignment and control structures — and hence may lead to overspecification, one of the capital sins of requirements.

No one forces us, however, to use the prescriptive parts of a language. Programming languages also offer powerful descriptive mechanisms. This observation is particularly applicable to modern object-oriented languages, with their abstraction constructs including classes, genericity, inheritance, information hiding and contracts, as presented in the previous chapter.

9-E EXERCISES

9-E.1 Formal family

Write the definitions requested in exercise 4-E.3, page 69 as formal specifications.

9-E.2 Concatenation

The "+" operation on sequences, denoting concatenation, was introduced informally in section 9.2.6, page 166, with the help of an example. Define it formally on the basis of the definition of sequences: "A (finite) sequence s over A is a total function from an interval $1..n$, for some integer $n \geq 0$". State and prove useful properties of concatenation.

9-E.3 Disjointness

Adapt the relocation-statistic specification (9.3) to state that the people who move are different every year. (*Hint*: you can keep the given specification in its second form, F2, and add a clause.)

9-E.4 Alphabetical order

Give a formal specification of the notion of alphabetical order between words. A word is a sequence of letters, and you can assume that the order between letters (as in "E is before I") is known. You can start from the second (informal) definition in "The difficulty of abstracting", 4.7.2, page 57.

9-E.5 Minimization

Prove the minimization lemma (9.5.6). (*Hint*: use the mathematical property that a finite set of numerical values has a minimum.)

9-E.6 The words and breaks of a text

Give formal definitions of *WORDS* (t), and *breaks* (t), respectively the sequences of words and breaks of a text t, used in T3 and T4, page 175. (*Hint*: prove that t can be written in exactly one way in the form $b_0 + \sum_{i=1}^{n} (w_i + b_i)$ for words w_i, all non-empty, and breaks b_i, all non-empty except possibly b_0 or b_n or both, and Σ refers to the "+" concatenation operator. The proof can use induction on the length of t.)

9-E.7 Theorems about a formal specification

Prove properties T5 to T7 (page 176).

9-E.8 Expressing formal properties informally

Express properties T2 to T4, page 175, and T8, page 177, in English, along the lines of the picnic versions of T1 (page 173) and T5 to T7 (page 176).

9-E.9 Do not just recast: right-justify

Adapt the formal specification of the text formatting problem (9.5) to specify that output lines must all be of exact size M, through the addition of intermediate spaces if needed. (*Hint*: you do not need to restart from scratch. The output may — conceptually — be "recast" and mini-mized first, then right-justified though the addition of spaces. In the formal specification, **compose** the *recast* relation — using the composition operator ";" introduced on page 165 — with another which adds the needed spaces.)

9-E.10 Right-justify in an evenly distributed fashion

With the requirements of exercise 9-E.9, the extra spaces used to right-justify a line can appear in any one of its breaks, as in a line of the form "as␣␣␣␣␣␣you␣like␣it". Justified text should be more eye-pleasing. Adapt the formal specification to express that spaces will be evenly distrib-uted: the length of breaks within a line must vary by one at most. Prove that the specification is feasible.

9-E.11 Right justification, in English

From the formal specification obtained in your answer to 9-E.9 or 9-E.10 or both, produce a precise natural-language version, applying the "formal picnic" idea (9.3.4). You can use the specification of 9.5.7 as a guide.

9-E.12 A not terribly efficient text-formatting program

(Programming problem; free choice of programming language.) Starting from the formal spec-ification of the text-formatting problem (9.5.4, page 175), write and test a program that imple-ments it literally, by computing all the "recasts" of the original text then looking for the ones that minimize the number of lines while satisfying the maximum-line-length condition. Make sure to guarantee that the program always terminates. (In this respect, note that the relation *recast* as defined is not symmetric and can only yield a text that is shorter, but also possibly the same, since it results from a reflexive transitive closure.)

Analyze the performance of that program and compare it to that of a more traditional imple-mentation (which you should also program).

9-E.13 Error handling

In the error-handling formal specification (9.5.8), prove that there is only one maximum-length prefix of *in* with word length of at most M (in the set P), and that the resulting output text *out* cannot be empty.

9-E.14 A different semantics for error handling

Adapt the error-handling specification of 9.5.8 (both the formal version and the picnic English version) to stop the output before the first oversize word rather than the first overflowing letter. Make sure to state and prove any relevant properties.

BIBLIOGRAPHICAL NOTES AND FURTHER READING

[Bruel et al. 2021] is a detailed survey of formal approaches to requirements.

The notion of "formal picnic" comes from [Meyer 2018]. The word-processing example was first analyzed in *"On Formalism in Specifications"* [Meyer 1985].

On the Intel 1994-1995 bug, the Wikipedia page en.wikipedia.org/wiki/Pentium_FDIV_-bug is a good starting point, with numerous references.

References on the formal requirements languages cited in 9.6 are: for Z, [Spivey 1989] and, for the original concepts, [Abrial et al. 1980]; for Alloy, [Jackson 2019]; for VDM, [Jones 1990].

The foundational article on temporal logic is [Pnueli 1977]. See also Lamport's original paper on TLA (Temporal Logic of Actions), part of the TLA+ page [Lamport 2021]. On the Promela model-checking language see [Ben-Ari 2008], a book on the SPIN model checker (for which Promela is the specification language), which also serves as an introduction to temporal logic.

10

Abstract data types

Abstract data types serve two different purposes, establishing the link between the preceding two chapters. They are both:

- A *formal requirements specification technique*, using mathematical principles to describe systems, as discussed in chapter 9.

- The conceptual basis for the object-oriented *architectural technique* introduced in chapter 8.

The present chapter explains both the theory of abstract data types and its applications to requirements. (While this Handbook generally eschews acronyms for clarity, it will in this case rely on the widely used abbreviation "ADT".)

10.1 AN EXAMPLE

Consider a type representing integer counters. An instance of this type is a simple device which displays a current value or "item", initialized to 0, and two buttons, "up" and "down", for incrementing and decrementing the value. (Devices of that kind are used to hand-count visitors entering an airplane or a sports venue.)

An up-and-down counter

In the state shown, if you click on the up arrow the display will change to "18"; if you then click on the down arrow it will again show "17"; and so on. For a new counter the display shows "0".

The counter supports four operations:

- One **creator**, called *new*. Its effect is to create a counter and initialize its value to 0.

- One **query**, called *item*. Its effect is to yield the current counter value, "17" in the figure.

- Two **commands**, symbolized by the up and down buttons in the figure. Their effect is to increase and decrease (respectively) the value by 1. Normally, names for commands should be verbs in the imperative (as in "*increment_item*"), but here we choose the names *up* and *down* as they are short and clear.

B. Meyer, *Handbook of Requirements and Business Analysis*, https://doi.org/10.1007/978-3-031-06739-6_10

10.2 THE CONCEPT OF ABSTRACT DATA TYPE

The essence of the ADT concept is that the operations, together with their properties (such as "after *new*, the value of *item* is 0" and "*up* increases the value of *item* by one"), define the type. They do not just *characterize* the type but constitute its **definition**: a counter is not an object implemented in some specific way or other in hardware or software, but is any structure to which we can apply the given operations in a manner satisfying the given properties.

This approach to specification takes an **external** view of the objects being specified: tell me not how they are made, tell me what I can do with them. (Along with "external", another applicable word is "selfish": I am not interested in who you *are* but in what you *have* — for me.)

Applying this discipline to requirements is a guarantee against *overspecification* (4.7.3, page 59). When you want to describe a new type of objects — belonging to the project, the environment or the system — the ADT approach allows you to limit yourself to the strict minimum necessary: describe only *what can be done* with these objects.

This view is not only pragmatic: it is also a protection against the effects of change. As projects proceed, many properties will come and go. "*What objects are*" (actual contents) changes much more often than "*what objects have*" (the applicable operations and their properties). By forcing other parts of a system to rely on these external properties only, you guard against the nightmare scenario of changes in individual components triggering chain reactions of changes throughout the others, leading to a messy and unstable development process.

10.3 FUNCTIONS AND THEIR SIGNATURES

Abstract data type specifications express the preceding concepts mathematically, using functions and associated concepts such as "signature", introduced in the previous chapter (particularly "Functions", 9.2.4, page 164).

An ADT specification for a type *T* consists of the following three parts:

- A list of **functions**, with their **signatures**, modeling the operations on instances of the type.
- A list of **axioms**, expressing the properties of the operations.
- A list of **preconditions** expressing constraints on the functions.

The first version of the example does not need preconditions, only functions and axioms. Preconditions will come later (10.7).

Here is the list of functions with their signatures for the *COUNTER* example:

Functions and signatures for *COUNTER* (with total functions only)			
new:	$\rightarrow$	*COUNTER*	-- Creator
item: *COUNTER*	$\rightarrow$	*INTEGER*	-- Query
up: *COUNTER*	$\rightarrow$	*COUNTER*	-- Command
down: *COUNTER*	$\rightarrow$	*COUNTER*	-- Command

(List marked "*total functions only*" in anticipation of being extended to partial functions in 10.7.)

An ADT specification defines a new type T, here *COUNTER*, and may use already defined types, which we call **previous types**. The example needs only one previous type: *INTEGER*, whose specification is not given but assumes the usual operations on integers (particularly addition) and their usual properties. Another frequently needed previous type is *BOOLEAN*.

The three kinds of operation, in the definition of an ADT T, can now be defined precisely:

- A function whose signature includes T only on the right of the arrow is a **creator**. A creator yields a new element of T. (An alternative term for "creator" is *constructor*.)

  The sole creator in the example, *new*, takes no argument. In the general case a creator can have arguments, as long as they are of previous types. Instead of initializing every counter to zero, we could have a creator *init* of signature *INTEGER* $\rightarrow$ *COUNTER* such that *init* (n) is a newly created counter whose "item" value is n.

- A function whose signature has T only on the left is a **query**. A query makes it possible to obtain information on values of the new type, here counters, in terms of values of previous types, here integers.

  The sole query in the example is *item*, which yields information on a counter in the form of its value, an integer.

- A function whose signature includes T on both sides of the arrow is a command. A command yields new elements of type T in terms of given elements of the same type.

  Here the two commands, *up* and *down*, only take one argument of type *COUNTER*, but in the general case a command may also have arguments of previous types. For example we could have a command *add* of signature *COUNTER* $\times$ *INTEGER* $\rightarrow$ *COUNTER* such that *add* (c, n) is a counter of "item" value *item* $(c) + n$.

To be useful, an ADT specification generally needs functions of all three kinds:

- Without creators, we might be able to talk about values of type T (through queries) and get new ones if we already had some (through commands), but we would not be able to produce any such values (from values of previously known types) in the first place.

- Without queries, we would not be able to extract usable information about values of type T.

- Without commands, the only values we would get for type T would be the initial elements produced by the creators. (As in a theory of integers that had only a few constants such as 0 and 1 but no operations to obtain new integers.) There can actually be legitimate examples of this situation: think of a type with a fixed set of predefined values, such as an ADT *PLANET* representing the planets of the solar system. It will have creators *Earth*, *Jupiter*, *Neptune* etc., and no commands. Outside of this very specific case, however, every ADT need commands.

10.4 Axioms

The list of functions with their signatures gives structural information about the ADT, but does not suffice to define its actual *semantics*, that is to say the behavior of the corresponding objects (such as counters). In the example, it says nothing about the effect of *up* and *down* on *item*. An implementation in which *up* actually decreases that value, or sets it to zero or to 1000, would still meet the specification as long as all functions return results of the announced types.

We need to specify that the functions live up to their names. The second part of the ADT specification, Axioms, fills this role:

Axioms for COUNTER		
A1	*item* (*new*) = 0	
	∀ *c*: *COUNTER* |	-- A2 and A3 are applicable to any counter *c*.
A2	*item* (*up* (*c*)) = *item* (*c*) + 1	
A3	*item* (*down* (*c*)) = *item* (*c*) − 1	

Axiom A1 tells us that a newly created counter — remember from 9.2.4 that we write it just *new* as an abbreviation for *new* () — has value 0. A2 and A3 express that *up* and *down* respectively increase and decrease that value by 1.

Thanks to these axioms, the ADT specification of *COUNTER* now fully reflects the intuitive presentation of the concept at the beginning of this chapter (10.1, page 187). "Fully" in the sense of "*necessary and sufficient*" properties:

- Necessary: capturing the concept requires all the elements. In particular, if we remove any one of the axioms, it will no longer be possible to prove all expected properties of counters.

- Sufficient: there is no need to add any other element, in particular any other axiom, to allow proving all relevant properties of counters.

The "necessary" part is easy to demonstrate: we expect the specification to be strong enough to prove (for example) that creating a counter then applying "up" once and "down" once will leave an "item" of zero. Formally, this property is *item* (*down* (*up* (*new*))) = 0. Removing either of the axioms A2 and A3 would make its proof impossible.

The "sufficient" part is less obvious: how do we know we have expressed *all relevant properties*? 10.6 will address this matter through the notion of "sufficient completeness".

10.5 ADT Expressions as a Model of Computation

The expression *item* (*down* (*up* (*new*))) is an example of how to describe a computation through a "well-formed expression" or WFE (also called "well-formed formula") built out of the functions of an abstract data type specification. "Well-formed" means that the expression must satisfy the obvious syntactic rules on parentheses and commas and use the right number and types of arguments. For example the following are **not** well-formed:

- *down* (*new*)): too many closing parentheses.
- *new* (1): wrong number of arguments (*new* takes none).
- *up* (1): wrong type of argument (*up* takes a *COUNTER*, not an integer).

The concept comes from mathematics, where the objects of discourse are WFEs built out of mathematical functions. An example mathematical WFE is

plus (*square* (*cos* (*plus* (3, 1))), *square* (*sin* (*square* (2))))

using the basic parenthesis notation $f(x, y, \dots)$ to denote the application of a function f to arguments x, y, ... Such an expression is usually written more concisely as $cos^2 (3 + 1) + sin^2 (2^2)$ since mathematical notation uses other syntax forms such as superscripts to avoid accumulating parentheses. One can define similar abbreviations for ADT functions and expressions, but for the present discussion the parenthesis form will suffice.

A WFE built from the functions of an ADT describes a computation with objects (instances) of this ADT and previous types. Consider for example the following WFE on counters:

item (*down* (*up* (*new*)))   -- We call this Well-Formed-Expression *e1*.

e1 represents a computation which a programmer would describe, in an operational style, as: create a new counter; then increment it; then decrement it; finally, return the counter's value. Or, in a programming language notation:

```
create c
c.up
c.down
e1 := c.item
```

It is a result of theoretical computer science that any meaningful program — such as can be modeled, for example, in the "Turing machine" mathematical framework, or in the "lambda calculus", another theory — can also be described as a WFE built out of the appropriate abstract data types, as with the expression *item* (*down* (*up* (*new*))) above. (Writing the code of the Windows operating system as a WFE on the appropriate ADTs is left as an exercise.)

10.6 SUFFICIENT COMPLETENESS

An interesting consequence of expressing a specification through ADTs is the possibility of formally defining a notion of completeness. As noted in the more general discussion of completeness (4.3 and chapter 11), the question "*are my requirements complete?*" appears at first to be self-defeating since it leads to the retort "*complete with respect to what?*", to which the answer could only be "*with respect to some other, higher-level specification*", raising the next question, "*then how do we know whether that specification is itself complete?*", with seemingly no end. This paradox is not, however, the whole story.

10.6.1 A workable notion of completeness

A meaningful variant of the completeness question is

> *"Do the requirements provide a way to predict the correct answer to any legitimate question about the system?"*

Sufficient completeness formalizes this idea thanks to the mathematical framework of abstract data types. We formalize "*legitimate questions*" as "correct query expressions".

To understand the concept, let us use, in addition to *e1* — defined as *item* (*down* (*up* (*new*)))) — another example WFE, *e2*:

> *item* (*up* (*up* (*down* (*up* (*new*)))))   -- -- We call this Well-Formed-Expression *e2*.

Both *e1* and *e2* have the query *item* as their outermost function, and return an integer. The reasoning leading to the concept of sufficient completeness is the following:

- Given an ADT specification, we can write expressions out of its functions, such as *e1* or *e2*.

- The only expressions of interest are well-formed (right number and types of arguments).

- Of those, we consider *query* expressions, where the outermost function is a query function. Both *e1* and *e2* are examples, since they are applications of the function *item* (to simpler WFEs) and *item* is a query function.

- Then the "sufficient completeness" of the ADT specification is the property that the axioms are **sufficient to yield the value of any such expression** in terms of values of previous types, that is to say, types we knew prior to the definition of the ADT.

Here is the precise definition of this concept:

> **Sufficient completeness of a (total) ADT specification**
> **(with total functions only)**
>
> A specification of a type T as an abstract data type is **sufficiently complete** if and only if its axioms make it possible to obtain, for any well-formed query expression built out of these functions, a value not involving T.

(The definition is for "*total functions only*" in anticipation of being extended to partial functions in 10.7.4.)

As an example of computing the value of a query expression, consider *e2*, defined above as *item* (*up* (*up* (*down* (*up* (*new*)))))). The axioms of the *COUNTER* ADT do indeed make it possible to obtain its value in terms of a previous type (*INTEGER*):

- By axiom A2, $e2 = f + 1$, with *f* defined as *item* (*up* (*down* (*up* (*new*))))).

- By axiom A2 again, $f = g + 1$, with *g* defined as *item* (*down* (*up* (*new*))).

- By axiom A3, $g = h - 1$, with h defined as *item* (*up* (*new*)).
- By axiom A2 again, $h = item$ (*new*) + 1.
- By axiom A1, *item* (*new*) = 0.
- So $h = 1$, hence $g = 0$, $f = 1$ and $e2 = (((0 + 1) - 1) + 1) + 1$, that is to say, $e2 = 2$.

This derivation of the value of *e2* is called a **reduction**: we start from an expression involving some elements of the type under definition, here *COUNTER*, and use the axioms to reduce it to a form that only involves elements of previously defined types, here *INTEGER*.

Note that the axioms of the ADT *COUNTER* do not actually yield the value 2 for the final result: they only yield the expression $(((0 + 1) - 1) + 1) + 1$, good enough for sufficient completeness since it involves no value of type *COUNTER*, only integers. Reducing it to 2 requires axioms (not given here) on the abstract data type *INTEGER*.

10.6.2 A proof of sufficient completeness

The reduction of *e2* to an integer expression is only one example. Sufficient completeness means that the axioms are strong enough to reduce **any** query expression q on counters to an integer expression. The specification satisfies this property; here is the proof, included for the benefit of readers interested in the theoretical basis. (Others may go straight to the next page.)

Since *item* is the only query function of the ADT specification, q is of the form *item* (*r*) where r is an expression of type *COUNTER*. The proof is by induction on the number n of parenthesis pairs in r. (Note that q has $n + 1$ parenthesis pairs.)

If n is 0, the only possibility for r is to be the expression *new*, since both of the other functions yielding a *COUNTER*, *up* and *down*, take an argument and hence will have at least one parenthesis pair, as in for example *up* (*s*). So the expression q is *item* (*new*), which from axiom A1 has value 0, an integer. This result takes care of the base step of the induction.

For the induction step, assume that the property has been proved for r having up to $n - 1$ parenthesis pairs ($n > 0$) and consider $q = item$ (*r*) where r has n parenthesis pairs. Then:

- r has to be of type *COUNTER* as required for the argument of *item* in q. Since it cannot be *new* (which has no parentheses), and the only other functions returning a *COUNTER* are *up* and *down*, r can only be of the form *up* (*s*) or *down* (*s*) for some expression s of type *COUNTER*. Since r has n parenthesis pairs, s has $n - 1$ parenthesis pairs.
- By axioms A2 and A3 respectively, q can be reduced to *item* (*s*) + 1 in the first case and *item* (*s*) −1 in the second case.
- Since s has $n - 1$ parenthesis pairs in either case, *item* (*s*) can, by the induction hypothesis, be reduced to an expression v involving only integers.
- As a consequence, q can be reduced to either $v + 1$ or $v - 1$. These too are integer-only expressions, which proves the induction step.

We saw above this reduction process at work for the special case of the expression *e2*, defined as *item* (*up* (*up* (*down* (*up* (*new*))))), which it reduced to $(((0 + 1) - 1) + 1) + 1$. The proof generalizes it to an arbitrary query expression.

10.7 PARTIAL FUNCTIONS AND PRECONDITIONS

Abstract data type specifications as seen so far use only *total* functions, which (as we saw in their definition on page 164) represent operations that are always applicable, regardless of their arguments. This assumption is too optimistic if we want to model realistic systems. Many specifications will require *partial* functions with *preconditions*.

10.7.1 The need for partial functions

In practice, not all operations are possible all the time. You cannot divide by zero; you cannot transfer from a bank account more than it actually holds; you cannot increase an object's velocity beyond the speed of light or (more prosaically) increase a message's transmission rate beyond what the available bandwidth permits.

Consider a variant of the *COUNTER* example in which counters are constrained to remain between 0 and a maximum, 10 in the figure below.

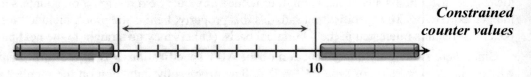

Constrained counter values

ADT models for such situations use functions that can be *partial*. Remember (9.2.4) that the set of partial functions from A to B is written $A \nrightarrow B$; unlike its counterparts in the set of total functions $A \rightarrow B$, a partial function f is not necessarily defined for all elements of A. The condition under which $f(x)$ is defined is called the *precondition* of f, and the subset of A on which the precondition holds is (as we saw in 9.2.3) written **domain** f.

It is convenient for generality to define the precondition of a *total* function as the condition **True** (which holds everywhere). This way, we can always talk about "the precondition of f" for any function f, partial or total.

10.7.2 Partial functions in ADT specifications

To account for constrained counters, the functions *up* and *down* must become partial. The new signatures are as follows, where the only changes (highlighted) are the arrows for the functions *up* and *down*:

Functions and signatures for *COUNTER* (constrained version)		
new:	$\rightarrow$	*COUNTER*
item: *COUNTER*	$\rightarrow$	*INTEGER*
up: *COUNTER*	$\nrightarrow$	*COUNTER*
down: *COUNTER*	$\nrightarrow$	*COUNTER*

As soon as a specification includes partial functions, it **must** also include their preconditions. Without the specification of its precondition, a partial function f is unusable, since we can no longer be certain that the function application notation $f(x)$ — the basic way of using functions — means anything at all. Writing $f(x)$ would become a kind of wager: a bet that x satisfies the precondition of f. (If not, $f(x)$ denotes nothing at all.)

Hope is not enough. To use the notation we need a guarantee that it makes sense, as defined by the precondition. The guarantee follows from observing the following obligation:

Partial Function rule

Any specification involving a partial function must state its precondition.

Another way of stating this rule is that whenever you write $f(x)$ — or more generally $g(x, y, \ldots)$ since the discussion applies to functions with any number of arguments — you have imposed on yourself a *proof obligation*: you must prove that the arguments satisfy the precondition.

Any ADT specification must follow the Partial Function rule: if it includes any partial functions, it must define their preconditions (hence their domains) in a separate *Preconditions* paragraph. That paragraph is one of the three components of the ADT specification along with *Functions and signatures* (10.3) and *Axioms* (10.4).

For the revised *COUNTER* example the preconditions are as follows:

Preconditions for *COUNTER* (constrained version)

up (*c*)	**require**	*item* (*c*) < 10
down (*c*)	**require**	*item* (*c*) > 0

The **require** notation for specifying preconditions is self-explanatory: in this example *up* is applicable to an arbitrary *c* (which, from the signature of the function, must be of type *COUNTER*) if and only if the *item* value for *c* is at most 9, and correspondingly for *down*.

10.7.3 The nature of preconditions

Technically, what exactly is a precondition? We need an expression of boolean type (with value true or false), and we want it to be always defined. Hence the rule:

ADT precondition rule

The precondition of a partial function in an abstract data type specification must be a well-formed query expression of type *BOOLEAN*, involving only total functions.

It assumes a predefined ADT *BOOLEAN* with the expected functions corresponding to the operations of boolean logic — "and", "or", "not" … — with their usual properties.

To keep things simple, the rule requires preconditions to be built only out of *total* functions: then it is always possible to determine whether a precondition is satisfied, without further ado. We should not have to fret about the precondition itself being defined. Such is the case with the above preconditions of *up* and *down*, which use *item*, a total function on *COUNTER*, and the total functions "<" and ">" on integer pairs.

10.7.4 Expression correctness

Sufficient completeness remains applicable in the presence of partial functions and so does the proof of the example (10.6.2), but they must be adapted to account for the notion of *correctness*:

> **Correct expression**
>
> A well-formed expression is **correct** if and only if every application of a function in its subexpressions satisfies the function's precondition.

The "subexpressions" of an expression are the expression itself and (recursively) the subexpressions of its arguments. For example, *item* (*up* (*new*)) has three subexpressions: the whole expression itself; *up* (*new*); and *new*.

The definition of "correct" adds to the requirement of well-formedness the requirement that in any function application $f(x, y, \ldots)$ occurring within the expression, where f is partial, the arguments $x, y, \ldots$ satisfy the precondition of f. (The requirement holds by default if f is total, thanks to the convention that the precondition in this case is **True**.)

An equivalent definition is that a function application $f(x, y, \ldots)$ is correct if and only if its arguments $x, y, \ldots$ are all (recursively) correct and satisfy the function's precondition.

Here are examples of correct and incorrect expressions, in reference to the revised version of the *COUNTER* specification (the one involving preconditions):

- *new* is correct (total function — hence **True** as its precondition — with no argument).
- *up* (*new*) is correct (the argument *new* is correct as just seen, and it satisfies the precondition *item* (*c*) < 10 of *up* since *item* (*new*) is equal to 0 from axiom A1.)
- *item* (*up* (*new*)) is correct (*item* is a total function, and its argument is correct as just seen). Note that from axiom A2 the value of this expression is 1.
- *down* (*new*) is not correct since the argument *new*, while itself correct, does not satisfy the precondition of *down*, evaluating here to *item* (*new*) > 0, which A1 tells us has value false.
- As a consequence, neither is *item* (*down* (*new*)) since the argument of *item* — a subexpression — is itself not correct.

How does the concept of correctness affect sufficient completeness? Remember that the purpose of sufficient completeness is to guarantee that the axioms of a specification are strong enough to make it usable in practice. More precisely, they must enable us to reduce query expressions to values of previously defined types. With functions now possibly being partial, we need only care about *correct* query expressions. This is the only change to the sufficient completeness rule. The rule (given in full with the changed words highlighted) becomes:

> ### Sufficient completeness of an ADT specification
> ### (possibly involving partial functions)
>
> A specification of a type T as an abstract data type (**possibly involving partial functions**) is **sufficiently complete** if and only if its axioms make it possible to obtain, for any **correct** query expression built out of these functions, a value not involving T.

The original on page 192 talked about *well-formed* query expressions, but the new version drops this qualification since "correct" implies well-formed.

10.7.5 Ascertaining correctness

(Readers less interested in theory may skip this subsection and the following one, and continue with 10.8 on the next page.) How can we determine that a specification is correct?

This property does not require a separate rule but follows from being able to determine sufficient completeness. For an expression to be correct, arguments in every function application $f(x, y, \ldots)$ in it must satisfy the function's precondition. Such preconditions are well-formed expressions; being of type $BOOLEAN$ (a "previous type"), they are query expressions. Since (by the "ADT precondition rule", page 195) they are built out of total functions, they are correct. Sufficient completeness guarantees that we can evaluate them, and hence determine whether the function application is correct. For example, to find out whether *down* (*new*) is correct:

- We need to evaluate the precondition of *down* on the argument *new*; it is *item* (*new*) > 0.

- Being sufficiently complete, the specification makes it possible to evaluate *item* (*new*). (Specifically, axiom A1 tells us that it evaluates to zero.)

- As a consequence, it also makes it possible to evaluate the precondition *item* (*new*) > 0. The result is False.

So the original expression *down* (*new*) is not correct.

10.7.6 No vicious cycle

The preceding argument — that being able to prove sufficient completeness implies being able to prove correctness — requires care since the relationship is mutually recursive:

1   To prove an expression correct, one needs to evaluate the arguments of its function applications, which (the reasoning goes) is possible because the specification is *sufficiently complete*.

2   Sufficient completeness is a property of *correct* expressions built out of the specification.

Fortunately, the recursion does not lead to a vicious cycle. In going from case 1 to case 2, sufficient completeness is applied to an *argument* in a function application, with one fewer parenthesis-pair than the original (in the example, we went from *down* (*new*) to *new*). The other way around, to ascertain that an expression is correct as part of proving sufficient completeness in case 2, we retain its number of parentheses. So any sequence of mutual references between the two cases will decrease the number of parentheses at every iteration and hence will be finite.

10.8 USING ABSTRACT DATA TYPES FOR REQUIREMENTS

Learning about abstract data types in this chapter after having read about object-oriented concepts in chapter 8 inevitably raises impressions of similarity. They are justified:

- Abstract data types provide the theory behind object technology; specifically, an abstract data type is the mathematical equivalent of a class, the key OO concept.

- Conversely, the notation introduced in chapter 8 to specify classes (and to implement them, a secondary aspect in a discussion of requirements), the Eiffel language, can be used to specify abstract data types.

10.8.1 Turning an ADT into a class

As an illustration of the second observation, here is a restatement of the *COUNTER* ADT example in the form of a class:

```
deferred class COUNTER feature

    Min: INTEGER = 0 ; Max: INTEGER = 10

    item: INTEGER
            -- Counter value.

    up
            -- Increment counter value.
        require
            item < Max
        deferred
        ensure
            item = old item + 1
        end

    down
            -- Decrement counter value.
        require
            item > Min
        deferred
        ensure
            item = old item + 1
        end
invariant
    item ≥ Min
    item ≤ Max
end
```

Out of the "The seven kinds of class", 8.8, page 154, this one is a Requirements class and more specifically a Concrete Environment class (8.8.1). As usual with Requirements classes, it is deferred and makes use of deferred features. Recall ("Relations between classes and the notion of deferred class", 8.3, page 139) that a deferred feature is an operation that the class specifies but does not implement (and that a class is itself deferred if it has at least one deferred feature).

The most remarkable property of this class declaration in relation to the ADT specification of the previous sections is how close they are. Under different notations — one closer to standard mathematical conventions, the other inspired by programming languages — they essentially express the same information.

10.8.2 Functional and imperative styles

Aside from the different notational styles, a difference of substance does exist between the class and the earlier ADT specification. A class uses an *imperative* approach in contrast with the *functional* approach of ADT definitions. These terms mean the following:

- A specification is functional if it simply defines functions, in the mathematical sense of this term, defined in 9.2: a mechanism defining the correspondence between certain values. For example the square function defines the correspondence between certain numbers (such as 0, 1, 2, 3, 4, ...) and others, their squares (0, 1, 4, 9, 16, ...). An ADT specification as introduced earlier in this chapter, using functions such as *new*, *item*, *up* and *down*, does not imply that anything "changes"; in particular, it simply models "commands" through functions (*up* and *down*) which use the same type T on both the left and right side of the signature (10.3). If c is a counter, *up* (c) does not change c or anything else, but simply denotes another abstract counter, whose "item" value is one higher than c's counter value. The functional style is characteristic of mathematics, where a fundamental practice is to use known values to define other values by applying functions, as in sin (x).

- A specification is imperative if it includes "orders" to an underlying machine to change something. The imperative style is characteristic of programming, where a fundamental practice is to change the values of variables, for example through assignment instructions.

Even though a deferred class is not entirely implemented, it can still use an imperative style, telling for example a *COUNTER* object, in the *up* operation, to increase its *item* value. The operation was introduced functionally as:

up: *COUNTER*   →   *COUNTER*

meaning that it is a *function* that takes a counter as argument and returns another counter as its result. The OO description of the corresponding feature, in class *COUNTER* on the previous page, defines *up* instead as a *procedure* that does not create a new counter but modifies an existing one. It specifies that modification through a postcondition: *item* = **old** *item* + 1, where **old** *item* denotes the value before the modification.

This notion of modifying an existing object has no direct equivalent in mathematics (computing the square of 2 does not change the number 2).

10.8.3 From an ADT to a class

The correspondence between the functions of an ADT and the features of a class, based on the three categories of function (defined in 10.3) in the specification of an ADT *T* follows from the preceding discussion:

- A command (a function of the ADT where *T* appears on both sides of the arrow, as with *up*) yields a procedure of the class (a feature returning no result).

- A query (where *T* appears only on the left of the arrow, as with *item*) yields a function or attribute of the class.

- A creator (*T* only on the right, as with *new*) yields a creation procedure, also called a constructor in many object-oriented languages. The above *COUNTER* class has no explicit creation procedure since it uses the default one, which initializes all fields to default values such as 0 for integers.

10.9 ADTs: LESSONS FOR THE REQUIREMENTS PRACTITIONERS

Understanding the basic abstract data type theory as presented in this chapter, and its relationship to object-oriented methodology, is essential to understanding requirements engineering.

Beyond the mathematical notation, you should remember the practical conclusion, which is also apparent in other parts of this Handbook. The most effective form of system specification is also the simplest:

- List commands, which change the system. (Also, creators, which initialize it.)

- List queries, which return information on the system.

- Specify how commands (and creators) affect queries.

If you are able to fill in this information, you have learned a lot about your system, and in fact are getting close to defining its functionality for the System book.

By bringing a formal analysis (chapter 9) to the concept of object-oriented requirements (chapter 8), abstract data types provide requirements engineers with a powerful conceptual framework which they can apply throughout their work.

10-E EXERCISES

10-E.0A Access control system: assumptions

(This part does not include any question but defines the assumptions shared by exercises 10-E.1 to 10-E.6.) An access control system for a building supports the following facilities:

- Admit a person in.
- Let a person out.
- Find out how many people are in.
- Find out if a given person is in or out.

Initially there is no one "in".

We want to define an abstract type *ACCESS* covering these concepts. (*Hint 1*: you may need another ADT, *PERSON*. *Hint 2*: whether Jill goes in or out does not affect the in/out status of Joan, if Joan is a different person.)

10-E.1 Access control: functions

Relying on the preceding assumptions, write the functions of the *ACCESS* ADT, with their signatures, in the precise notation illustrated for *COUNTER* in section 10.3.

10-E.2 Access control: axioms

Relying on the specification from the previous exercise and the above informal description of the operations, write the axioms of the *ACCESS* ADT, in the style of 10.4.

10-E.3 Access control: definition of sufficient completeness

Assume that someone asks whether your specification from the previous two exercises is sufficiently complete: what would be the property or properties to prove? (You are not yet asked to *prove* sufficiently completeness, only to state what it means for this particular specification.)

10-E.4 Access control: proof of sufficient completeness

Based on the result of the preceding exercise, now prove that your specification of the *ACCESS* ADT is sufficiently complete. (If it is not, update the specification to ensure that you can prove its sufficient completeness.) *Hint*: you can use the proof of 10.6.2 as a guide.

10-E.5 Introducing partiality

Adapt the specification obtained in the preceding four exercises to account for a rule that limits to 100 the number of persons who may be "in" the building at any given time. (*Hint*: in the style of 10.7, make some functions partial and express all needed preconditions.)

10-E.6 Sufficient completeness with preconditions

Adapt your sufficient-completeness proof from 10-E.10 to the constrained version with pre-conditions of 10-E.11. (*Hint*: make sure to prove expression correctness where needed.)

10-E.0B Trackpad: assumptions

(This section does not include any question but defines the assumptions shared by all the exercises that follow.) We consider the notion of a trackpad, which defines a position in two-dimensional space, and can be moved, scaled and (with respect to the origin) rotated. At any time it is possible to know the following:

- x and y: Cartesian coordinates.
- ρ and θ ("ro" and "theta"): polar coordinates (distance to the center and angle from the horizontal axis).

It is also possible to:

- Move the joystick by a horizontally, b vertically. (For example if it is at Cartesian coordinates $[0, 1]$, moving it by $[5, 3]$ will take it to $[5, 4]$.)
- Rotate it around the origin by θ' (so that the new angle will be $\theta + \theta'$).
- Move it closer to or further from the origin, scaling it by a given factor.

The following "trigonometric properties" tell us that the two kinds of coordinates, Cartesian and polar, are related:

- $\rho = \sqrt{x^2 + y^2}$.
- $\theta = \text{arctg}\,(y/x)$ for $x \neq 0$ where arctg, also written $\tan^{-1}$, is "arc-tangent" or "inverse tangent".
- $x = \ \cos(\theta)$.
- $y = \ \sin(\theta)$.

All the values are real numbers, of type *REAL*. You need not worry about floating-point approximations (all the operations are assumed to be exact). We initially assume that the trackpad can go anywhere in the plane (exercise 10-E.11 will remove that assumption).

The following exercises will address the various parts of the specification of an abstract data type *TRACKPAD* covering the notion just described.

10-E.7 Trackpad as an ADT: functions

Relying on the preceding assumptions, write the functions of the *TRACKPAD* ADT, with their signatures, in the precise notation illustrated for *COUNTER* in section 10.3.

10-E.8 Trackpad: Axioms

Relying on the specification from the previous exercise, write the axioms of the *TRACKPAD* ADT, in the style of 10.4. You may rely on the trigonometric properties given above, and assume appropriate functions on the abstract data type *REAL*, such as *square_root*, *square*, *plus* and *divided*, with their standard properties.

10-E.9 Definition of sufficient completeness

Assume that someone asks whether your specification, from the previous two exercises, is sufficiently complete: what would be the property or properties to prove? (You are not yet asked to *prove* sufficiently completeness, only to state what it means for this particular specification.)

10-E.10 Proving sufficient completeness

Based on the result of the preceding exercise, prove that your specification of the *TRACKPAD* ADT is sufficiently complete. (If it is not, update the specification to ensure that you can prove its sufficient completeness.) *Hint*: you can use the proof of 10.6.2 as a guide.

10-E.11 Introducing partiality

Adapt the specification obtained in the preceding four exercises to account for a trackpad that can move not anywhere in the plane (as assumed so far), but only within a 100×100 area. (*Hint*: in the style of 10.7, make some functions partial and express all needed preconditions.)

10-E.12 Sufficient completeness with preconditions

Adapt your sufficient-completeness proof from 10-E.10 to the constrained version with preconditions of 10-E.11. (Hint: make sure to prove expression correctness where needed.)

BIBLIOGRAPHICAL NOTES AND FURTHER READING

[Liskov-Zilles 1974] introduced abstract data types.

The notion of sufficient completeness comes from [Guttag-Horning 1978], which also shows that sufficient completeness is an undecidable problem, in the sense that there is no general procedure to decide whether an ADT specification satisfies the property. It is of course possible to prove it in specific cases as done in 10.6.2.

11

Are my requirements complete?

Chapter 4, devoted to requirements quality, pointed out that one of the key quality factors is completeness: how do we know that requirements cover all that should be covered? The discussion then (4.3), a preview of the present chapter, presented the paradox of requirements completeness:

- At first sight, completeness seems impossible to define, let alone assess: you want my requirements to be complete in relation to *what*? The "what" could only be another statement of project, environment, goals and system properties; in other words, another set of requirements, at a higher level but subject to the same question: how do we know whether it is complete? No end in sight.

- And yet, if we ignore the philosophical dilemma and focus on concrete signs of completeness, each modest but significant, we actually get a useful set of criteria.

Section 4.3 already listed these criteria, six of them, which we will now examine: document completeness (11.1); goal completeness (11.2); scenario completeness (11.3); environment completeness (11.4); interface completeness: (11.5); command-query completeness (11.6). As in the discussion of other quality factors in chapter 4, the presentation of each completeness factor includes hints on how to *ensure* the property and how to *assess* it on proposed requirements.

11.1 DOCUMENT COMPLETENESS

The first criterion is of a mundane, almost bureaucratic nature, but projects should satisfy it as part of good practices. Document completeness is a property of requirements *texts*:

Document completeness
A set of requirements is document-complete if it includes all expected elements:
1   If the requirements are devised to follow a template, such as the PEGS plan (chapter 3) or IEEE-830, all parts required by the template.
2   Appropriate front matter including names of authors and endorsers, table of contents and any other needed meta-information as may be required by organizational standards, such as a table of figures, a bibliography and an index.
3   Proper numbering of all elements such as paragraphs and figures, with a unique identification of every element, allowing it to be referenced unambiguously.
4   All figures and formal elements announced in texts.
5   Up-to-date values for all cross-references between requirements elements.

© The Author(s), under exclusive license to Springer Nature Switzerland AG 2022
B. Meyer, *Handbook of Requirements and Business Analysis*, https://doi.org/10.1007/978-3-031-06739-6_11

> 6   The precise references to all other documents, such as articles from the technical literature or industry standards, cited in or used by the requirements.
>
> 7   If any TBDs ("To Be Determined") remain, application of the TBD rule (5.8), including the presence of a TBD list.

Document completeness guarantees nothing about the value of the contents. But it enforces a basic level of professionalism, a prerequisite for other forms of completeness.

Endorsements (clause 2) may need to include a signature.

In electronic forms of requirements, tables (clause 2) will contain hyperlinks; cross-references (clause 5 and, whenever possible, 6) will be hyperlinks.

Clause 7 refers to "To Be Determined" elements. It is sometimes inevitable to mention some properties, so that they are not forgotten, but leave the details to later. This possibility is in practice overused and misused. The chapter on writing requirements introduced the **TBD rule** (5.8) which restricts the use of TBDs and removes their main drawbacks.

Enforcing and assessing document completeness: the above statement of document completeness is precise and relies on clearly defined properties of the requirements document, making it possible to check objectively whether requirements satisfy this property. Some of the checks can be carried out automatically by software tools.

11.2 GOAL COMPLETENESS

> **Goal completeness**
>
> A set of requirements is goal-complete if for every goal there exist project or system requirements ensuring the achievement of that goal.

Goal completeness involves three of the four PEGS. It expresses how the System and (to a lesser extent) Project parts meet the Goals. Unless addressed in the system and project, goals would remain wishful thinking.

On first encountering the name "goal completeness", one might misunderstand this criterion as demanding that requirements (particularly the Goals book, 3.4) include all the organization's goals. Such a criterion, however, would be elusive. While you can and should apply the requirements elicitation techniques of chapter 6 to ensure that stakeholder discussions leave no stone unturned ("Ask effective questions", 6.10.4, page 119), it is impossible to guarantee that the process uncovers all relevant goals. Goal completeness as discussed here is a different criterion, enforceable and assessable: goal *fulfillment* completeness.

Ensuring goal completeness: make sure that the Goals book remains up to date throughout the project, and that all project members are familiar with it; remind them to go back to it regularly to check that goals are being addressed. (Not enforcing these rules means that the project has lofty goals that impress high-level management, but the development progressively steers away from them; and that as the inevitable obstacles arise the project and system are updated but not the goals, causing further divergence between the high-level picture for the organization and the reality in the field.)

A key notion in helping achieve goal completeness is **traceability**, which was discussed in 4.8. Traceability tools can help record relations between requirements elements, within a book or across books. An example of such a relation is "*f* helps satisfy *g*" where *f* is a functionality element from S.2 (the Functionality chapter in the System book) and *g* is a goal from G.3 (the Expected Benefits chapter in the Goals book).

Ensuring goal completeness: make sure that the project members are aware of the Goals book, particularly G.3, and regularly consult it. It frequently happens in practice that statements of goals get written — in advance of the actual project start — with the primary objective of gaining the support of management and other key stakeholders, but then developers largely ignore them. The project should instead pay constant attention to goals, and update them when new circumstances lead to departures from the original project focus.

Assessing goal completeness: check that project documents, in particular in the System book, as well as design elements and code, refer to the Goals and remain consistent with them.

11.3 SCENARIO COMPLETENESS

> **Scenario completeness**
> A set of requirements is scenario-complete if for every identified scenario the specification of functionality includes enough information to support the scenario.

"Scenario" is a general term for requirements specification techniques, covered in chapter 7 and describing typical paths of execution of the system by a user. The most important kinds are use cases and user stories.

Here too we must avoid a possible confusion: "scenario completeness" is not about ensuring that the scenarios themselves are "complete" in the sense of covering all possible behaviors. Such a goal would be meaningless: the set of possible scenarios for any realistic system is extremely large and in many cases infinite. The scenarios identified in the requirements (chapters G.5 and S.4 of the Standard Plan, respectively in the Goals and System books) can only cover some of the most important interaction paths of a user with the system. Scenario completeness is about something else: making sure that the specification of system functionality (chapter S.2) includes all the functions necessary to support the requested scenarios.

Enforcing and assessing scenario completeness: check every step of the scenarios (G.5 and S.4) to ensure that there is enough specification elsewhere (particularly S.2) to realize it.

11.4 ENVIRONMENT COMPLETENESS

Environment completeness

A set of requirements for a system is environment-complete if it identifies, as part of the environment's specification, all constraints, assumptions, effects and invariants relevant to the system.

The four categories listed correspond to the constituents of the environment, specified in respective chapters E.3 to E.6 of the Environment book. It is essential to understand the relationship of the system with these features of the environment; as reviewed in earlier chapters:

- Constraints define environment properties imposed on the system, setting bounds on the developers' work.

- Assumptions, in contrast, facilitate the developers' task by explicitly allowing them to take certain properties for granted.

- Effects describe the consequences of the system's operation on the environment.

- Invariants describe environment properties that the system must maintain (and hence are both constraints and effects).

Ensuring and assessing environment completeness:

- Systematically examine the results of stakeholder interviews and workshops (chapter P.7 in the Project book) for properties of the environment that might have been missed.

- Perform a similar check on other requirements sources such as meeting minutes and legal contracts (see "Preparatory discussions", page 106).

- Check that environment properties are characterized as such and appear in book E, as it is a common mistake to mix them up with system properties. (Remember the rule, from "Distinguishing system and environment", 1.1.2, page 2: if it is something that you decide to build, it is a system property; otherwise, it is an environment property.)

11.5 INTERFACE COMPLETENESS

Interface completeness

A set of requirements for a system is interface-complete if it identifies all required technology elements and all the interfaces it will offer to other systems.

"Interfaces" in this definition includes both:

- Interfaces *expected from* the rest of the world, enabling the system to benefit from existing technology elements, and covered in the Project book, chapter P.5.

- Interfaces *provided to* the rest of the world so that it can use the system's functionality; they may include user interfaces and program interfaces (API), and appear in chapter S.3 as part of the System book.

Ensuring and assessing interface completeness: make sure to identify all needed technology elements in P.5 (see "Risk assessment and mitigation", 6.11.7, page 126); think of all the possible ways in which the system's functionality can be useful. It is in particular a common mistake to think only of a graphical (desktop) user interface or web interface, whereas a successful system will have to lend itself to other forms of use such as: a mobile phone interface; an API, so that other programs can call its functions directly; a web-services interface, to make these functions available to other systems communicating with it through the World-Wide Web.

11.6 COMMAND-QUERY COMPLETENESS

Command-Query Completeness Principle

Ensure, and check, that the System requirements make it possible to determine, after the application of any Creator and Command on any object, the value of any Query applicable to the object.

Ensuring command-query completeness can be an essential step towards a satisfactory system.

The theoretical basis is the notion of command and query in Abstract Data Types, studied in the previous chapter: "Sufficient completeness", 10.6, page 191 (with complements in 10.7.4). The idea can be explained to people who have not had the benefit of this theoretical discussion. It simply states that a good requirements specification should make it possible to determine the effect of every *action* of the system in terms of visible changes in the answers to *questions* that we may ask of the system.

The basic observation from the discussion of ADTs is that operations on the objects of a system belong to three categories:

- Queries, which return information about objects.

- Commands, which modify objects.

- Creators (or "constructors"), which initialize objects.

For example, in a customer relationship management system (CRM), a relevant type of objects is *PROSPECT*. It is possible on *PROSPECT* objects to:

- Obtain information such as identification, relevant products to be pitched to the prospect, target date for a possible sale (queries).

- Perform update operations such as promoting a prospect to a higher priority for possible sales (commands).

- Add new prospects with initial values for the associated information (creators).

Command-query completeness — more properly, command-query-creator completeness, but for simplicity the name bundles creators with commands — expresses a natural expectation on the requirements: that they allow to determine, for every operation that can change objects (command or creator), how exactly it changes them, in terms of its effect on queries.

This notion lends itself naturally to a tabular form of specification, where rows represent commands and creators, columns represent queries, and table entries represent effects. As an illustration, chapter 10 had (see the informal presentation in 10.1) a simple example of counters with a creator *new* to initialize a counter, a

query *item* to find out its current value, and two commands *up* and *down* to update it. The command-query completeness table looks like this (with just one column since this simple example has only one query):

	item
new	0
up	**old** *item* + 1
down	**old** *item* − 1

An entry in the row for a given command may use the **old** notation to express the command's effect on a query in reference to the query's value before execution of the command. Command *up*, for example, increases the value of *item* by 1. Entries for creators such as *new* do not need such a notation, since a creator simply sets the query's initial value.

For the sketched CRM example, the table might start like this:

	id	*products*	*target_date*	*priority*
new (i)	*i*	*default_range*	today + 6 months	1
promote	**old** *id*	**old** *products*	max (today, **old** *target_date* − 3 months)	**old** *priority* + 1
register_ interest (p)	**old** *id*	**old** *products* ∪ {*p*}	**old** *target_date*	**old** *priority*

Filling the entire table (with *m . n* entries for *m* commands and *n* queries) can be tedious. But it helps *ensure* and *assess* that the requirements specify the effect of all the system's operations on all its observable properties.

BIBLIOGRAPHICAL NOTES AND FURTHER READING

On the notion of sufficient completeness, see the bibliographical notes to chapter 10 (page 203).

12

Requirements in the software lifecycle

Requirements are not a goal in themselves but a tool for producing quality systems ("Requirements Effort Principle", page 31). The preceding chapters have explained how to develop good requirements; it is also necessary to understand how they will fit into the rest of the development lifecycle, along with other activities such as design, implementation, verification, deployment and maintenance.

The "Requirements Elaboration Principle", page 25, provides general guidance by directing us — away from both unrealistic extremes, all-upfront Waterfall and no-upfront Agile — to produce a first version of the requirements at the start and then update it throughout. This chapter explores further the relationship of requirements to the rest of the process.

It begins by analyzing what needs to be discarded, and what needs to be retained, from each of the extremes (as well as interesting intermediate variants, Spiral and RUP). It then introduces important lifecycle concepts: seamless and cluster-based development. Combining the best ideas from all these approaches, while discarding their more dubious ones, leads to a modern lifecycle model giving requirements their due place.

12.1 RESCUING THE WATERFALL

The following properties of the Waterfall model explain why it serves as frequent fodder for criticism:

See original diagram on page 23

- **Late appearance of code**. Many seemingly attractive ideas fall apart when you try to implement them. Code is the essential product of software development, what bread is to a baker. It is essential to produce some of it early and often (and not stay with flour).

- **Rigidity**. The model leaves little room for on-the-fly rescheduling when a task turns out to take more time, or less, than planned.

- **Synchrony**. The model assumes that each of the successive steps is performed at the same time on the entire system. This assumption is not realistic; any significant system must be split into pieces, each with its own process integrated in a greater scheme.

- **Gaps**. Each step uses its own notations and tools, for example UML for design and a programming language for implementation, introducing risks of mismatches between steps.

- **Directionality**. The model assumes that activities proceed linearly, down from the top of the figure, and has little room for updating elements from an earlier stage, for example if suggestions of better functionality (affecting the requirements) arise at the time of implementation. As a result, the implementation often diverges from what requirements documents describe.

B. Meyer, *Handbook of Requirements and Business Analysis*, https://doi.org/10.1007/978-3-031-06739-6_12

The Waterfall model, however, is not all bad. It introduces some crucially beneficial concepts:

- The model prescribes a set of tasks, from requirements to deployment. If we stop seeing them as *steps* to be executed in a strict order, they remain important as *activities* of system construction. This idea will be discussed further in connection with the RUP model below.

- The ordering constraints are meaningful. An initial version of the requirements should precede design. An initial version of the design, defining the overall architecture, should precede implementation. Even if verification occurs throughout the development rather than just as a separate step, there will remain a need for an overall verification phase (such as acceptance testing) after partial or full implementation. Deployment should only occur if verification gives the green light.

- More generally, the Waterfall model promotes the sound idea that one should perform some initial thinking before jumping into code.

12.2 RESCUING THE SPIRAL MODEL

An influential alternative to the Waterfall is the Spiral model, whose purpose is to reduce the principal risk associated by the Waterfall, called "late appearance of code" above. The Spiral produces a first version of the system through an initial iteration, evaluates the result, then produces a second iteration and so on. The non-final iterations are not meant to be shippable. A pictorial representation of the Spiral model, devised by its inventor, appears below.

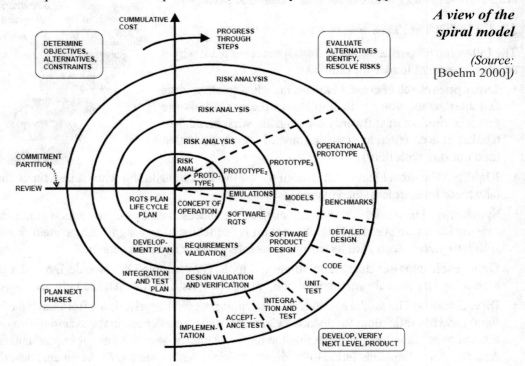

A view of the spiral model

(Source: [Boehm 2000])

Through its promotion of iterative development, the Spiral has strongly influenced agile methods.

The notion of prototype comes in part from a famous line in Fred Brooks's *Mythical Man-Month*, a classic book on software project management: "*Plan to throw one away; you will anyhow*" (see exercise 6-E.1, page 126). His observation was that it is difficult to get things right the first time around, so you might just as well try a first version intended to teach you some lessons and then to be discarded. The Spiral model generalizes this notion to a succession of initial versions: "throwaway prototypes" (6.11.3, page 123), not meant to be shipped.

This scheme follows from good intentions but can have detrimental consequences:

- About the good intentions: teams build throwaway prototypes to avoid the risk of jumping into design and implementation decisions without having enough information. Building initial versions can reveal important details that an abstract requirements or design effort might miss. "Just do it", in the sense of attempting an implementation, and draw the lessons.

- About the potentially unpleasant consequences: if an iteration was not designed for shipping, project events can decide otherwise. The pressures of deadlines, competition and limited budgets can be such that at some stage the project will have to ship whatever it has. If what it has is a prototype, shipping it is risky. Since the goal of throwaway prototyping is to produce a runnable version quickly, it is natural for a prototype to sacrifice certain aspects: ignore performance ("*we'll make it fast later*"); compromise on reliability ("*we'll fix the bugs later*"); skimp on usability ("*we'll make it user-friendly later*"); forget about security ("*we'll make it secure later*"). The difficulty of software engineering comes from the need to reconcile such diverse quality factors. Trying *after a full development cycle* to correct inefficient choices of algorithms and data structures, bug-prone development practices, poor choices of user interface or built-in security holes may be an insurmountable task.

Throwaway prototypes were more attractive in an earlier era when an actual development cycle, envision-specify-design-code-compile-fix-test-debug, could be heavy and take weeks or months. Building a prototype was tempting then, as a cheap way to try out some ideas without making a firm commitment. With today's advances in programming languages, methods and tools, it is often possible to produce an implementation of some essential functionality in a few days. Why build a prototype when you can build the real thing (and then decide whether to keep or discard it)? This observation also provides a strong argument in favor of *feasibility* prototypes (6.11.5, page 123) and tracer code (page 128).

It is important, however, to retain the long-lasting contributions of the Spiral model:

- The usefulness of certain kinds of prototype, other than throwaway prototypes of an entire system. Prototyping retains its value as a way to obtain information about *specific* aspects. We saw the principal examples as techniques for requirements elicitation ("Prototypes: tell or show?", 6.11, page 122): user interface and feasibility prototypes.

- The general notion of iterative development.

- Preserving elements of Waterfall-like order as part of a more flexible development scheme.

12.3 RESCUING RUP

The Rational Unified Process or RUP, introduced in the early 2000s, is not just a lifecycle model but a comprehensive framework for project organization, also including a toolset and a collection of best practices for development. For the present discussion, focused on the lifecycle and the requirements' role in it, RUP introduced an important concept: in looking at the Waterfall, distinguish *steps* from *activities*. Plotting steps against activities yields a two-dimensional model and, more generally, a model family from which a project can define its own variant.

Consider again the final observations (page 212) in the discussion of the Waterfall (the part that attempted to rescue it from its reputation as the big bad guy of lifecycle models). We saw that the components of that model, from requirements to design and so on, describe meaningful tasks, even if one does not accept the strict *order* of these tasks, to be performed synchronously on the entire system one after the other. RUP distinguishes two dimensions:

- The activity dimension. The activities could be those of the Waterfall, although RUP uses a slightly different classification from the one in section 12.1: Business modeling, Requirements, Analysis and Design, Implementation, Test, Deployment. Rather than activities, they are known in RUP as the **six engineering disciplines**.
- The project progress dimension, that is to say, the time dimension. Here RUP recognizes **four phases**: Inception, Elaboration, Construction, Transition.

Progress through each of the disciplines follows a sequential process (reminiscent of the Waterfall) through the phases. RUP can hence be described as a two-dimensional scheme:

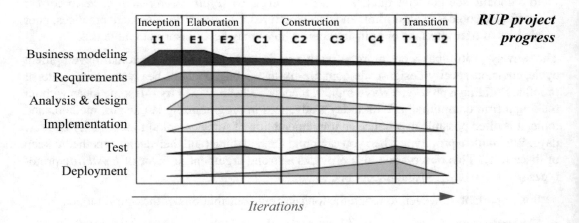

Iterations

The sizes of the colored areas suggest the respective importance of the engineering disciplines at various stages through the project: initially (Inception and Elaboration), Business Modeling and then Requirements are paramount. At Elaboration time, Analysis and Design take up an important role. With Transition starting, Deployment becomes the major concern. Testing (which in the context of this Handbook would be "verification", a more general concept) has peaks towards the end of every phase after the first two.

The sizes in the figure, showing the respective weights of each discipline at each phase, are just representative examples. By varying the distribution, one can use specific variants of RUP. As a consequence, RUP defines a family of models rather than a single model.

A full definition of such a model requires filling in 24 parameters (disciplines times phases), which may appear too complicated. Some of the combinations appear more theoretical than reflecting the reality of projects: for example, Business Modeling and requirements go well with Inception and Elaboration, but it is not clear why they should be subject to a later phase of Construction; conversely, the concept of Inception seems to make little sense for Implementation, as the inception of implementation sounds suspiciously like design! While intellectually pleasing, the orthogonality of the theory does not quite match the practice of most projects.

RUP, however, brings in a number of seminal ideas worth retaining in any effective model:

- The decoupling of activities and steps, which the Waterfall coalesced into a single concept.
- The flexibility brought in by the model's two-dimensional nature.
- A key insight: that the core activities ("*disciplines*") of software development need both to proceed throughout the project and to vary their share of the effort.

For example, as we will see in the final model of this chapter (12.7), both requirements and implementation should happen throughout the project. Towards the beginning there will be lots of requirements and little implementation (maybe just a user interface prototype to get feedback from users); towards the end it will be the other way around.

12.4 RESCUING AGILE AND DEVOPS

While the many followers of agile methods may not think that the approach needs to be "rescued", it has, like all others, its merits and limitations.

12.4.1 An agile lifecycle

As the name suggests, agile methods favor a flexible style of development, not characterized by a strict lifecycle model such as the Waterfall or the Spiral. Unlike other approaches they do not usually specify an explicit lifecycle model supported by a picture, but if they did it would look something like this:

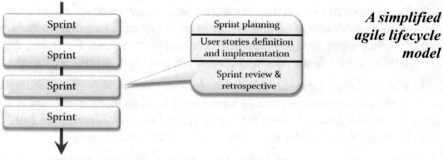

A simplified agile lifecycle model

One can indeed talk of an agile lifecycle model, characterized by a sequence of iterations often called "sprints" (the term introduced by the most widely used agile method, Scrum). Each sprint involves both requirements (typically in the form of user stories) and implementation; it starts with a "sprint planning" phase and ends with a "sprint review". The process dedicates steps to introspection and improvement, including a "sprint retrospective", which addresses the process itself (whereas the sprint review addresses its product).

12.4.2 Agile damage, agile benefit

In the agile method's influence on the lifecycle model, the worst part is the blanket rejection of upfront requirements, considered to be "waste" and replaced by as-you-go production of user stories. This absurd idea (not shared by the more level-headed part of the agile literature) has damaged many projects. As noted in an earlier discussion ("Requirements Elaboration Principle", page 25), the effective approach is to produce an upfront version — however partial — at the beginning of the project and continue revising it throughout.

Several other agile ideas are, in contrast, beneficial contributions. Particularly worth retaining in a modern lifecycle model are:

- The concept of iterative development: produce a system by successive extensions.
- The concept of short iterations. A sprint should take a few weeks at most.
- The idea of producing an executable system (even a very partial one) early on and maintaining a running version at all times. (Remember the related notion of "tracer code", page 128.)
- The emphasis on constant testing, which we may extend to constant *verification* (a more general notion than just testing, including other techniques such as static analysis).

12.4.3 DevOps

The DevOps model of software development is an extension of agile ideas, which dramatically reduces the conceptual and temporal distance between the two components of the name, development and operation.

DevOps has spread together with World-Wide Web applications, which often need to deploy changes to a system in a matter of hours or even minutes. As a sign of the novelty of this paradigm, whereas users of a traditional text-processing system (such as Microsoft Word) can point to the product version they are using, which they retain for months and years, users of a cloud-based collaborative editing system such as Google Docs seldom have such information; and when they come back from lunch to continue working on a document, they may well, without knowing it, be using a new version that has just been silently deployed.

In pre-DevOps lifecycle models, development and deployment (leading to operation) are distinct phases: developers produce a system; system administrators deploy it on as many platforms as needed; operations engineers run it. The jobs are different, and call for different skills. With DevOps, they become intertwined or even merged.

The discipline of frequent deployment has important consequences on system architecture: rather than monolithic applications, it favors independent parts, deployable separately. These individual elements run in separate operational environments or "containers", with strong isolation mechanisms protecting them from each other, and well-defined communication paths through "microservices".

Although there is still little literature on the topic of requirements for DevOps processes, it is clear that the principles of good requirements apply, if anything, even more strongly to DevOps than to more traditional forms of development: with immediate deployment, the consequences of errors and misunderstandings are immediate too, and can be felt on a large scale. The form of requirements that is appropriate for such processes is in line with the "Requirements Evolution Principle", page 23 and other related principles: maintain the requirements as a continuously evolving resource of the project, kept up to date at all times.

12.5 THE CLUSTER MODEL

Another model, the "Cluster model", is intended to remedy the synchronous nature of the Waterfall (with its activities applied simultaneously to the entire system). The idea is to retain a sequential process but apply it to subsystems, or "clusters", rather than to the entire product. In the illustrative diagram below, individual steps are labeled with abbreviations of specific activities Requirements, Design, Implementation, Verification and Generalization (the last one explained in the next section). The model can also accommodate different choices of steps.

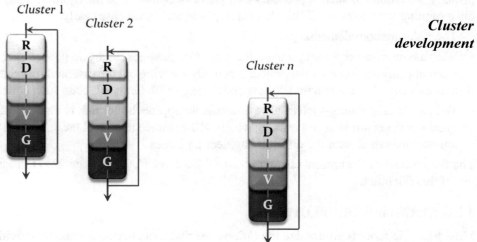

Cluster development

There is an initial step of division into clusters, not shown in the diagram; it is straightforward since any experienced project leader knows what the main divisions of the system will be. For example an interactive system built with the MVC (Model-View-Controller) design pattern will have a View cluster covering the user interface, a Control cluster covering the management of user interactions, and a Model cluster, or several in the case of a complex system, covering the logic of the system. Other typical cluster examples are a Data Management cluster and a Network Communication cluster. It is possible to fine-tune the division into clusters (for example, adding a new cluster, or merging two existing ones) as the project develops.

The main characteristic of the Cluster model is its mix of sequential and concurrent engineering. As suggested by the diagram, the clusters can start at various times and proceed partly in parallel and partly after each other. Such flexibility, not supported by the Waterfall, is precious, since in practice, even with careful planning, there will be activities taking more time than expected, but also (not all project news is bad news) others taking less than planned. The project can then reschedule the start and continuation of cluster developments accordingly.

The recommended order of starting clusters is from more fundamental and hardest to more user-oriented and easiest. This strategy decreases risk:

- In modern software development, the user interface part is typically not hard, thanks to the many available tools and libraries; it is also easy to change it if test users react negatively.
- Core components (particularly those in the Model part of MVC) are, in contrast, the most difficult and carry the highest risk. For example, bad performance in computationally-intensive parts of the system or inability to handle large data or communication loads can ruin a project. It is essential to work on these risk areas early so as to build a solid basis.

This bottom-up strategy (build the foundations before you build the decoration) is the most logical and follows engineering principles, but is also difficult to accept for some stakeholders, who are eager to see "something that works". The ability to fulfill that expectation is one of the primary attractions of such approaches as agile development and the Spiral model, which produce running versions (possibly only prototypes in the Spiral case) early.

The risks are complementary:

- With a bottom-up approach, stakeholders can lose patience if they do not see executable versions appearing — even if the project is actually carrying out the essential foundational work successfully. (Note again that "tracer code", page 128, helps alleviate such concerns.)
- With a partial-running-system-always-available approach, the risk is that everything looks great but the result is only a mirage, which will not scale up to real usage since it focuses on appearance rather than the difficult engineering issues.

The final model of the present chapter ("A unifying model", 12.7, page 221) introduces a way out of this dilemma.

12.6 SEAMLESS DEVELOPMENT

Most lifecycle models emphasize the *differences* that exist between various activities of software development, such as requirements, design and so on. The Waterfall goes furthest by actually making each of these activities a step in a rigid sequence. Seamless development instead emphasizes the *similarities*.

12.6.1 The unity of software development

These similarities are indeed striking. The activities mentioned raise many of the same issues, and we can address them through many of the same techniques, notations and tools. Similarity is not identity: the differences stand out — requirements are definitely not the same thing as implementation — but exaggerating them harms system development by leading to representations of the system expressed in different notations and causing a risk of discrepancy. A typical example is a specification or design expressed in a graphical notation such as UML, against code in a programming language such as Java or Python. Such discrepancies are also known, using a metaphor from electrical engineering, as *impedance mismatches*. Even modern ideas such as "Model-Driven Development" reinforce such gaps by enjoining the development to produce a high-level model first, to be translated into an actual program.

What makes impedance mismatches particularly harmful is the phenomenon of change, so central to software engineering (the reason for the "*soft*" part of the name "software"). Change can occur at any level, beginning with requirements ("Requirements Evolution Principle", page 23). One of the main challenges confronting a software engineering project is to keep the various levels of description in agreement. This goal is hard to meet if the notations and concepts are different at each level. Tools for so-called "roundtrip engineering" (transferring changes made at one level to the description at another one) have limited ability, particularly when going backward, for example from implementation back to design and requirements.

Seamless development tackles this issue by promoting the use of a single set of structuring concepts, a single notation and a single set of tools throughout the development. Seamless ideas appeared at the same time as the object-oriented approach (chapter 8) did, since the basic OO technique of modeling a system through its types of objects, characterized by the applicable operations, is as productive for high-level system descriptions (requirements, design) as for implementation. The Eiffel object-oriented language (8.5) was specifically conceived as a notation applicable at all levels, not just programming.

12.6.2 A seamless process

The following diagram captures the basis for a seamless process. Note that it does not model the development of an entire system, as the Waterfall does; instead it describes a "mini-lifecycle" covering the development of a *cluster*.

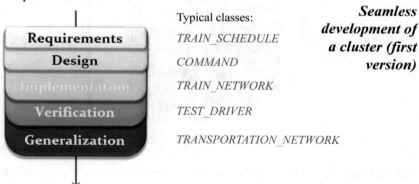

Typical classes:

TRAIN_SCHEDULE

COMMAND

TRAIN_NETWORK

TEST_DRIVER

TRANSPORTATION_NETWORK

Seamless development of a cluster (first version)

The steps are some of those found in a typical Waterfall, complemented by a *generalization* step intended to improve the result with a view to making the software elements easier to change and to reuse in future developments. (Generalization involves *refactoring*, the questioning and improvement of design choices.)

The symbolism in the figure expresses a key difference with the Waterfall: the activities shown are not successive steps but successive developments of a core product, which starts out as a requirements specification and, through a process of successive augmentation, yields a design, an implementation and a verified system amenable to extension and reuse. What is being augmented is the set of classes:

- Design, implementation, verification or generalization classes inheriting from requirements classes (under the rules discussed above, 12.6.2) to add detail.

- Entirely new classes at any of those levels. Examples are: an implementation class introducing a data structure used in the algorithmic solution; a design class corresponding to a chosen design pattern; a verification class introducing test drivers.

- Generalization classes which may not be indispensable for the current project but take advantage of its results to benefit other projects. (The previous figure assumes a train control system with a class *TRAIN_NETWORK*. Generalization might provide a more general class *TRANSPORTATION_NETWORK* describing transportation structures of any kind.)

12.6.3 Reversibility

One of the main goals of adopting a seamless model is, as noted, to support change. Using a single notation and a single set of concepts makes it possible to integrate change at any level much faster and more simply than with traditional one-directional models. The depiction of a seamless cluster-level mini-lifecycle should reflect this property:

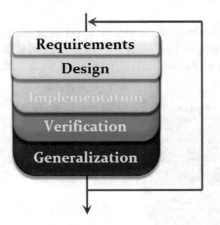

Seamless development of a cluster (revised version with reversibility)

The backward arrow reflects the iterative nature of the process not only for the entire lifecycle (as with the Spiral and agile models) but also within the development of every cluster. Iterativeness continues to exist at the overall level, through a notion of sprint retained from agile methods (see below), but also permeates the individual steps: it is often the case that implementing a function of the System reveals a better form of that function, previously neglected properties of the Environment, or a change to the tasks of the Project.

12.7 A UNIFYING MODEL

Consideration of the strengths and weaknesses of the preceding models leads to a general model which integrates the best of each, and devotes special attention to requirements and to the needs of the modern development world (the world of Web and mobile applications, of ubiquitous computing, of virtual reality and the Metaverse, of immediate deployment, of cloud-based architectures, of the Internet of Things…) which these other models predated.

Its name, in reference to the theme running through this Handbook, is the "PEGS model". We successively review the overall scheme, variations in the setup of sprints, a typical instance of the model, and the structure of individual sprints.

12.7.1 Overall iterative scheme

The model is iterative. It retains from agile methods the notion of sprint: development proceeds in successive iterations, with a typical duration of a few days to a month. While it varies with projects, that duration is fixed for any given project (this "time-boxing" principle is a keystone of agile development, and experience has shown that it is an excellent idea). An overall view of the process is as follows:

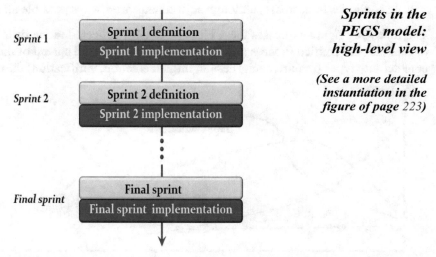

Sprints in the PEGS model: high-level view

(See a more detailed instantiation in the figure of page 223)

Each sprint consists of two parts: sprint definition and sprint implementation. Here the model departs significantly from typical agile practice: each sprint is a mini-Waterfall, with not only implementation (including verification) but also definition, including requirements and design. This concept follows in particular from the Requirements Elaboration Principle (2.1.5, page 25): "*Produce an initial version of the requirements at the start of the project. Update and extend them throughout the project*", a rule that also applies to design.

12.7.2 Not all sprints are created equal

The above view only introduces the overall scheme, but the nature of sprints (not their duration) can vary considerably. The agile view of a single scheme for all sprints (collect user stories, implement, reflect) does not measure up to the reality of a significant project: the beginning differs a lot from the middle and the middle differs a lot from the end. Here the Waterfall got it (partly) right:

- At the beginning, the emphasis is on definition. You should also (unlike in the waterfall) perform some implementation, if only to reinforce the stakeholders' trust, as discussed next; but requirements and design — *upfront* requirements and design, to which a dogmatic agile view would object — will command most of the effort. In addition, some *verification* work will already take place, in particular verification of the requirements themselves (chapter 4).

- In the middle, it will be implement, implement, implement — but with constant efforts to keep the requirements and design up to date, in line with the Requirements Elaboration and other principles of this Handbook. In addition, verification should constantly accompany implementation, and re-verification when parts of the requirements and design change.

- Towards the end, the role of verification grows. Implementation proceeds towards its finalization, but increasingly yields to further verification of what has already been built. Unless the requirements and design were really messed up (in which case the project is, too), their role continues to decrease, although adjustments are always possible all the way to the end.

The following figure expresses these ideas — already reflected in the distribution of activities of the Rational Unified Process (12.3) — by showing a typical spread of the effort among four core activity types (requirements, design, implementation, verification) through the lifecycle.

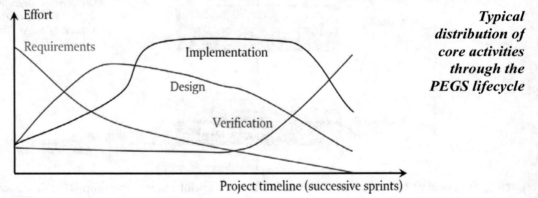

Typical distribution of core activities through the PEGS lifecycle

This general scheme, inspired by RUP, is an application of the following "NASACE" Principle:

Not-All-Sprints-Are-Created-Equal ("NASACE") Principle
1   Every sprint includes a definition phase and an implementation phase.
2   Both of these phases involve verification.
3   Definition dominates early sprints, decreases afterwards.
4   Implementation starts on a small scale with the earliest sprints, increases afterwards.
5   Verification becomes dominant in the latest sprints.

12.7.3 An example sequence of sprints

A typical PEGS-lifecycle project might, as a result of the NASACE Principle, look like this:

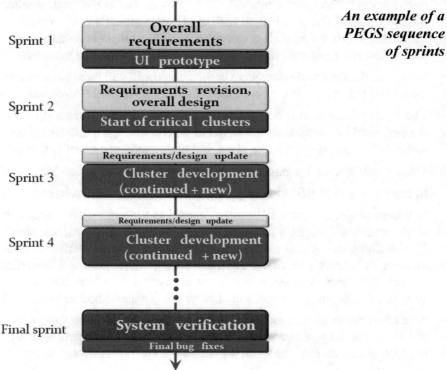

*An example of a
PEGS sequence
of sprints*

To understand this figure, note the following:

- It is a specific instance of the general PEGS lifecycle from the figure of page 221. Each such instance will have a variable number of sprints (all, however, of the same duration).

- Per the general PEGS model and the NASACE Principle, every sprint consists of two parts, definition and implementation. Both parts include verification activities. (Scrum sprints similarly consist of a planning meeting and implementation, plus a review and retrospective.)

- In the figure, the relative height of these two components of each of the sprints varies, reflecting points 3 and 4 of the NASACE Principle. Initially the green parts (definition) dominate and the blue parts (implementation) are small; as the project progresses, the ratio of their importance is gradually reversed. At the end, verification (specifically, in this case, validation against requirements) takes over.

In the particular PEGS-model instance illustrated here:

- The first sprint is devoted mostly to requirements, but there is already a first implementation step, labeled in this case "UI prototype" (see 6.11.4). Other kinds of prototype, such as feasibility prototypes (6.11.5), may also be appropriate here. See next about the importance of starting implementation early.

- In the second sprint, part of the effort remains devoted to refining the requirements, but we also define the overall design (the system's architecture), implying in particular a division into clusters ("The Cluster model", 12.5, page 217). On the implementation side, we start the fundamental clusters. In line with the Cluster model's principles, the work on clusters should begin (after a possible prototyping of UI and other elements as in the first sprint) with the hardest and most critical clusters, progressing towards the more user-visible parts.

- In each of the third and subsequent sprints, there will still be a phase of refining the requirements and the design, but most of the effort will go towards implementation.

- The final sprint is mostly devoted to verification (acceptance testing). Of course, this being the real world and not a mythical world where all bugs are detected and corrected early, some final bug-fixing will take place, but no implementation of new functionality.

The figure only shows one possible instance of the PEGS lifecycle. Variants will exist:

- In large projects, verification may extend over several final sprints rather than just one.

- In a large project, "Sprint 1", mostly devoted to upfront requirements with only prototype implementations, might actually be spread over several sprints, and similarly with "Sprint 2" if defining the overall architecture is a complex matter. Verification too will often take up more than one sprint. In such cases, we are getting closer to a Waterfall-style approach, but key differences remain: every sprint has both a definition part and an implementation part, and development proceeds in clusters (as discussed further in 12.7.5 below).

- At another extreme, the model also accommodates a variant very close to the textbook definition of agile project management: upfront work, while present, is limited, and right from the first sprints most of the work (although not 100%) is devoted to implementation.

- Many other variants are possible.

As noted in the presentation of the Cluster model, the division into clusters normally remains stable, but it can be adjusted after each sprint.

12.7.4 Implement early and often

Even in a variant that is closest in spirit to a Waterfall style of development, early sprints should, per the NASACE Principle, already contain an implementation element. The reason for this rule is simple: the project must manage stakeholders' expectations properly.

The ideal order for cluster development is often, as noted in 12.5, bottom-up: from the most fundamental clusters to the more user-oriented ones. This approach minimizes risk, since the fundamental clusters — such as those implementing the core business operations, or networking, or synchronization, or data management — are usually the hardest ones, requiring the most advanced technical knowledge and subject to failure, from which it will be hard to recover, if incorrect technical decisions are made. In contrast, clusters that are closer to users' direct view, while potentially demanding as well, are less critical. With a good technical architecture, you can correct a bad user interface. However good the user interface may be, it will not make up for a bad set of architectural choices.

The problem with a bottom-up ordering of clusters, however, is the risk of losing customer confidence. You may be working on the fundamental parts, in the customers' best interest, but if you are not able to show something usable the customers, particularly those without an IT background, may grow suspicious. The benefit of showing something that works, or seems to work, is an advantage of approaches that produce working systems right from the start, such as the Spiral (and others that rely on developing initial prototypes) and agile development.

The risk here, as we have seen, is to demonstrate to the customer a system that seems to work impressively but does not have the infrastructure that will enable it to scale up to real usage — a kind of Potemkin village.

How do you reconcile the two goals: focusing on the really difficult stuff, while having something to show to the customer at all times?

The answer is not to prototype the entire system, a costly approach whose risks we saw in the discussion of the Spiral model. The answer is to build some parts that will directly demonstrate progress, without affecting the core development.

A user interface prototype, as in the example illustrated earlier, is one such technique. It should clearly be presented for what it is, a prototype of the interface, and not as a first version of the entire system.

Building such a part of the system in the initial sprints also forces the team to engage in implementation (and not just upfront work of requirements and design) right from the beginning, avoiding the Waterfall's "analysis paralysis" syndrome.

12.7.5 Detailed view of a sprint

The discussion of the PEGS model has not yet described in detail what happens in each sprint.

The figure on the following page illustrates the individual sprint structure, developing the two parts that appeared without further details in the preceding figures (pages 221 and 223): definition, in green (the color of hope), and implementation, in blue.

What exactly are "definition" and "implementation"?

The scope of the "definition" part is a consequence of the distinction between the four PEGS: Project, Environment, Goals and System. Definition is about analyzing these four elements, at the beginning of the project, and later on to refine such earlier analyses. Some activities can be performed in parallel, whereas others have to happen in sequence:

D1 The Goals and Environment, or parts of them, can be analyzed in parallel.

D2 It is also possible to for the planning of the Project or some of its steps, to proceed in parallel with the overall design of the System or some of its components.

D3 The tasks listed under D1 must, however, precede those under D2. To plan project steps and design system components, you need to have at your disposal the relevant goals from the enterprise and the relevant constraints, effects and invariants from the environment.

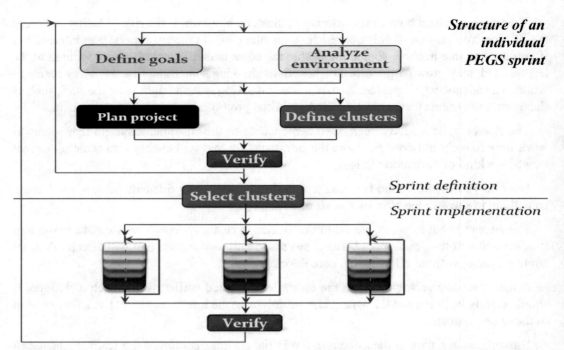

Structure of an individual PEGS sprint

From these observations, the top part of the individual cluster lifecycle follows, as pictured. After that first part follows a Verification effort. It might uncover problems in the work done so far, hence the upward arrow: at that level too, even within a given sprint (specifically, the first part of that sprint), the process is iterative.

Part of the result of the work on the System aspect is to define the clusters on which the implementation phase will work. The definition phase concludes, as a consequence, with a selection of these clusters. Some might be clusters to be started in this sprint; others, clusters initiated in previous sprints and to be continued in the current sprint.

The implementation phase follows the mini-lifecycle scheme of the Cluster model, each applied, in parallel, to the selected clusters. While step-by-step verification occurs throughout the process, the implementation phase concludes with a general verification effort for all the developments of the current sprint.

12.7.6 A combination of best practices

It was noted at the beginning of this discussion that the PEGS model retains some of the best elements of all preceding models. Specifically:

- The general order of activities (requirements then design and so on) comes from the Waterfall. It is applied both to the process as a whole (see the distribution of activities in the figure of page 222) and within the implementation phase for each sprint and each cluster.

- The variable weight of these activities as the project develops is similar to the Rational Unified Process concepts.

- Short fixed-time sprints come from agile methods.

- The insistence on having a working system throughout, including at the very start, is also a key agile influence.

- The division of the system into clusters and the mini-lifecycles for each cluster (with a role for generalization, to prepare for reuse) come from the Cluster model.

- So does the mix of sequential and concurrent engineering.

BIBLIOGRAPHICAL NOTES AND FURTHER READING

The Waterfall model was first described in [Royce 1970], an article — still good reading — whose purpose was actually to criticize the Waterfall, thereby introducing a long tradition.

The notion of prototype and the advice to "throw one away" appear in [Brooks 1975-1995]. The observation (on page 213) that modern technology has made it much more realistic to build actual partial implementations, rather than prototypes, follows from a comment to the author by Mike Cohn.

The Spiral model is described in [Boehm 1986], with a more detailed analysis and report on its application in [Boehm 2000]. The principal reference on the Rational Unified Process is [Kruchten 2003].

A general framework for describing lifecycle schemes and other standardized practices is the CMMI model, "Capability Maturity Model Integration"; see [CMMI 2010] and [SEI 2005].

[Meyer 2014] is an analysis of the advantages and deficiencies of agile methods. Generalization is presented and discussed in [Meyer 1995], which covers the Cluster model and seamless development (see also the corresponding chapters in [Meyer 1997]).

Bibliography

All URLs checked September 2022.

[Abrial et al. 1980]

Jean-Raymond Abrial, Stephen A.Schuman and Bertrand Meyer: *A Specification Language*, in *On the Construction of Programs*, eds. R. McNaughten and R.C. McKeag, Cambridge Univ. Press, 1980, available at se.ethz.ch/~meyer/publications/languages/ Z_original.pdf.

[Alexander 2003]

Ian Alexander: *Misuse Cases: Use Cases with Hostile Intent*, in IEEE *Software*, vol. 20, no. 1, January 2003, pages 58-66, DOI 10.1109/MS.2003.1159030.

[Bair 2005]

Bettina Bair: example requirements document from a course at Ohio State University, course CSE 616, *Object-Oriented Systems Analysis*, Autumn 2005, available online at web.cse.ohio-state.edu/~bair.41/616/Project/Example_Document/Req_Doc_Example.html. (Copy available on the site for this Handbook at requirements.bertrandmeyer.com.)

[Beck 2005]

Kent Beck, with Cynthia Andres: *Extreme Programming Explained — Embrace Change*, Addison-Wesley, 2005. (Second edition.)

[Ben-Ari 2008]

Mordechai Ben-Ari, *Principles of the Spin Model Checker*, Springer, 2008, see book page at www.springer.com/gp/book/9781846287695.

[Berry 1995]

Daniel M. Berry: *The Importance of Ignorance in Requirements Engineering*, in *Journal of Systems and Software*, Vol. 28, No. 1, February 1995, available at bit.ly/2BWKYES.

[Boehm 1986]

Barry W. Boehm: *A Spiral Model of Software Development and Enhancement*, in *Computer* (IEEE), vol. 21, no. 5, May 1986, pages 61-72.

[Boehm 2000]

Barry W. Boehm (edited by Wilfred J. Hansen): *Spiral Development: Experience, Principles, and Refinements*, Report CMU/SEI-2000-SR-008, July 2000, available online at resources.sei.cmu.edu/asset_files/SpecialReport/2000_003_001_13655.pdf.

[Brennan 2015]

  Kevin Brennan, *Business Analysis Body of Knowledge (BABOK guide) v3*, slides from a
  webinar, available at www.iiba.org/contentassets/a566a72f87314878bbed046681829fb8/
  business-analysis-body-of-knowledge-babok-guide-v3.pdf.

[Brooks 1975-1995]

  Frederic P. Brooks: *The Mythical Man-Month*, Addison-Wesley, 1975 (revised edition, 1995).

[Bruel et al. 2021]

  Jean-Michel Bruel, Sophie Ebersold, Florian Galinier, Alexandr Naumchev, Mariya
  Naumcheva and Bertrand Meyer, *The Role of Formalism in System Requirements*, in
  ACM *Computing Surveys*, vol. 54, no. 5, June 2021, pages 1-36, preprint available at
  se.ethz.ch/~meyer/publications/requirements/formalism.pdf.

[Bruel et al. 2022]

  Jean-Michel Bruel, Sophie Ebersold and Mariya Naumcheva: *Effective Requirements:
  Complete Examples and Practical Material* (companion to this Handbook), 2022 , to appear.

[Christel-Kang 1992]

  Michael G. Christel and Kyo C. Kang: *Issues in Requirements Elicitation*, Software
  Engineering Institute, CMU/SEI-92-TR-012, September 1992, available online at
  cupdf.com/document/201107011101-issues-in-requirements-elicitation.html.

[Chung et al. 2000]

  Lawrence Chung, Brian Nixon, Eric Yu and John Mylopoulos: *Non-functional requirements
  in software engineering*, Springer, 2000

[CMMI 2010]

  CMMI Product Team: *CMMI for Development, Version 1.3, Improving processes for
  developing better products and services*, Tech. Report CMU/SEI-2010-TR-033, Software
  Engineering Institute, November 2010, available at www.sei.cmu.edu/reports/10tr033.pdf.

[Cockburn 2001]

  Alistair Cockburn: *Writing Effective Use Cases*, Pearson Education, 2001.

[Derby 2010]

  Esther Derby: *Building a Requirements Foundation with Customer Interviews*, at,
  www.estherderby.com/building-a-requirements-foundation-with-customer-interviews/.

[DOSE 2007-2015]

  Bertrand Meyer, Martin Nordio et al.: *A Distributed Project for a Globalized World*, course
  page and publication list at se.inf.ethz.ch/research/dose/.

[EIS 2021]

  Eiffel Information System (EIS), online documentation available at eiffel.org/doc/
  eiffelstudio/Eiffel_Information_System.

[Gamma et al. 1994]

Erich Gamma, Richard Helm, Ralph Johnson and John Vlissides: *Design Patterns: Elements of Reusable Object-Oriented Software*, Addison-Wesley, 1994.

[Ghezzi et al. 2002]

Carlo Ghezzi, Mehdi Jazayeri, Dino Mandrioli: *Fundamentals of Software Engineering*. 2nd Edition. Prentice Hall, 2002.

[Gilb 2005-2022]

Tom Gilb: *Planguage Basics and Process Control*, pages 1-34 of *Competitive Engineering* by Tom Gilb, ed. Lindsey Brodie, originally published in 2005, available (together with recent PLanguage documentation) at gilb.com.

[Glinz 2000]

Martin Glinz: *Problems and Deficiencies of UML as a Requirements Specification Language*, in *Proc. of 10th International Workshop on Software Specification and Design* (IWSSD 10), Nov. 2000, available at files.ifi.uzh.ch/rerg/amadeus/publications/papers/IWSSD-10.pdf.

[Goodenough-Gerhart 1977]

John B. Goodenough and Susan Gerhart: *Towards a Theory of Test: Data Selection Criteria*, in *Current Trends in Programming Methodology*, ed. Raymond T. Yeh, pages 44-79, Prentice Hall, 1977.

[Gotel-Finkelstein 1994]

Orlena C. Z. Gotel & Anthony C. W. Finkelstein: *An Analysis of the Requirements Traceability Problem*, in *Proceedings of 1st International Conference on Requirements Engineering*, IEEE Computer Society Press, 1994, pages 94-101.

[Gottesdiener 2002]

Ellen Gottesdiener: *Requirements Workshops: Collaborating to Explore User Requirements*, in *Software Management*, 2002, available at www.ebgconsulting.com/Pubs/Articles/ReqtsWorkshopsCollabToExplore-Gottesdiener.pdf.

[Guttag-Horning 1978]

John V. Guttag and Jim J. Horning: *The Algebraic Specification of Abstract Data Types*, in *Acta Informatica*, vol. 10, 1978, pages 27-52.

[Harish 2021]

Ajay Harish: *When NASA Lost a Spacecraft Due to a Metric Math Mistake*, online article at www.simscale.com/blog/2017/12/nasa-mars-climate-orbiter-metric/.

[Hull, Jackson and Dick 2011]

Elizabeth Hull, Ken Jackson and Jeremy Dick: *Requirements Engineering*, Springer, 2011.

[Hull, Jackson and Dick 2011-a]

Elizabeth Hull, Ken Jackson and Jeremy Dick: *DOORS: A Tool to Manage Requirements*, chapter 9 of previous entry, also at link.springer.com/chapter/10.1007/978-1-4471-3730-6_9.

[IBM 2021]

IBM: *DOORS Next Generation*, online material at jazz.net/previews/#dng.

[IEEE 1998]

IEEE: *IEEE Recommended Practice for Software Requirements Specifiations*, IEEE Standard 830-1998 (revision of IEEE Std 830-1988), available at ieeexplore.ieee.org/iel4/5841/15571/00720574.pdf?arnumber=720574.

[IEEE 2005]

IEEE: *IEEE Standard for Application and Management of the Systems Engineering Process*, Standard 1220-1005, September 2005, available at ieeexplore.ieee.org/stamp/stamp.jsp?tp=&arnumber=1511885.

[IEEE 2014]

IEEE: *Guide to the Software Engineering Body of Knowledge (SWEBOK)*, version 3.0, eds. Pierre Bourque and Dick Fairley, IEEE Computer Society, 2014, available online at ieeexplore.ieee.org/document/1511885.

[IfSQ 2016]

Institute for Software Quality (IfSQ): *SPM, Single Point of Maintenance*, collection of articles at www.ifsq.org/single-point-of-maintenance.html.

[IIBA 2004-2022]

International Institute of Business Analysis: BABOK (Business Analysis Book Of Knowledge) documents, available at iiba.org.

[IIBA 2006]

International Institute of Business Analysis: BABOK (Business Analysis Book Of Knowledge) version 1.6, 2006, documents available from Australian National University site at comp.anu.edu.au/courses/comp3120/public_docs/BOKV1_6.pdf.

[Isaacson 2011]

Walter Isaacson: *Steve Jobs*, Simon & Schuster, 2011.

[ISO 2018]

International Standards Organization: *Systems and software engineering — Life cycle processes — Requirements engineering*, international standard ISO/IEC/IEEE 29148, second edition, November 2018.

[Jackson 1995]

Michael Jackson: *Software Requirements and Specifications: A Lexicon of Practice, Principles and Prejudices*, Addison Wesley / ACM Press, 1995.

[Jackson 2000]

Michael Jackson: *Problem Frames: Analysing & Structuring Software Development Problems*, Addison-Wesley, 2000.

[Jackson 2019]

Daniel Jackson: Alloy: *A Language and Tool for Exploring Software Designs*, in *Communications of the ACM*, Vol. 62 No. 9, September 2019, pages 66-76, available at cacm.acm.org/magazines/2019/9/238969-alloy/fulltext.

[Jacobson 1992]

Ivar Jacobson: *Object-Oriented Software Engineering: A Use Case Driven Approach*, Addison-Wesley, 1992.

[Jacobson-Spence-Kerr 2016]

Ivar Jacobson, Ian Spence and Brian Kerr: *Use Case 2.0, The Hub of Software Development*, in ACM *Queue*, Vol. 14, no. 1, 5 April 2016, at queue.acm.org/detail.cfm?id=2912151.

[Jézéquel-Meyer 1997]

Jean-Marc Jézéquel and Bertrand Meyer: *Design by Contract: The Lessons of Ariane*, in *Computer* (IEEE), vol. 30, no. 1, January 1997, pages 129-130, available online at se.ethz.ch/~meyer/publications/computer/ariane.pdf.

[Jones 1990]

Cliff B. Jones: *Systematic Software Development using VDM*, Prentice Hall 1990. Available online at eprints.ncl.ac.uk/158505.

[Kotonya-Sommerville 1998]

Gerald Kotonya and Ian Sommerville: *Requirements Engineering: Processes and Techniques*, Wiley, 1998.

[Kruchten 2003]

Philippe Kruchten: *The Rational Unified Process: An Introduction*, Addison-Wesley, 2003.

[Lamport 2021]

Leslie Lamport, The TLA+ Home Page, at lamport.azurewebsites.net/tla/tla.html. (Includes extensive TLA+ documentation, in particular a PDF version of Lamport's book *Specifying Systems: The TLA+ Language and Tools for Hardware and Software Engineers*, Addison-Wesley, 2002.)

[Laplante 2018]

Philipp A. Laplante, *Requirements Engineering for Software and Systems*, Third Edition, CRC Press, 2018.

[Leffingwell 2011]

Dean Leffingwell: *Agile Software Requirements — Lean Requirements Practices for Teams, Programs, and the Enterprise*, Addison-Wesley, 2011.

[Liskov-Zilles 1974]

Barbara H. Liskov, Steven N. Zilles: *Programming with Abstract Data Types*, in *Proceedings of ACM SIGPLAN Symposium on Very High Level Languages*, SIGPLAN Notices 9, 1974, pages 50-59.

[Lutz 1993]

Robyn Lutz: *Analyzing Software Requirements Errors in Safety-Critical, Embedded Systems*, in ISRE 93 (Proc. Int. Symposium on Requirements Engineering), IEEE, 1993, also available at ieeexplore.ieee.org/document/324825.

[Mannion-Keepence 1995]

Mike Mannion and Barry Keepence: *SMART Requirements*, in ACM SIGSOFT Software Engineering Notes, vol. 20, no. 2, pages 42-47, April 1995, available online at www.researchgate.net/publication/2937339_SMART_requirements.

[McConnell 2006]

Steve McConnell: *Software Estimation: Demystifying the Black Art*, Microsoft Press, 2006.

[Meyer 1985]

Bertrand Meyer: *On Formalism in Specifications*, in *Software* (IEEE), pages 6-26, January 1985, available at se.ethz.ch/~meyer/publications/ieee/formalism.pdf.

[Meyer 1995]

Bertrand Meyer: *Object Success: A Manager's Guide to Object Orientation, Its Impact on the Corporation and its Use for Reengineering the Software Process*, Prentice Hall, 1995.

[Meyer 1997]

Bertrand Meyer: *Object-Oriented Software Construction*, 2nd edition, Prentice Hall, 1997.

[Meyer 2012]

Bertrand Meyer: *Salad Requirements, Requirements Salad*, blog article, 10 August 2012, at bertrandmeyer.com/2012/08/10/salad-requirements-requirements-salad/.

[Meyer 2012a]

Bertrand Meyer: *A Fundamental Duality of Software Engineering*, blog article, 14 October 2012, at bertrandmeyer.com/2012/10/14/a-fundamental-duality-of-software-engineering/.

[Meyer 2013]

Bertrand Meyer: *Multirequirements*, in *Modelling and Quality in Requirements Engineering* (Martin Glinz Festschrift), eds. Norbert Seyff and Anne Koziolek, MV Wissenschaft, 2013, available at se.ethz.ch/~meyer/publications/methodology/multirequirements.pdf.

[Meyer 2014]

Bertrand Meyer: *Agile! The Good, the Hype and the Ugly*, Springer, 2014, book page at se.ethz.ch/~meyer/books/agile/.

[Meyer 2018]

Bertrand Meyer: *The Formal Picnic Approach to Requirements*, blog article, 17 December 2018, available at bertrandmeyer.com/2018/12/17/formal-picnic-approach-requirements/.

[Meyer et al. 2019]

Bertrand Meyer, Jean-Michel Bruel, Sophie Ebersold, Florian Galinier and Alexandr Naumchev: *The Anatomy of Software Requirements*, in TOOLS 50+1, Innopolis, Russia, Oct. 2015, Springer Lecture Notes in Computer Science 11771, pages 10-40 , available at link.springer.com/chapter/10.1007/978-3-030-29852-4_2.

[NASA 1999]

NASA: *Climate Orbiter Mishap Investigation Board Phase I Report*, 10 November 1999, available at llis.nasa.gov/llis_lib/pdf/1009464main1_0641-mr.pdf.

[Naumchev-Meyer 2016]

Alexandr Naumchev and Bertrand Meyer, *Complete contracts through specification drivers*, in Proc. of TASE 2016 (10th Int. Symp. on Theoretical Aspects of Soft. Eng.), Shanghai, 17-19 July 2016, se.ethz.ch/~meyer/publications/requirements/sd.pdf.

[Naur 1969]

Peter Naur: *Programming with Action Clusters*, in BIT, vol. 3, no. 9, pages 250-258, 1969.

[Nuseibeh-Zave 2010]

Bashar Nuseibeh and Pamela Zave (eds): *Software Requirements and Design: The Work of Michael Jackson*, lulu.com, 2010.

[Parnas 2001]

David L. Parnas: *The Tabular Method for Relational Documentation.* Electronic Notes in Theoretical Computer Science, vol. 44, no. 3, 2001, pages 1-26.

[Pfleeger-Atlee 2009]

Shari Lawrence Pfleeger and Joanne M. Atlee: *Software Engineering: Theory and Practice.* 4th Edition, Prentice Hall, 2009.

[Pnueli 1977]

Amir Pnueli, *The Temporal Logic of Programs*, in *Proceedings of 18th Annual Symposium on Foundations of Computer Science*, 1977, available online at various URLs including ieeexplore.ieee.org/document/4567924.

[Poppendieck 2003]

Mary and Tom Poppendieck: *Lean Software Development — An Agile Toolkit*, Addison-Wesley, 2003.

[Poppendieck 2010]

Mary and Tom Poppendieck: *Leading Lean Software Development*, Addison-Wesley, 2010.

[Popper 1959]

Karl Popper. *The Logic of Scientific Discovery*, Routledge, 1959 (original German edition was published in 1934).

[Royce 1970]

Winston W. Royce: *Managing the Development of Large Software Systems*, in *Proceedings of IEEE WESCON*, August 1970, pages 1–9.

[Rubens 2007]

Jason Rubens: *Business Analysis and Requirements Engineering: the Same, only Different?*, in *Requirements Engineering* (Springer), vol. 12, pages 121–123, 2007, available at link.springer.com/article/10.1007/s00766-007-0043-3.

[Scharer 1981]

Laura L. Scharer: *Pinpointing Requirements*, in *Datamation*, vol. 27, April 1981, pages 139-151.

[Schwaber and Sutherland 2012]

Ken Schwaber and Jeff Sutherland: *Software in 30 Days: How Agile Managers Beat the Odds, Delight Their Customers, And Leave Competitors In the Dust*, Wiley, 2012.

[SEI 2005]

Software Engineering Institute: *CMMI for Software Engineering*, Version 1.1, Staged Representation (CMMI-SW, V1.1, Staged), 2005, available online at www.sei.cmu.edu/publications/documents/02.reports/02tr029.html.

[Southwell et al. 1987]

K. Southwell, K. James, B. A. Clarke, B. Andrews, C. Ashworth, M. Norris, and V. Patel, *Requirements Definition and Design, The STARTS Guide*, Second Edition, Vol.1, National Computing Centre, pages177-313, Chapter 5, 1987 (as cited in [Christel-Kang 1992]).

[Spivey 1989]

J. Michael Spivey: *The Z Notation: A Reference Manual*, Prentice Hall, 1989.

[Stakeholder maps]

Stakeholder Mapping site, at www.stakeholdermap.com.

[Strunk-White]

William Strunk Jr. and E.B. White: *The Elements of Style*, 4th edition, Turtleback, 1999 (1st edition is from 1935 and White's revision from 1959).

[Thomas-Hunt 2019]

David Thomas and Andrew Hunt: *The Pragmatic Programmer: Your Journey To Mastery*, 20th Anniversary Edition (2nd Edition), Addison-Wesley, 2019.

[Van Lamsweerde 2008]

Axel van Lamsweerde: *Requirements Engineering*, Wiley, 2008.

[Wake 2003-2017]

William C. Wake: *INVEST in Good Stories: The Series*, 2003-2017, e-book available (after registration) from xp123.com/articles/invest-in-good-stories-and-smart-tasks/.

[Wiegers-Beatty 2013]

Karl Wiegers and Joy Beatty, *Software Requirements*, third edition, Microsoft Press, 2013.

[Winant 2002]

Becky Winant: *Requirement #1: Ask Honest Questions*, online article, 2002, available at www.stickyminds.com/sitewide.asp?Function=edetail&ObjectType=COL&ObjectId=326.

[Wikipedia: OSI]

Open Systems Interconnection (OSI), Wikipedia page at en.wikipedia.org/wiki/OSI_model.

[Wikipedia: SOA]

Service-Oriented Architecture, Wikipedia page at en.wikipedia.org/wiki/Service-oriented_architecture. Figure (reproduced on page 80 of this Handbook) credited to Loïc Corbasson based on original by David S. Linthicum, under GNU Free Documentation License.

[Young 2002]

Ralph Young: *Recommended Requirements Gathering Practices*, in *CrossTalk, the Journal of Defense Software Engineering*, April 2002, available at www.semanticscholar.org/paper/Recommended-Requirements-Gathering-Practices-Young-Grumman/2cf07cba67d011474 3fcc9e626f5aab9ac7b9fcb.

[Zave-Jackson 1997]

Pamela Zave and Michael Jackson: *Four Dark Corners of Requirements Engineering*, in ACM *TOSEM* (*Transactions on Software Engineering and Methodology*), vol. 6, no. 1, January 1997, pages 1-30.

Index

Printed in the United States
by Baker & Taylor Publisher Services